ADVANCE PRAISE
FOR *DANCING ON BONES*

"Dancing on Bones is an engaging account of how leaders in China, Russia, and North Korea re-moulded, re-tooled, and retrofitted postwar history to turn it into an unforgiving bulwark of support for today's regimes. Its value lies not just in illuminating how this happened, but why it matters for the rest of the world, as the powerful and aggrieved nationalism constructed on this new historical foundation spills out into the rest of the world."

—**Richard McGregor**, author of *The Party: The Secret World of China's Communist Rulers*

DANCING ON BONES

HISTORY AND POWER IN CHINA,
RUSSIA, AND NORTH KOREA

KATIE STALLARD

OXFORD
UNIVERSITY PRESS

OXFORD
UNIVERSITY PRESS

Oxford University Press is a department of the University of Oxford. It furthers
the University's objective of excellence in research, scholarship, and education
by publishing worldwide. Oxford is a registered trade mark of Oxford University
Press in the UK and certain other countries.

Published in the United States of America by Oxford University Press
198 Madison Avenue, New York, NY 10016, United States of America.

CIP data is on file at the Library of Congress
ISBN 978–0–19–757535–2

DOI: 10.1093/oso/9780197575352.001.0001

1 3 5 7 9 8 6 4 2

Printed by LSC communications, United States of America

Who controls the past controls the future; who controls the present controls the past.

— GEORGE ORWELL, *Nineteen Eighty-Four*[1]

CONTENTS

ACKNOWLEDGMENTS

I'VE HEARD IT SAID that writing a book is like giving birth. Having recently done both, I can say this is not the case. For childbirth, they give you drugs and you're surrounded by highly qualified medical professionals telling you exactly what to do. Writing a book is more like those first few weeks of being a new parent, when you get home from the hospital and realize you have absolutely no idea what you're doing. You stumble around in the dark trying to figure it out and wondering how anyone has ever managed to do this before. The answer, as with writing this book, is with the love and support of family and friends, and with the kindness and wise counsel of those who have been there before you—and coffee.

There are so many people who contributed to this book in one way or another that I could fill another book just with thanks, but let me try to get down at least some of my gratitude. I started at Sky News as a runner two weeks out of university and I was lucky to spend the next fifteen years working alongside so many amazing people and some of the most talented professionals in the industry. Nick Pollard gave me that first job; Simon Cole gave me my first shot as a reporter; and Dan Williams, Jonathan Levy, Sarah Whitehead, and John Ryley gave me the opportunity to go to Russia, and later China, and I am truly grateful for all the adventures and life-changing experiences that followed. There are too many wonderful people to list here individually, but I'm particularly grateful to all the camera operators, satellite engineers, sound technicians, and field producers who stood outside courts and in snowdrifts with me over the years—thank you for your camaraderie, encouragement, patience, and expertise. The fantastic foreign and home desk teams work hard day and night, as do the talented production teams, archivists, and digital teams, and I'm grateful for your friendship and support. A special mention has to go to the edit corridor, whose soundproofed booths functioned as confessionals and emotional support facilities for me and countless others, and whose editors perform feats of wizardry and high-speed creativity every day.

In Moscow, I worked with the incredible Vadim Nechaev and Yulia James, as well as Anastasya, Nataliya, Roman, Gena, and Svetlana. Vadim, I'm sorry I quoted the part where you swore, but also not sorry as you are truly one of the world's best and most artful deliverers of profanities, and nobody can talk their way through a checkpoint like you. I don't know where to start with all the kindness, humor, and amazing pictures you came up with on all those crazy adventures, so let me just say thank you. When I once got very sick in Crimea, Yulia checked herself into the hospital too and kept me company on a neighboring camp bed on the ward; thank you for your friendship, expertise, and endless ability to source "just one more" glass of red wine.

In Beijing, I worked with the amazing Kevin Sheppard and Michael Greenfield, as well as others whose names I'm not including here but who know who they are and I hope know how grateful I am. Kev is not just a terrific camera operator but also a warm, kind, and wonderful friend (I know this will embarrass him and I'm not sorry) and the sort of person who can find the funny side (eventually) of spending six days at sea in a small wooden boat with no bathroom facilities. There are few people in the world as organized and indefatigable as Michael, or as able to talk about football, who brought the humor and enthusiasm (and sometimes an entire bushel of bananas) on all manner of adventures. Thanks to Jen Kwon for all her help and fantastic work in South Korea. Thank you to H, Y, and P for all your hard work, friendship, knowledge, and camaraderie. I am really lucky to have worked with you. I joined the *New Statesman* as I was finishing this book, and I'm so grateful to be working for such a fantastic publication and to be part of such an incredible team.

This book would not exist without the Wilson Center in Washington, DC. When I needed a place to research and write, the amazing Wilson fellowship program gave me time and space, and an office with a door that closed, as well as endless encouragement, expertise, and library loans. I remember being nervous before my first day after looking at the caliber of people I would be working alongside—my office was just down the hall from Stapleton Roy—but everyone I met was gracious, welcoming, and happy to help. I am so lucky to have had the chance to learn from and work with you all, and grateful that this extraordinary program exists. Thank you to Robert Litwak, Abraham Denmark, Jean Lee, Michael Kugelman, Shihoko Goto, Robert Daly, Stapleton Roy, Rui Zhong, Christian Ostermann, Charles Kraus, Pieter Biersteker, Matthew Rojansky, Izabella Tabarovsky, Congresswoman Jane Harman, Ambassador Mark Green, Kim Conner, Lindsay Collins, Beverly Thomas, Elinor Harty, Alex Roberts, Ivan Yurov, Samuel Wells, Kent Hughes, Diana Negroponte, Ryan McKenna, John Milewski, Janet Spikes, Michelle Kamalich, and Katherine Wahler.

Cindy Gyungmin Bae and Eliana Hubacker provided invaluable research help and I know have exciting careers of their own ahead.

Thank you to my fellow fellows for your camaraderie, thought-provoking conversations, and friendship: Amy Austin Holmes, Felix Boecking, Patrick Liddiard, Hazel Smith, Michael Davis, Ruslan Garipov, Benjamin Creutzfeldt, Natalia Ruiz Morato, Louise Young, Bradley Jardine, Hannes Grassegger, Jonathan (Yoni) Shimshoni, Sarah Oates, Catherine Schuler, Lindsay Benstead, Todd Buchwald, Dalton Conley, Brad Simpson, and Quito Swan.

This project gave me the cover to approach some of my scholarly heroes, who were kind and gracious enough to submit to interviews and take the time to offer guidance and share their hard-won insights with me. Thank you for your scholarship and your continuing work. In particular, I'm grateful to Felix Boecking, Seth Center, John Delury, Darcie Draught, Sandra Fahy, Sheena Chestnut Greitens, Jeremy Hicks, Nikolay Koposov, Jean Lee, Patrick McEachern, Rana Mitter, B. R. Myers, Sergey Parkhomenko, Stapleton Roy, Gilbert Rozman, Blair Ruble, Benjamin Katzeff Silberstein, Hazel Smith, Balázs

Szalontai, Izabella Tabarovsky, Joseph Torigian, Nina Tumarkin, Jeffrey Wasserstrom, Samuel Wells, Yafeng Xia, Daqing Yang, and Lijia Zhang. Gil Rozman also commissioned me to write on this topic for the *Asan Forum* and a section of chapter two and chapter ten is adapted from the resulting article with his kind permission.

For ploughing through drafts of chapters and providing wise comments and valuable feedback, I am extremely grateful to Sarah Beran, Jude Blanchette, Felix Boecking, John Delury, Darcie Draught, Sandra Fahy, Anna Fifield, Elinor Harty, Frank Hersey, Ben Hoyle, Isobel Hoyle, Jeff Kearns, Michael Kugelman, Jean Lee, Patrick Liddiard, Peter Martin, Jessica Meyers, Rana Mitter, Blair Ruble, David Stallard, Rosemary Stallard, Joseph Torigian, Rick Waters, Edward Wong, Lijia Zhang, and Rui Zhong. Your thoughtful insights and suggestions added so much to these pages, and the responsibility for any errors that remain is of course my own.

Thank you to David McBride at Oxford University Press for understanding the idea behind this project straight away and shaping it for the better with thoughtful and incisive edits. I am grateful to Holly Mitchell, Emily Mackenzie Benitez, Gabriel Kachuck, and Sarah Green for patiently and expertly shepherding this project through the publication process, and to the two anonymous reviewers for their helpful early comments. Kevin Sheppard, Rory Challands, Dan Franklin, and Matt Reynolds generously shared their amazing photographs and helped source images.

Many long-suffering friends provided moral support and pep talks and endured long explanations about this book. For this and for everything over the years, thank you to Amy Austin Holmes, Sarah Beran, Paul Bouanchaud, David Bowden, Charlotte Boyer-Millar, Bethanie Brady, Maria Byrne, Rory Challands, Michelle Clifford, Teresa Collinson, Jane Dougall, Anna Fifield, Frank Hersey, Ben Hoyle, Izzie Hoyle, Mollie Hoyle, Rosie Hoyle, Yulia James, Jeff Kearns, Christina Larson, Sarah Larson, Peter Martin, Jessica Meyers, James Palmer, Andrew Polk, Erin Polk, Alex Pomeroy, Kevin Sheppard, Vicky Waller, Rick Waters, Ian Woods, and Lijia Zhang.

And this book would definitely not exist without my even more long-suffering family. I was very fortunate to marry into the wonderful Blanchette clan and could not ask for a more loving, warm, and supportive family than the one Peg, Joe, Josh, Sue, and the wider Blanchette network immediately welcomed me into. I am so lucky to have such a kind, funny, and brilliant (and intrepid) brother and sister-in-law as Michael and Marie-Claire, who also showed me how much fun parenting could be, casually carting their kids up mountains and on paddle boards and mountain bikes as though it was no big deal. Ailsa and Struan, I love you so much and I can't wait to see all the adventures you go on.

My own parents, Rosemary and David, taught me to be interested in the world and to believe I could go anywhere and do anything, so they really only had themselves to blame when I told them I was moving to Russia, and then China, and they gamely visited me and threw themselves into every available activity wherever I was. It was my mother who first got me interested in Russia with tales of her own travels to the Soviet Union as a student, traveling through Checkpoint Charlie in a minibus, visiting Lenin on Red Square, and getting flagged down by officials waving party cards when they got lost and ended up in a village they weren't meant to see. My father gave me my enduring love of books and history and taught me to just keep putting one foot in front of the other and chipping away, an approach he has taken to his own ridiculous and truly bloody-minded feats of hill-walking and endurance. Both my parents devoted their own careers to improving the world around them and measure their success in the difference they can make to others, the friendships they have built, and the love and support they give their children, and now grandchildren. If I can be a fraction of the parent either of them is, I'll be very proud.

Finally, this book would not even have been started without Jude. We discussed the idea on our first date in Beijing because that's the level of nerds we are, and I still have the little stack of bar receipts where he sketched out the first notes. Whenever I was unsure if I could do this (which was all the time), he cheered me on, talked me down, read my drafts, snuck the proposal to David McBride, bucked me up, and told me that I definitely could. He read every word, assuaged every doubt, and cooked up great vats of stir fry and vegetable stew, all while pretending not to mind and being the most incredible father to our new baby. I am so lucky to be married to such an amazing, kind, and remarkable man—and more importantly, to still be married to him at the end of this: you are the love of my life and partner in crime and I couldn't have done this without you. And because I promised I would put this in writing, here it is: writing a book is really hard. I don't know how you did it with such limited time. Our very good dog Shackleton kept me company and enforced walk breaks when he could. But the last word must go to Hamish, who changed our lives in the best possible way and wields his own power with absolute benevolence. You were your own extraordinary person from the very beginning, and we love you more than you could ever know.

Introduction

Make the past serve the present.

—MAO ZEDONG[1]

Southern Ukraine

There's a man with a gun by the side of our car. It's dark, close to midnight, on the main road to Crimea. He's wearing a mask and combat gear.

It's February 2014. Ukraine's president, Viktor Yanukovych, has fled into exile in Russia and protesters in the capital are declaring victory after a long winter of demonstrations in Kyiv. But something ominous is happening here in the south. Unidentified soldiers have seized control of the airport and surrounded military bases in Crimea, the peninsula that juts out into the Black Sea from southern Ukraine. They won't answer questions about where they're from and they've removed the identifying patches from their uniforms, so people are calling them "little green men." Alongside what are clearly professional soldiers, local volunteers are forming "self-defense" militias and setting up checkpoints like this one.

The man with the gun yanks open the front passenger door and grabs my colleague Vadim's camera, who swears at him in his best Soviet army Russian. The man's whole posture relaxes. He says he's sorry, he didn't know where we were from. We hold up our press passes. Producer Yulia deploys her most reassuring smile. We're based in Moscow as journalists for Sky News, so we have accreditation from the Russian foreign ministry, which apparently is good enough for him.

"I'm a peaceful citizen. I'm a pensioner," an older man in a camou-flage mask and hooded anorak who is helping to operate the check-point tells me. "I'm just making sure everything is in order here." He says he's from Sevastopol, a famous port city in Crimea that was desig-nated a "Hero City" by Stalin after the Great Patriotic War, as World War II is known in Russia. "Fascists" have taken over the Ukrainian capital, he says, so they are out here guarding the approach to Crimea to make sure they don't get through.

They order the man and the woman out of the car behind us at gun-point. He is pale and skinny, maybe in his early twenties, wearing a striped sweatshirt. She is crying, pleading with the men to let them go. They tie his hands behind his back and lead him out of sight.

They're searching all of the vehicles, ostensibly for weapons being smuggled into Crimea, but two of the men are already sporting flak jackets marked "Press" they've clearly taken from other journalists, and they seem to be making up the rules as much as following them. Members of the elite—and notoriously violent—riot police unit the in-terim government has just disbanded are out here on the roadblock in their uniforms as though the transfer of power hasn't happened. They show me rifles, shotguns, and an axe they say they've recovered from passing cars—proof, they claim, of a plot by armed gangs in Kyiv to seize the peninsula by force.

"These are barbarians and fascists," one man says, gesturing to the guns as if this should be all the evidence I need. "They are trying to turn our Slavic world into hell." His eyes are dark and serious and they're all I can see, because he's pulled his green balaclava up over his nose to hide his face. But on his shoulder is the orange-and-black ribbon of St. George. Most of the others are wearing it too. It represents the Soviet victory in 1945 and it's become a popular symbol in Russia in recent years as Vladimir Putin ramps up commemoration of the Great Patriotic War. He wears the ribbon himself during annual Victory Day celebrations to mark the anniversary of the end of the conflict, and people pin them to their lapels and tie them to car aerials in the weeks beforehand. The ribbon becomes so ubiquitous among the rebels in eastern Ukraine that the government in Kyiv later bans it as a symbol of extremism.

"This is the land of our ancestors, who spilled their blood in the Great Patriotic War," another of the checkpoint guards tells me. "Now the fascists are on the rise again, and we are here to show that it's not going to work." He says there has been a coup in their country and Russia should send troops to help them fight back.

* * *

In fact, Russian troops were already there. But Putin wouldn't admit this until the annexation of Crimea was complete. Meanwhile, the Kremlin stoked fears of the new government in Kyiv and stirred up memories of the wartime past. Russian marines and paratroopers seized control of the territory, but Moscow's political operatives followed close behind.

Ahead of the hastily organized referendum on joining Russia—which international observers declared illegal—huge billboards went up across the peninsula showing two images of Crimea side by side. The territory was colored red and stamped with a black swastika on one side and in the red, white, and blue of the Russian flag on the other. "We Choose," said the accompanying text. Another re-created the famous Soviet recruiting poster from the Great Patriotic War with the red figure of Mother Russia summoning her citizens to battle and the slogan "Everyone to the Referendum!"

Russian state television, which was widely watched in Crimea, carried regular reports of the fascists supposedly marauding through Kyiv and reminders of how Ukrainian nationalists had collaborated with Hitler during the war. It is true that there were far-right factions among the protesters, but they were a small minority, and the idea that a "fascist junta" had taken power was a fiction created in Moscow.

Still, it was effective. I met a young mother in Sevastopol who told me she wasn't happy about all the soldiers on the streets, that it wasn't safe for the children to have so many guns around. But some older women who had stopped to listen in to our interview interrupted to set her straight. She should be grateful for the brave men out here protecting them, they said, crowding around her with their shopping bags. One of the women took hold of her arm and shook it for emphasis. Didn't she watch TV? Didn't she know what sort of people they were up against?

By Victory Day that year—May 9, 2014—Russia had annexed Crimea. Putin celebrated the holiday in Sevastopol with the orange-and-black St. George's ribbon on his chest. Just as their ancestors defeated Hitler during the Great Patriotic War, he said, so once again they had repelled the fascist threat and won a glorious victory.

"Exactly 70 years ago, this city was liberated from the German fascist invaders," he told a crowd of veterans and troops from Russia's Black Sea Fleet. "I am sure that 2014 will also become part of the city's chronicle and of that of our entire country as the year in which the peoples here expressed their firm desire to be together with Russia."[2] He left out the part about the masked men patrolling the streets outside the polling stations with assault rifles, the campaign of harassment against the Tatar minority, and the absence of any real choice.

From those first uncertain days of guns and checkpoints in Crimea, the Great Patriotic War and its symbols were used to signal which side you were on. The history of that past war was the lens through which the Kremlin framed the contemporary struggle. According to that narrative, now as then, fascists threatened Crimea and the Russian-speaking citizens of southeastern Ukraine, and you were either with them or with the brave self-defense groups—and what were later revealed to be Russian troops—standing against them. The world on Russian television was divided into good and evil, patriots and traitors, us and them.

The annexation of Crimea was genuinely popular in Russia. The territory had been part of the Russian Empire since 1783, and it was transferred from Russia to Ukraine in 1954, when both were republics of the USSR. Putin claimed he was merely righting a historical wrong, "returning" land that had always belonged to Russia, rather than illegally annexing part of a neighboring state. As he presented it, he was standing up for Russia's interests and standing up to the West after far too long of being pushed around. He was reclaiming Russia's rightful status as a great power. As he put it in a speech to mark the annexation: "If you compress the spring all the way to its limit, it will snap back hard."[3]

In the heady days before the international sanctions and the cost of absorbing the territory kicked in, you could see T-shirts, commemorative mugs, and car bumper stickers all over Moscow with the slogan

"Crimea Is Ours!" Putin's approval rating soared to 88 percent in independent polls.[4] Even Mikhail Gorbachev, a staunch critic of his author-
itarianism, applauded the move as a "happy event."[5] It was something
to celebrate at last after the long decades in the doldrums of the Soviet
Union's decay and ultimate collapse. "Crimea's reunion with Russia,"
remarked one state television anchor, "is the second most important
event in Russian history, after victory in the Second World War."[6]

The euphoria wouldn't last, but the Kremlin's focus on the glorious
history of the Great Patriotic War was here to stay. As the economy
stalled and the cost of living spiraled during Putin's second decade in
office, he turned increasingly to the past to shore up support for his
regime, elevating the memory of the Soviet victory to the status of
a national religion. He denounced anyone who tried to challenge his
version of events as "falsifiers of history" and threatened to "stuff their
filthy mouths with documents."[7] Stripped of its complex realities and
the extent of the suffering and strategic blunders involved, the memory
of the conflict became a sacred myth to rally the country behind. It was
a tale of heroism, sacrifice, and resolute leadership, and a reminder of
the enemies they faced now as they had in the last century.

I was based in Russia as a foreign correspondent for Sky News at
the time. As I traveled back and forth to both sides of the front line
in Ukraine and returned home to Moscow to see the parallel reality
playing out on television, I became fascinated by the power of history
to shape our understanding of the present. These narratives could inspire people to pick up guns, man checkpoints in the middle of the
night, and rally behind a repressive regime. When I moved to Beijing
and saw how Chinese leader Xi Jinping was using some of the same
tactics to enforce the Communist Party's version of history and began
reporting on and from North Korea—where Kim Jong Un bases his
claim to rule on a partly fictional past—I embarked on what has turned
out to be a multiyear quest to understand how autocrats exploit history
to stay in power.

Since Xi took office in 2012, Beijing has almost doubled the official
length of the Second World War in China. The conflict is now said
to have lasted fourteen years, instead of eight, and to have started in
1931, not 1937 as was previously the case. There are new memorial days,
new laws to protect the party's narrative, and a new crackdown on

dissenting views—or what the party calls "historical nihilism." Censors enforce the official account in newspapers and big-budget movie productions, on television, on social media platforms, and even in video games. People have gone to prison for challenging the party's version of history.[8] Just as Mao Zedong once instructed his officials to "make the past serve the present," so Xi is determined to make the country's history serve the party's current needs.

But nowhere does the past play a more important role in contemporary politics than North Korea, where the Kim dynasty's version of history dominates daily life. From their earliest days in kindergarten, children learn how the current leader's grandfather, Kim Il Sung, "liberated" the country from Japanese rule in 1945 before "defeating" the United States in the Korean War in 1953, which they are told the United States and South Korea started. This isn't true, but three generations of North Korean leaders have brandished this make-believe history as proof of why they must be in power—and latterly, why they must have nuclear weapons and the means to deliver them—as they claim to be defending their citizens, instead of the truth that their actions are isolating and impoverishing them.

Russia, China, and North Korea consistently top lists of threats to US and European security and the post-1945 international order. They have nuclear weapons, advanced cyber capabilities, and some of the largest standing armies in the world. And yet the stories the ruling regimes tell their own people are about how they are threatened, how their enemies (chief among them the United States) seek to keep them down and keep them weak and contained, how they are the true guardians of peace and the global order. They invoke the wars of the last century—specifically, World War II and the Korean War—to remind their citizens how they struggled and prevailed against foreign aggression then, and why they must have strong leaders and the strength to defend their interests again now.

At its heart, this is a story about power. It's a history of how successive authoritarian rulers have co-opted and manipulated the past to serve their political needs. This book traces that story from the end of World War II to the current day. From the founding myths of the Kim dynasty in North Korea to the reality of victory in China and the Soviet Union, the early chapters examine the political utility of external enemies and the regime's efforts to control popular memory and remind citizens how their country has been victimized and made to suffer in the past. Later chapters explore the political risks of allowing too close an examination of the truth and the potency of lies, stringent legal controls, and strict limits on public discourse as those in power present themselves as heroes and patriots.

Let me add a few important caveats. First, and perhaps obviously, it's much more complicated than this. These regimes are more than just the man at the top, and staying in power means managing multiple resources and constituencies. Putin, Xi, and Kim wield repressive security forces, crush opposition to their rule, control access to information, and cultivate the loyalties of the regime elite. But they also go to great lengths to generate popular support, or at least the appearance of it, which is where these historical narratives come in. Apart from the fact that force alone is a brittle and expensive way to rule, maintaining the impression that the leader is popular helps to reinforce the message that their position is secure, so their backers don't start looking for a new patron and their rivals don't risk trying to topple them.[9] Casting themselves as patriots and defenders of the nation also helps frame their opponents as traitors and enemies of the state.

Second, this doesn't mean that everyone in these countries believes what they are told. The citizens of North Korea, Russia, and China are no more automatons than people anywhere else in the world, and it's important not to confuse the views someone might express publicly in an authoritarian system—especially to a foreign reporter—with private and truly held beliefs. The purpose of examining these stories is to understand the popular narratives these regimes promote and how they enforce the boundaries of acceptable discourse, historical research, and education to advance their political goals. Dissenting and diverse views can and do endure even under the most severe social controls.

Finally, the impulse to manipulate history for political purposes is not a uniquely authoritarian trait. It is not just autocrats who appeal to nostalgia and cultivate crises. Plenty of democratically elected leaders distort and draw selectively from the past to rally popular support and advance their own political aims, and the history of the Second World War remains a potent cultural touchstone among all the Allied powers. In the United Kingdom, where I grew up, both sides in the

2016 Brexit referendum marshaled imagery from the conflict to appeal for votes, and newspaper headlines regularly summon Churchill and the "Blitz Spirit" for everything from soccer tournaments to inclement weather. Similarly, in the United States, political leaders frequently invoke the attack on Pearl Harbor, the heroism of the "Greatest Generation," and the shared sacrifice of World War II. Donald Trump waded into his own history wars as he tried to hold on to power in 2020, calling for patriotic education in American schools and setting up a "1776 Commission" to oversee the teaching of history, which Joe Biden promptly dissolved on his first day in office.[10]

But in Russia, China, and North Korea, the official version of history is becoming the only version of history and it is getting harder and more dangerous to push back. This matters beyond their borders as these narratives are wielded to justify expansive military ambitions and aggressive foreign policy, and to frame contemporary rivalries and territorial disputes. And this approach to history won't end with Putin, Xi, and Kim. Whoever comes next may be even more dependent on stoking these historical grievances and finding an external enemy to blame for domestic difficulties.

This book argues that if we want to understand where these countries are heading, we must understand the stories they are telling their citizens about the past. This is not about remembering history as it actually was, but as those in power need it to be—making the past serve the present as Mao once urged, or as one Russian activist put it more recently: "dancing on bones."[11]

I

Myth

Because the regime is captive to its own lies, it must falsify everything. It falsifies the past. It falsifies the present, and it falsifies the future.

—VÁCLAV HAVEL[1]

Demilitarized Zone (DMZ), North Korea

As we left Pyongyang, the color drained away. Pastel-painted high-rises faded to the dirt of open farmland, the world around us shades of muddy brown. It was spring in North Korea and there were people working in bare feet, but the wind was bitterly cold and in a few hours it would snow. In the hills above us, huge red and white letters spelled out: "We are following our Leader wherever he goes."

I could list all the clichés at this point: how closed and secretive this country is, how mysterious and dangerous its ruler—inferred, how brave am I for going there—but the truth is journalists like me travel to North Korea every year, or at least they did until it sealed its borders at the start of the coronavirus pandemic, and they surely will again once the restrictions lift. Instead of repeating the stereotypes and the caricatures, I want to take you there with as little melodrama as I can, to take you through the version of history you would hear if you grew up in North Korea and how it shapes this country and serves the interests of those in power.

Much of that history is heavily distorted and highly selective—in parts wholly fictional—but the ruling Kim regime presents it to its citizens as fact. Over the last seven decades, successive leaders have held up this account as evidence for why they must be in power, why they must build up the country's military strength, and why they must have nuclear weapons and long-range missiles that can reach the United States.

At the heart of this story are two big lies: that Kim Il Sung (the current leader's grandfather) liberated the country from Japanese rule in 1945, and that North Korea was invaded by the United States and South Korea at the start of the Korean War in 1950. The mythology has become more elaborate over time, with the first Kim's heroism and the supposed barbarism of the country's enemies intensifying with the passing years. The greater the difficulties the regime perceives in the present, the more it relies on this narrative and stoking fears of external threats. Even as I write this, a new generation of schoolchildren will be learning how their country was attacked and subjugated before the Kims took control, and how the dynasty defends North Korea from its enemies. It doesn't matter whether they really believe this; the regime just needs them to memorize these stories and pass them on, always remembering that the Kim family leaders are the heroes and their tireless protectors, and North Korea's problems are all someone else's fault.

Out of the window of the minibus, I watched two men using an ox to plow a field. An old lady squatted nearby, pulling up weeds by hand. There was no modern farm machinery in sight. We were only just outside the vast capital you see on television, with its military parades, amusement parks, and towering monuments. But only the elite—the most trusted citizens—are allowed to live there, in a city ringed by checkpoints and armed guards.

If you never left Pyongyang, you might almost believe the hype: that this is a powerful nation whose latest supreme leader, Kim Jong Un, is following in his predecessors' footsteps and working hard to improve the lives of his people and keep them safe. But in reality, the Kim regime's priority is, as it always has been, the survival of the Kim regime.

Out here in the countryside life is hard and desperately poor. There is often not enough to eat or safe water to drink. According to the United Nations, 40 percent of the population was classed as "food insecure" in 2020, meaning they regularly lacked enough food and nutrition to meet their daily needs. One in five children was found to be stunted, an irreversible condition that limits their growth caused by chronic malnutrition.[2]

But still the regime has pumped money and manpower into building one of the world's largest standing armies—with more active-duty personnel than Russia or Iran—and developing nuclear weapons and an advanced missile arsenal.

Along the otherwise deserted highway we passed concrete guard posts at regular intervals. Sometimes I could make out the outline of a soldier staring back from inside the rectangular observation slit. As we traveled farther south, soldiers patrolled the roadside with rifles in hand.

We were heading for the Demilitarized Zone—or DMZ—the border between North and South Korea and ground zero for one of the Kim dynasty's most important myths. This is where the regime tells its citizens they were invaded in a surprise attack in June 1950 at the start of the Korean War, and that another attack could come at any time. The site serves as a memorial to the imperialist aggression the regime claims to have faced down in the past, and still claims to be defending the country against. It's the front line of a war that hasn't ended, just been frozen in time.

"This is the most dangerous place in the world," a Korean People's Army (KPA) officer in a tall, peaked cap warned us as we approached the entrance to the DMZ. He said we would be escorted by his men from that point on for our security. Thatched screens dotted the hillside behind us, presumably to conceal some of the thousands of artillery pieces and rocket launchers ranged on the South Korean capital along this border. Repeated signs warned about the danger of mines buried on either side of the road.

There was a small, squat museum preserving North Korea's version of the conflict's history and the site where the armistice was signed in July 1953, bringing a halt but not a formal end to the hostilities. The original desks and chairs were set out in the center of the room, complete with their flags. One of the guides pointed out the faded UN flag and said the United States had used it to "hide the shame of their defeat," which is how they presented the truce. But mostly the museum, as with so much else in this country, was about the Kim family. There were pictures of the leaders on every wall, and not just those who were adults or even alive at the time of the war. All three generations—the first president, Kim Il Sung; his son, Kim Jong Il; and his son, Kim

Jong Un—were pictured visiting the border, staring down the enemies they insisted were plotting against the country on the other side.

"No countries have leaders like ours," said the guide, "who went to the front line."

As we approached the front line ourselves, I could hear soothing Korean folk music, which was not what I had expected at what I had just been told was the most dangerous place on Earth. It was part of a campaign, which has since been suspended, where the two Koreas blasted each other with propaganda from dueling loudspeakers along the border, which was at least better than the alternative. The North kept up a steady barrage of rousing marching songs and ballads about their great leaders, while the South pumped out salvos of the South Korean pop music known as K-pop and information about the Kim family's lavish lives.

Looking out across the demarcation line into South Korea, I noticed our military escort drawing himself up to his full height now that we were in view of the other side. His shoulders were squared. His face was serious and unsmiling. He appeared to be clenching his jaw. I wondered how much of this was real—whether he truly believed that North Korea had been attacked here in 1950, and that their enemies were out there preparing to strike again. Because what he had just told me was not true. There was no surprise invasion of the North at the start of the Korean War. It was North Korea that invaded the South.

* * *

The lies started years before the fighting, with Kim Il Sung's foundation myth.

To understand the version of history the Kim regime tells its citizens—including that soldier at the DMZ—we need to go back to the beginning, before there was even a North Korea, and the early years of the first leader's life.

Kim Il Sung was not his real name. The future president was born Kim Song Ju in 1912, when the Korean peninsula was under Japanese colonial rule. Korea had been annexed by Japan in 1910 and the struggle to regain independence would shape the young Kim's childhood and form the foundation of his later claim to power. He adopted the nom de guerre Kim Il Sung, which roughly translates as "becomes the sun," as a guerrilla fighter in the anti-Japanese resistance in the mid-1930s.[3] But he claimed to have been active in the movement from the start.

Kim's family home on the outskirts of Pyongyang has been turned into a vast complex that is part museum, part shrine, and a non-negotiable stop on every visiting journalist's itinerary. Gentle melodies play from speakers concealed somewhere among the trees as elegant guides in traditional silk dresses lead you around the perfectly mani-cured grounds, relaying the great leader's youthful exploits in hushed, reverential tones. Among the exhibits was an enormous gold-framed painting depicting the young Kim joining a mass uprising against Japanese rule in 1919, when he was just seven years old. He was the only child in a scene filled with angry men brandishing sticks and scythes, striding along in a pink shirt and dark waistcoat, his gaze fixed firmly ahead. One of the guides gestured proudly to the image during my visit and declared that from this moment on, Kim's life's course was set. He resolved to devote himself to liberating Korea and vowed that he would not rest until his country was free. Apparently, he took this seriously and literally, wrestling older boys to build up his strength and prepare for his later battles against Japan.[4]

But soon afterward, Kim and his family fled the country, following the path of many other Korean exiles across the border to the north-eastern Chinese region of Manchuria. They drifted, he later wrote, "like fallen leaves to the desolate wilderness."[5] It was the start of almost a quarter of a century on the move for Kim and the last time either of his parents would see their homeland.

When Kim's father died in 1926, his mother strapped her husband's two pistols to the fourteen-year-old boy and urged him to fight for Korean independence, or so the official story goes. The details of what followed have been lost to the propaganda, but it seems Kim served a brief sentence in a Chinese prison for belonging to a Communist youth group in his late teens and joined the anti-Japanese guerrillas fighting in Manchuria in the early 1930s.

Kim fought alongside and at times under the leadership of com-manders from the Chinese Communist Party, an organization that was then in the early stages of its own struggle for power, as they battled the Japanese invasion in northeast China. But that part has been erased from the North Korean account. Instead, Kim is portrayed leading his own band of fighters, subordinate to no one, and founding the Korean People's Revolutionary Army (KPRA), which in turn became the Korean People's Army (KPA), as North Korea's military is known today, although there is no evidence the first organization actually existed.[6]

According to the regime's account, Kim and his guerrillas established a secret base on the slopes of Mount Paektu, an extinct volcano that is revered both north and south of the modern-day border as the mythical birthplace of the Korean people. This is also where his son, Kim Jong Il, would later claim to have been born.

As the older Kim's memoirs describe the fighting, the guerrillas staged daring raids on Japanese positions before disappearing back into the forests, and of course, he was utterly fearless under fire.

"Comrades, we must seize the fort at any cost. Let us fight for the revolution to the last drop of our blood!" he claims to have shouted during one battle. "Then, mowing the enemy down with Mauser fire, I charged forward. . . . The rain of machine gun bullets from the fort grazed my ears. A bullet pierced through my cap. But I dashed forward without pause for breath. The men sprang to their feet and followed me."[7] Kim reported that they had overwhelmed the Japanese defenses and won the battle in less than an hour.

If this sounds like a scene from an action movie, that's because it might actually be one. Kim's memoirs were crafted by the same writers who worked on some of North Korea's biggest films, which at least, commented former ideology secretary Hwang Jang-yop, "made for very interesting reading."

"When Part I [of the memoirs] was published it was a huge hit," Hwang said after defecting to South Korea. "This was only natural, since its contents were literally scenes straight out of the movies that had been made for the same purpose."[8]

Like all the best action movie heroes, Kim was portrayed enduring great suffering and overcoming repeated obstacles on his journey to victory. "Under the banner of anti-Japanese struggle," he wrote, "I had to endure hardships going hungry and sleeping outdoors in the deep forests of Mount Paektu, push my way through endless snowstorms and wage long bloody battles convinced of national liberation, fighting against the formidable enemy scores of times stronger than our forlorn force."⁹

But eventually the long years of struggle paid off as he led the charge to free his homeland in August 1945.

"At last, on August 9, he ordered all KPRA units to commence the final attack for the liberation of the homeland," another official publication explains. "From the first moment of the operations for the liberation of the country, all commanders and soldiers of the KPRA displayed matchless courage, self-sacrificing spirit and mass heroism."[10] The early versions of this story credited the Soviet army with leading the offensive against Japan. But their role receded over the decades as Kim claimed more of the glory for himself. Later editions depict Kim and his guerrillas leading the attack, as in this account, which was published in 1983.

"The fierce attack of our units and stubborn anti-Japanese resistance of the people dealt a mortal blow to the Japanese imperialists and brought them to surrender unconditionally in great haste on August 15, 1945," readers are told. "That is only a week after the start of the operations for liberating the country."[11] The text does not mention the nuclear bombs the United States dropped on Japan that same week, and there is only the most fleeting reference to the idea that any of the Western powers were fighting in the Pacific theater at all. Kim Il Sung is then depicted returning home in triumph.

"The great leader Comrade Kim Il Sung led the glorious anti-Japanese armed struggle to brilliant victory and thus liberated the Korean people from under the colonial yoke of imperialism," the regime's historians claim. "Our people who had been impatiently waiting for the day of national liberation fervently welcomed the KPRA, shouting 'Long live General Kim Il Sung!' and 'Long live [the] independence of Korea!'"[12]

It was an epic tale of courage and endurance, filled with daring battles and narrated with cinematic flair. Over the years, the story of Kim's guerrilla heroism would be used to fuel an extraordinary cult of personality and to explain why he alone—and then his son, and his grandson—deserved to rule North Korea. There was just one problem. He had made most of it up.

* * *

Kim Il Sung did not return home at the head of a victorious army, nor was he even in Korea, let alone leading a great battle to liberate it from Japanese colonial rule in August 1945. In fact, at the time he was around 500 miles away at a Red Army base near Khabarovsk in the Russian Far East, where he sat out the last four years of the war and where his son, Kim Jong Il, was really born.[13]

Japan surrendered control of Korea because it was defeated by the Allied powers in the Second World War and stripped of its colonial territories, not because it was vanquished by Kim and his guerrillas.

There were glimmers of truth among the lies. The broad outline of Kim's early life was accurate, even if some of the details and the stories were apocryphal. It was true that he fled with his family to Manchuria as a child, that he loathed colonial rule, and that he really was a guerrilla fighter who took part in the anti-Japanese resistance. But he fought primarily in Manchuria in China, not Korea, and his efforts petered out long before the end of the war.

"He suffered many defeats, but he also scored some impressive victories and made a name for himself—indeed, he became the most wanted guerrilla leader in Manchuria," wrote Suh Dae-sook in his 1988 biography of the North Korean leader. "He persisted in the hopeless fight without much support, but he endured and did not surrender or submit to the Japanese."

Suh summed up Kim's guerrilla struggle as "brief," but nevertheless "solid . . . and deserving of recognition."[14]

But that struggle was over by the winter of 1940–1941 when Kim was forced to flee again as Japanese forces consolidated their control of Manchuria. This time he crossed the border from northern China into the Soviet Union.[15]

Kim reemerged in the Red Army in 1941 as a battalion commander in an intelligence unit based in Khabarovsk, according to documents from the Russian archives.[16] The unit was composed of Chinese, Korean, and Soviet-Korean soldiers and nominally tasked with gathering information on Japanese troop movements. But in practice it seems to have spent most of its time training and seen little action. Kim's interpreter, Yu Song-ch'ol, who worked alongside him in the unit from 1943, said he couldn't fairly assess his abilities as a soldier because he had never seen him in combat.

And what he did remember was less than impressive.

"Kim was lean and weak, and his mouth was always open, perhaps because he was suffering at the time from hypertrophic rhinitis [chronic inflammation of the nasal passages]," Yu later wrote. "During outdoor ski training, he was forced to tie himself to one of his troops using ropes to move, being too physically exhausted to move on his own."[17]

Although Yu was not an impartial witness—he wrote this account in exile in the Soviet Union after being purged by Kim Il Sung—Soviet military advisers in North Korea have confirmed its validity, and he does also offer praise.[18]

Kim's Soviet superiors thought highly of Kim, Yu noted, who was "regarded as being exceptionally smart and possessive of leadership qualities." He was also popular among his fellow Koreans, enjoying "considerable authority among the 25 partisans who, with Kim, had risked their lives conducting anti-Japanese resistance operations."[19] He had a reputation for self-discipline, too, and strict rules against heavy drinking.

It was not quite the stuff of legend, but it was enough to get him noticed by his commanding officers and would prove critical when the Soviets came to choose a leader for North Korea in the years to come.

For the time being, though, Kim was stranded. In the final days of World War II, as Soviet forces rolled into Korea and the fictional Kim Il Sung leaped into action, leading his heroic charge to victory, the real one was stranded in the forests of Khabarovsk, where his brigade was disbanded and unceremoniously disarmed. As he handed back his rifle, it wasn't clear when or in what capacity he might be going home.

It had looked for a while like Kim's unit might join the advance into Korea. In July 1945, the head of the Soviet Far East Command visited the camp and told them to get ready to join the invasion force. But the Soviet leader Joseph Stalin vetoed the plan, apparently concerned that the Koreans would demand too much after the war if they were allowed to play such a prominent role in the victory.[20]

Kim later tried to persuade a Soviet officer to write him back into the liberation story. "Commander, sir, please make it so that it appears as though the anti-Japanese partisans participated in the war of liberation," Major-General Nikolai Lebedev, who was part of the Soviet occupation force in the northern half of Korea, recalled the young man pleading. But he turned him down.[21]

In fact, Kim returned to Korea more than a month after the end of the war, on September 19, 1945, to no acclaim. Wearing a Red Army uniform and sailing on a Soviet naval ship, he traveled with other Korean exiles from his unit to the east coast port of Wonsan, where his grandson would one day build a vast palace and moor a luxury yacht. Instead of rapturous crowds, they were greeted by a delegation of the Soviet officials now in charge of the northern half of the peninsula. There was no great ceremony. Kim and his comrades spent their first night sleeping on the floor of a noodle restaurant.[22]

But from those very first steps back on Korean soil, Kim was already crafting a better story for himself. He introduced himself by his birth name, Kim Song Ju, and told the others to pretend they hadn't seen the real Kim Il Sung.

Yu Song-ch'ol, his interpreter, recalled the orders he gave them over dinner that first night as he warned them to keep a low profile. He told them not to go out and drink too much, and should anyone ask where he was, they were "to respond that we were the advance party and that Kim Il-song planned on returning later." He said he thought Kim was trying to "hide the truth of his shabby, humble return to Korea" as he cultivated the image of a great resistance hero. "Kim instructed us to insist that we knew absolutely nothing about Kim Il-song such as his age, place of birth or personal history," Yu said. Afterward, he remembers a colleague mumbling to himself, "He really is talking nonsense."[23]

When the men did venture out, they found a divided Korea. In the final hours of World War II, with the Allied victory imminent, the United States and the Soviet Union had agreed to split control of Japanese-occupied Korea between them. It was meant to be a temporary arrangement with the two halves of the peninsula later unified under Korean rule, but the two powers were less concerned with what was in the best interests of the Koreans themselves and more with how to stop the other from seizing control. The wartime alliance was already giving way to the enmity of the Cold War, and neither Washington nor Moscow was prepared to cede influence over the strategically important territory to the other, even if that meant splitting the country in two.

Working late into the night on the eve of the Japanese surrender with the help of a National Geographic map, two young US Army officers—one of them future secretary of state Dean Rusk—proposed dividing the peninsula along the thirty-eighth parallel, which would leave the capital Seoul in the US-controlled sector. It looked to the two men like a reasonable compromise, and anyway, it wasn't supposed to be permanent. To their surprise, the Soviets agreed.

The first task for the rival powers was to make sure that their Korea survived—that it wouldn't be the one to collapse and be subsumed by the other, now allied to their adversary.

In the South, the Americans had backed Syngman Rhee as leader. He was a well-known nationalist who had been president of the Korean provisional government in exile. The Soviets needed a similarly credible figurehead in the North, and in the autumn of 1945 that was not Kim Il Sung.

At first they tried to recruit the higher-profile Cho Man-sik. Sometimes referred to as "Korea's Gandhi" for his nonviolent opposition to Japanese rule, Cho had impeccable credentials as a Korean patriot. He even dressed the part, wearing traditional clothes and Korean-made shoes and handing out name cards printed on Korean paper to demonstrate his commitment to the cause. Cho rebuffed the Soviet advances, but he agreed to appear alongside Kim—whose own star now appeared to be rising—at a rally to introduce him to the public in Pyongyang in October 1945, conferring some of his authority on the younger man.[24]

A black-and-white photograph taken before the rally shows Kim smiling at the camera in an ill-fitting three-piece suit, the jacket too big and the waistcoat too small, buttons bulging under the strain.[25] Baby-faced and with a toothy grin, he looks much younger than his thirty-three years, an effect compounded by the older Soviet officer standing next to him, pointedly admiring the Red Army medal on his chest and looking like a proud father with his son before the high school prom.

Kim's Korean was rusty. He had spent his entire adult life outside the country and most of his schooling was in Chinese. But his Soviet advisers had drafted a speech and he had practiced reading it aloud. They advertised the event as a "Reception for the triumphant return of General Kim Il-sung."[26]

It did not go well.

When Kim took to the stage, Yu Song-ch'ol, who was there, said there was real excitement at first. "The crowd shouted out, 'Long live General Kim Il-song.' It seemed as though the stadium would collapse," Yu recalled. But as Kim's speech went on, the mood changed. "Whispers began to circulate through the crowd saying, 'This is a bogus Kim Il-song,' and some even cursed him, calling him a 'Ruskie stooge' as they began to leave the stadium."[27]

The problem was that the Kim they were expecting based on the newspaper reports was a battle-hardened resistance hero, not the nervous young man who appeared on stage.

"They saw a young man of about 30 with a manuscript approaching the microphone," O Yong-jin, Cho's personal secretary, later wrote. He "wore a blue suit that was a bit too small for him," and "he had a haircut like a Chinese waiter." The initial cheers gave way to jeers and shouts of "He is a fake!," O said, and an "electrifying sense of distrust, disappointment, discontent, and anger."

Not that Kim seemed to notice. "Oblivious to the sudden change in mass psychology, Kim Il-song continued in his monotonous, plain, and ducklike voice to praise the heroic struggle of the Red Army," O reported. He added that the content of the speech, with its extravagant praise of Stalin and the Soviet Union, was as unpopular as the speaker.[28]

Kim's Soviet handlers were disappointed with the reception, but not discouraged. Instead, they embarked on an intensive propaganda campaign to improve his image. They reframed his youth as an asset, arranging photo opportunities where he wielded a shovel alongside construction workers and rolled up his shirtsleeves to work with farmers in the fields—the epitome of a patriotic young man of the people, pitching in to help rebuild the nation.[29]

In any case, they didn't have a wealth of other options. Soviet relations with their first-choice leader, Cho Man-sik, had soured as he continued to push back against their plans. The exact sequence of events isn't clear, but Cho appears to have been arrested in January 1946 and then he disappeared. He is thought to have been executed four years later, during the early months of the Korean War.[30] By contrast, Kim had proven himself disciplined and obedient during his years in

Khabarovsk and his past service in the Red Army was a major selling point for the Soviet officials. He was a man who followed orders, specifically their orders, and who could be relied upon to do as he was told.[31] His guerrilla background gave them plenty of raw material for propaganda and, perhaps just as important, he had no significant power base of his own.

Unlike Cho, Kim would be dependent on his sponsors and therefore loyal. He was a known quantity for the Soviets, or so they thought. In any case, North Korea was not Europe, which was then at the forefront of Moscow's concerns.

"The name of KIM IL SUNG is known in broad sections of the Korean people," Soviet officials in Pyongyang reported to Moscow in December 1945. "He is known as a fighter and hero of the Korean people against Japanese imperialism," the report said. "With the creation of a popular democratic front, KIM IL SUNG will be a suitable candidate to head it." Immediately below that, they noted, "The Americans have brought in a well-known Korean émigré, SYNGMAN RHEE."[32]

Stalin himself made the final decision. "Korea is a young country. It needs a young leader," he reportedly said as he approved Kim's selection.[33]

Kim's and Stalin's interests now aligned. Stalin needed a popular hero to head up the northern half of Korea, and Kim needed Stalin's help becoming that popular hero. The Soviet propagandists were not prepared to go as far as the North Koreans later would in placing Kim at the head of the liberation force, but they were not exactly squeamish about exaggerating his accomplishments.

"They might have preferred a national hero known to all Koreans, but once they decided on Kim, they promoted and popularized him," wrote Suh Dae-Sook in his biography of Kim. "In the absence of any competing Communist groups and leaders in the North, it was not a difficult task. Kim's obscure past and lack of popularity mattered little."[34] Thanks to the Soviet campaign, Suh said, "A ballad about his heroic deeds in Manchuria, which schoolchildren were forced to sing, eventually became the most popular song in the North. A university was named after him, and poets were mobilized to write poems and stories about his partisan activities against the Japanese."[35]

At first, while he was still dependent on Moscow's support, Kim was careful to credit the Soviet army with leading the final offensive to liberate Korea from Japan. But from the outset he embellished his exploits as a guerrilla fighter and spun wild tales of his supposed feats. "Kim spent all his adult years from the age of nineteen fighting the Japanese," Anna Louise Strong, an American journalist known for her support of Communism, reported after interviewing him in 1947. "He built a guerrilla army of 10,000 men," she wrote, and "raided across the border into Korea, destroying Japanese garrisons." Kim also reimagined the story of his return to Korea, making good on the secrecy he had urged on his companions that first night when he told them to pretend they hadn't seen him. He told Strong he had returned undercover to conduct reconnaissance.

"Kim did not appear publicly in Korea in the first weeks after Japan's surrender," she explained. "Many of his band returned, and the people were asking: 'Where is he?' It was then discovered that Kim had been travelling under an assumed name, taking part in the organization of local governments, in order to get acquainted with his native land, from which he had been an enforced exile so many years." In this rendering, he was welcomed with a triumphant rally fit for a homecoming hero. "A tremendous ovation greeted his first public appearance in Pyongyang," Strong wrote. "He was unanimously chosen first provisional president at the first assembly of delegates from the northern provinces."[36]

This was just the beginning. Over the next four decades, Kim would continue to exaggerate his accomplishments until he was claiming credit for defeating Japan almost single-handedly. His cult of personality would exceed the heights even Stalin's cult reached. And he would build a dynasty that would outlast the USSR. But it all started with this first foundation myth—the idea that Kim Il Sung was a great guerrilla hero who had played a crucial role in the fight to free his country from colonial rule. His son and his grandson would draw on this story repeatedly in the years to come, and soon they would have a second purported victory to add to the family lore.

Back then, the first Kim's priority was simply staying in power. And he was about to take his new country to war.

2

Victory

Victory! For You we fought for almost four years, and now we will never give you up for anything, for anyone.

—*RED STAR* NEWSPAPER, 1945[1]

Nanjing, China

At the end of World War II, China was on the winning side, but not because it had defeated Japan. In fact, when the recording of Emperor Hirohito's surrender was played on the radio there on August 15, 1945, many frontline Japanese soldiers couldn't hear the broadcast clearly and assumed he was urging them on because, as far as they were concerned, they were winning. When the message was clarified, some threatened to kill their officers unless they were allowed to continue the war.[2] Landing at an airfield outside the capital Nanjing shortly afterward, a senior British officer reported a large Japanese military presence, vastly outnumbering their Chinese counterparts and struggling to comprehend the news that they had lost.

"The Japanese army gave me the impression of being extremely tough and dangerous as indeed it had proved itself in battle," wrote Major General Eric Hayes. "There is clearly no realization of the extent of the disaster Japan has suffered. It regards itself, with some reason, as an undefeated army which, to its regret, has been ordered by the emperor to lay down its arms."[3]

If the war was won elsewhere, the other major problem for the Chinese Communist Party (CCP) when it came to retelling this story in the years to come was that it was not involved in most of the fighting. It was the rival Kuomintang (KMT) forces, led by Mao Zedong's enemy Chiang Kai-shek, that bore the brunt of the conflict. And it was Chiang, not Mao, who sat alongside Roosevelt and Churchill in meetings of the Allied powers and presided over the end of the war. The crowds at the victory celebrations in the major cities waved KMT and American flags, not the red banner of the CCP.

"People abandoned their normal reserve and embraced on the streets," one young woman in the KMT's wartime stronghold of Chongqing recorded in her diary. "They danced and laughed. They sang patriotic songs . . . and cries of 'Long Live the Republic of China' [as China was known under the KMT] resounded through the heavens."[4] In Shanghai, US naval intelligence reported that "the Chinese national flag can be seen all over . . . even the U.S. flag had been hoisted. Crowds are welling in the streets and though preventive measures are being taken, apprehension is felt concerning maintenance of public order."[5]

But for Chiang the celebrations were short-lived. His forces had been decimated and the economy devastated by the war. Millions of his citizens were on the verge of starvation. "Armies of homeless, wandering people" were roaming the countryside as they attempted to return to the towns and cities they had fled, reported one aid worker, in many cases on foot because the railways had been so badly damaged. Thousands of miles of track had been torn up, with their wooden crossties burned for fuel and the rails themselves melted down for scrap metal.[6] The KMT had also lost control over large swaths of the northeast of China, which was now under the de facto administration of the CCP.

On paper, China was recognized as one of the victors and awarded one of the five permanent seats at the new United Nations Security Council (UNSC), which was meant to secure the peace, alongside the United States, the United Kingdom, the Soviet Union, and France.[7] But Chiang complained that the country was still being humiliated and treated as a "vassal" by its wartime allies, forced to give up territory without even the pretense of being consulted.[8] By 1945, China was divided, demoralized, and close to disintegration.

Still, the KMT government was determined to go through the rituals of victory. With history in mind, they set the Japanese surrender ceremony in China for nine o'clock on the morning of September 9, 1945—the ninth hour of the ninth day of the ninth month. It was a deliberate attempt to echo the First World War armistice, writes Hans van de Ven in *China at War*, which took effect at 11:00 a.m. on November 11, 1918—the eleventh hour of the eleventh day of the eleventh month—with a date and time that was meant to resonate through the country's collective memory for generations to come.[9] But it would soon be forgotten instead. Plans to hold an annual Victory Day celebration were similarly scrapped.[10] Chiang and the KMT were about to lose power in mainland China and with it, for several decades at least, their place in the country's wartime history.

* * *

Chiang and Mao had formed an uneasy alliance against Japan in 1937, known as the Second United Front, although in practice they fought separately and remained bitterly opposed. But as the foreign threat receded, that alliance collapsed, and China plunged back into civil war.

After the Communist Party's victory in 1949 and Chiang Kai-shek's flight with his remaining forces into exile in Taiwan, the new government in Beijing began to revise the story of the Second World War. Mao had no interest in glorifying Chiang or the KMT—who were presumed to be preparing an attempt to wrest back power from their new base across the Taiwan Strait—and every reason to blacken their names. Chiang was recast as a traitor who had tried to sabotage the Chinese resistance and collaborated with the Japanese, while his officials were depicted as corrupt and his troops ill-disciplined and reluctant to fight, leaving the country weak and vulnerable to attack. In the new version of history, the victory was attributed to the "leading role" of the CCP and Mao's revolutionary tactics.[11]

The gathering storm clouds of the Cold War also hung over official recollections of the conflict as growing hostility overshadowed the previous alliances. In practice, this meant the CCP now emphasized the Soviet role in defeating Japan and downplayed the contribution of the United States, whose troops had been stationed in China for several years. But this was hardly unique to Beijing. Across the former Allied powers, the story of the war was viewed through the prism of contemporary politics.

In the nascent People's Republic of China, Mao shifted the focus to building his new state and glorifying his revolution. The war memorial that had gone up in Chongqing in 1946, known as the Monument to Victory in the Anti-Japanese War, was renamed Liberation Monument after 1949, repurposed as a memorial to the CCP's victory in the civil war.[12] In Beijing, the new capital, memorials to the war with Japan simply weren't built, although there would soon be plenty of statues of Mao.[13] Commemorative ceremonies and local events still took place on the major anniversaries, but as long as Mao was alive the memory of the conflict would be eclipsed by the far greater attention paid to the Communist Party's rise to power.

* * *

This was not an abstract exercise. Real people and real lives were affected by these shifting historical narratives.

Peng Shiliang was about to turn thirty-three when the war started in July 1937. He had a wife and four young children at home, but his granddaughter told me he was determined to fight to defend the country. He had trained at the renowned Whampoa Military Academy and he rose quickly through the ranks to become a general. By 1943, he was in charge of a unit in the central Chinese province of Hunan tasked with slowing the Japanese advance; however, they were badly outnumbered, and it was soon clear they were about to be overrun. Peng volunteered to stay behind to cover his comrades' retreat, even though it would almost certainly mean his own death. He held out for as long as he could to allow them to escape before finally succumbing to his injuries. His granddaughter Zhao Yan showed me a newspaper clipping she had saved that described his actions as the "honorable embodiment of our nationalism" and said ten thousand people had turned out for his memorial ceremony. But Peng had fought for the KMT and after the Communist Party took power in 1949, his war hero status was revoked.

"Before the liberation, they [KMT soldiers] were all called 'national heroes' who died for the country, and for the nation, and its people," Zhao told me, but then, "from 1949 to 1985, he was called a counterrevolutionary."

We were talking in her tiny magazine store, tucked away in a back-street, just off People's Square in central Shanghai. The walls were bare concrete and there was no heat, so Zhao and her husband wore thick, puffy jackets to keep warm. But the lack of space hadn't stopped her from filling it. There were books and magazines piled on every surface and she had decorated every inch of the walls with photographs clipped from their pages. There were pictures of Queen Elizabeth II, Michelle Obama, Gandhi, Vladimir Putin, and Xi Jinping. Where some people might have been reticent to speak to a foreign reporter who showed up unannounced, claiming to be writing a book about the war, Zhao was unperturbed. She immediately ejected her husband from the black vinyl office chair that was clearly the prime seat and insisted I sit down, handing me a bottle of mineral water from a cardboard box and launching into her family's story as though we were old friends picking up where we had left off.

It had been hard for her to understand as a child, she explained. She knew she was supposed to keep quiet about her grandfather, but she wasn't sure what he had done wrong. He had joined the army of the government at the time and died in action during the war, but she was told not to talk about it. The worst years were after Mao launched his Cultural Revolution campaign in 1966, urging young supporters known as "Red Guards" to root out class enemies and anyone deemed to be standing in the way of the revolution. Zhao was in high school at the time. By her own account, she was a conscientious student and, until that point, one of the teacher's favorites, but then the Red Guards in her class found out about her family's KMT past. They singled her out for abuse, bullying her relentlessly, but when she went to the teacher to ask for help, she found that he had turned on her too.

"He said, 'Your grandfather was a counterrevolutionary; he was the Kuomintang,'" Zhao recalled. "The teacher told me, 'You hid deeply, you know, like a spy; you should go to the countryside to be reformed.' When I heard that, I said to myself, 'So I became a counterrevolutionary overnight.'"[14]

Her mother, Peng's daughter, suffered too. She was subjected to re-peated interrogations and self-criticism sessions at the hospital where she worked until she was eventually fired. The family moved around, trying to escape the shame of their past, but they were never quite able to shake the fear that their KMT links were about to be revealed. Zhao loved books and she had dreamed of studying at a top university, but the family's counterrevolutionary designation meant there was no hope of admission. Eventually she settled in Shanghai and came up with the idea of opening her magazine and bookstore instead.

But this wasn't the end of Peng or Zhao's story. In the decades to come, the way he was remembered would change again as the story of the war was rewritten for a second time after Mao's death.

* * *

After the Second World War in the Soviet Union, there was no civil war for Stalin to fight, no equivalent of the KMT to confront, but that didn't mean he was short of enemies. As the paranoid dictator entered his final decade, he saw new plots and potential challengers all around, new dangers at home and abroad. Victory did not bring security for the Soviet leader, but a world of new threats.

News of the German surrender crackled over the radio in Moscow in the early hours of May 9, 1945. Hitler was dead, listeners were told, and the war was finally over. People began pouring out into the still-dark streets to celebrate, embracing each other in joy and relief. The day was declared a national holiday, Victory Day, not that any encouragement was needed.

"May 9th was an unforgettable day in Moscow," British journalist Alexander Werth reported from the Russian capital. "The spontaneous joy of the two or three million people who thronged the Red Square . . . was of a quality and a depth I had never yet seen in Moscow before. They danced and sang in the streets; every soldier and officer was hugged and kissed." Young men, he said, were "so happy that they did not even have to get drunk."[15] At the American embassy, then–deputy chief of mission George Kennan recorded "a holiday mood so exuberant as to defy all normal disciplinary restraints," with an atmosphere of "almost delirious friendship" effectively trapping US diplomats inside the building. "If any of us ventured out into the street, he was immediately seized, tossed enthusiastically into the air, and passed on friendly hands over the heads of the crowd, to be lost, eventually, in a confused orgy of good feelings somewhere on its outer fringes,"

Kennan wrote. "Few of us were anxious to court this experience, so we lined the balconies and waved back as bravely as we could."[16]

The Victory Parade took place six weeks later, on June 24, 1945, with Soviet soldiers returning directly from the front to march through the capital. Stalin had planned to lead the procession on horseback, but after reportedly being thrown off during rehearsals, he opted for the solid ground of the Lenin mausoleum instead.[17] Two of his top commanders, Marshals Georgii Zhukov and Konstantin Rokossovsky, supplied the horsemanship in his place, riding into Red Square at the start of the ceremony on handsome black and white chargers.

"I could feel my heart beating faster," Marshal Zhukov, who had led the assault on Berlin, later confided. He recalled looking across at Rokossovsky as they waited for the signal to start, "who was, I am sure, as nervous as I." It was raining steadily that day, but nobody cared. Zhukov noted the "high spirits" and "elated faces" of the crowds, and his own pride as he studied the "war-scorched gallant faces" of his men. "As I reviewed the troops I could see little streams of rain trickling from the peaks of the men's caps," he wrote. "But the unanimous spiritual uplift was so great that no one bothered to notice it. A particular feeling of jubilation engulfed all those present."[18]

Zhukov praised the courage of the armed forces in his speech, declaring that the Red Army had secured its place in history with an "unfading halo of glory," but he was politically astute enough to add where the real credit lay: "We triumphed because we were led to victory by our great leader and brilliant commander, Marshal of the Soviet Union—Stalin!"[19]

Not that it mattered. The Red Army's halo was about to be snatched away, along with Zhukov's own reputation. Stalin, it turned out, was not prepared to share credit for the victory with anyone, least of all those who had actually fought and risked becoming popular figures in their own right and perhaps a threat to his leadership.

As in China, the losses were staggering. Almost twenty-seven million people died during the war, according to the most recent estimates, although the official figure under Stalin was seven million.[20] And the suffering didn't end with the fighting. Drought and famine ravaged the countryside. Factories, cities, and heavy industry lay in ruins. Families had been torn apart. During the war, it had at least been possible to believe that you were fighting for something—that there would be some future reward for all the hardship—but now that future was here and it was bleak. Living standards were much worse than they had been before the conflict, and all the Communist Party had to offer was more hard work and a new, even more grueling five-year plan to make up the ground they had lost. More worrying still for the leadership was that unlike Chinese troops, who had fought for the most part on their own territory, the Red Army had made its way across Europe to Berlin, exposing millions of its soldiers to living conditions outside the Soviet Union along the way. Stalin was all too aware of the precedent for what might happen when they came home.

"Stalin was a student of Russian history," explained Robert Service in his biography of the Soviet leader. "He knew that the Russian Imperial Army's entry into Paris in 1825 after the defeat of Napoleon had led to political unrest in Russia. Officers and troops who had experienced the greater civic freedom in France were never the same again, and in 1825 a mutiny took place which nearly overthrew the Romanovs."[21] That history could not be allowed to repeat itself. The returning soldiers and their commanders would need to be kept under tight control.

Less than a year after leading the victory parade in Red Square, Zhukov was stripped of his position in disgrace, accused of looting wartime goods for his personal use, and transferred to a remote posting in southern Ukraine. "It was about the same," one American observer said, "as if Mr Truman had sent Eisenhower to take charge of National Guard training in Oklahoma."[22] He was not alone. Senior officers, including aviation industry commissar Aleksei Shakhurin and air force commander Alexander Novikov, twice decorated as a Hero of the Soviet Union, were arrested, interrogated, and imprisoned.[23]

There was a perverse irony to the timing. Just as Stalin's officials were promoting Kim Il Sung as a war hero in North Korea based on his largely fictional accomplishments, at home Stalin was purging his own commanders and downplaying the real battles they had fought. But perhaps they were lucky to escape with their lives.

The Soviet intelligence services had been tasked with monitoring all military leaders after the war for signs of trouble, and on New Year's Eve 1946 they recorded a private conversation between two senior officers that raised serious concerns. General Vasily Gordov, who had served as a commander on the Stalingrad front, and his former chief of staff, General Fedor Rybalchenko, were caught complaining about conditions in the country in what they thought was the privacy of the latter's apartment. "People are angry about their life and complain openly, on trains and everywhere," Rybalchenko confided to his old friend. "Famine is unbelievable, but newspapers just lie. Only the government lives well, while people are starving." He predicted the Soviet Union would lose a war with the West and bemoaned their declining prestige. Gordov raised the possibility of moving abroad. The two men were arrested and later shot.[24]

Military heroes were disappearing from the pages of the Soviet newspapers, too. On the first anniversary of the end of the war, not a single officer's name was mentioned in *Pravda*, the party's mouthpiece. "The Soviet people know that the great victory won by our Motherland in the cruelest of wars that the history of mankind has ever known was above all a victory of our social and state system," the newspaper explained. "It was the result of the wise and far-seeing Stalinist policy of the Bolshevik Party, which prepared the country for active defense and created the powerful Red Army."[25]

Stalin held up the victory as proof of the strength of the Soviet political system, offering only qualified praise for the military. The armed forces should be commended, he said in a speech on February 9, 1946, for having "heroically withstood all the hardships of war . . . and emerged from the war the victor." At this point, according to the transcript, he was interrupted by a voice shouting, "Under Comrade Stalin's Leadership!" and "Loud and prolonged applause, rising to an ovation." But, he continued, "it would be wrong to think that such a historical victory could have been achieved without preliminary preparation by the whole country. . . . It would be still more wrong to assert that our victory was entirely due to the bravery of our troops."[26] Shortly afterward, the Red Army, as it had been known since 1918, was renamed the Soviet Army.[27]

The need to flatter the troops had ended with the conflict. Now the party needed them to get back to work. In April 1946, Andrei Zhdanov, Stalin's chief propagandist, issued a directive to propaganda workers instructing them to dispel the idea that "people should take some time to recover after the war."[28] Too much focus on the wartime past, it was feared, would only remind the population of the hardship they had suffered and the rewards that weren't coming and distract from the pressing issues of the day. On the morning after Victory Day that year, *Pravda* featured the story of a Soviet soldier who returned from the front and immediately devoted himself to working on a collective farm.[29] The message to readers was clear. This was the model they were expected to follow. It was time to move on from the war to the battle to build socialism at home.

The following year the Victory Day holiday was canceled. A short notice in the main newspapers in December 1947 announced that May 9 was now a normal working day.[30]

* * *

The war still had its political uses for Stalin, much more so than was the case for Mao. He didn't want the masses dwelling on their sacrifices or the heroism of individual commanders, but he was quite content to bask in the praise for his leadership.

He was hailed in the Soviet press as the "greatest commander of all ages" and credited with devising a "strategic counteroffensive" that amounted to the greatest contribution ever made to the science of warfare.[31] Presumably this hyperbole inspired some of the early paeans to Kim Il Sung's greatness in North Korea, where Soviet officials were helping to burnish the young leader's image. In Moscow, a new movie, whose screenplay Stalin reportedly edited, showed a defeated Hitler cursing, "Stalin! He brought everyone to their knees." The final scene showed the Soviet leader flying into the German capital in a pristine white uniform, where he was welcomed by crowds of ecstatic soldiers, including some waving American flags. It was, commented one scholar of Soviet propaganda, "the apotheosis of Stalin's Cult of Stalin."[32]

Maintaining the myth of Stalin's wartime heroism meant silencing those who had served under him in case they contradicted the official account. It was "too early to be writing memoirs so soon after these great events," Stalin told one commander, "at a time when passions were still too much aroused, and thus the memoirs would not have the required objectivity."[33] His words sent a chill through the publishing industry and would-be authors took the hint.

"Stalin's attitude not only prevented the publication of memoirs but also stopped people from even picking up their pens," explained Lazar Lazarev, a literary critic who had served in the Red Army during the war. "Everyone understood at once that it was not subjectivism which Stalin feared, but the truth."[34] Some veterans pushed back, publishing wartime diaries that challenged the official myth. "The defenders of the fatherland have the moral right to share with contemporaries these thoughts," argued one former partisan commander in a literary magazine in 1948.[35] But the authorities did not agree.

The censors enforced new restrictions. It was now forbidden to refer to wartime orders such as Stalin's notorious "not one step back" command, which banned soldiers and their units from retreating without explicit permission from higher command, even if it made tactical sense on the ground. Research on the conflict became increasingly difficult as access to the archives was limited. "Historians of the war found themselves in a particularly sorry situation," Lazarev said. "[They] quickly understood that their job was to embroider prepared patterns using beautiful materials to delight the eye, not to conduct research into facts."[36]

Those beautiful materials did not include the terrible realities of the war. The wounded veterans who had returned from the conflict with missing limbs and suffering grievous injuries, thought to number in the millions, began to vanish from the streets of the capital, where many had been reduced to begging to survive. Ahead of the celebrations for Stalin's seventieth birthday in 1949, they were rounded up by the authorities and packed off to live the rest of their lives out of sight, and often without adequate medical care, in "Invalids' Homes" in remote communities.[37] Those who were left were monitored by the security services for signs of political unreliability, in case they began to organize and sow dissent.

Stalin's paranoia and his purges intensified. The political arrests and the show trials resumed. "We thought that after the war everything would change. . . Stalin would trust his people," one woman told the Belarussian writer Svetlana Alexievich. But instead, she said, "After the Victory everybody became silent. Silent and afraid, as before the war."[38]

In Moscow, too, the emerging Cold War shaped how the past conflict was remembered as the atmosphere of "almost delirious friendship" George Kennan described on that first Victory Day in 1945 was replaced by hostility, at least at the official level. The Western allies were dropped from the victory commendations and transformed into "zealous warmongers" in the Soviet press.[39] With a new main enemy to focus on in the United States, the Soviet leadership had little interest in preserving the memory of their past alliance. And the animosity and suspicion went both ways.

The geopolitical fault lines were shifting and the outlines of a new conflict were taking shape. With the CCP in power in Beijing, the new young leader of North Korea petitioned Stalin for his blessing to invade South Korea and unite the peninsula under his control. The Americans wouldn't intervene, Kim assured him, and it would all be over in three days.[40]

3

Enemies

A state without an enemy or external peril is absolutely doomed.

—MENCIUS[1]

North Korea–South Korea Border

The attack started just before dawn on June 25, 1950. Shellfire shattered the darkness. Mortars pounded the ground. The artillery teams mounted a furious barrage as the first North Korean tank units stormed south. It was thirty-five miles from the border to the South Korean capital Seoul.

Kim Il Sung had personally approved the offensive. The plan was to combine the element of surprise with overwhelming force. They would capture Seoul and crush the government's resolve before there was time to summon help from the Americans. By the time it was over, Kim intended to control the entire Korean peninsula.

But that was not what he told his own citizens.

Twenty-four hours into the conflict, Kim addressed the nation in an emergency radio broadcast. In a black suit and a solemn voice, he delivered the grave news that North Korea was under attack. "On June 25, the army of the puppet government of the traitor Syngman Rhee started an all-out offensive against the areas of the northern half of the Republic," Kim said, referring to the leader of South Korea. He told listeners that their own "valiant garrisons" were now "fighting fierce battles to counter the enemy's invasion."

In fact, as Kim was well aware, it was his army that was invading the South. North Korean forces were bearing down on the South Korean capital as he spoke. But the story he told would at least have sounded credible to his listeners. They had lived under Japanese colonial rule until just five years earlier and Kim claimed they were facing another imperialist attack.

"The traitorous Syngman Rhee clique has sold off the southern half of our country as a colony and a military strategic base to the US imperialists," Kim said. They planned to turn the economy over to "US monopoly capitalists," he warned, and "make the entire Korean people slaves of US imperialism." He urged his countrymen to fight for their newly won liberty.

"The entire Korean people, if they do not want to become slaves of foreign imperialists again, must rise as one in the national-salvation struggle," Kim declared. "We must win ultimate victory at all costs."[2]

From those very first hours, Kim lied to his citizens about the war. But like the myth of his earlier guerrilla struggle against Japan, those lies became a critical component of his claim to power. Throughout the conflict and through the decades that followed, Kim claimed that it was a defensive war—that North Korea had been attacked, unprovoked, by its enemies.

Known as the Korean War in the United States, it was called the Fatherland Liberation War in North Korea and held up as evidence of the threats the country faced and the need to build up its military strength. It was North Korea's Pearl Harbor and 9/11 all in one. Seventy years after those first shots were fired, the dynasty's third leader Kim Jong Un would invoke his grandfather's fiction to justify his pursuit of nuclear weapons and missiles that could reach Seattle and Los Angeles as he insisted that they needed to be able to defend themselves.

And the Kims didn't just lie about the start of the war. They went much further than that.

* * *

The Kim Il Sung who took to the airwaves that day in June 1950 was thirty-eight years old and the leader of a country that had existed for less than two years.[3] This was his first real experience of large-scale combat. But as far as his audience knew, he was a battle-hardened guerrilla war hero who had played a crucial role in the fight to free Korea from Japanese control.

Soviet propaganda had flooded North Korea with tales of Kim's heroism since he was first installed as the leader of the young Kremlin-backed regime, as Stalin's officials sought to bolster their man's credentials so that he could hold his own against the better-known Syngman Rhee in South Korea.

Some of the claims were true. Kim really had been a guerrilla fighter—albeit based in China, not Korea—and he had spent the better part of a decade in the struggle against Japan. But the stories of his exploits that were now circulating were greatly exaggerated, although they would be embellished still further in the years to come.

Just as Kim's Soviet patrons were tamping down commemoration of World War II, the annual celebrations in North Korea were ramping up. In 1947, the same year Stalin cancelled the Victory Day holiday in the USSR, the anniversary of the end of the war was celebrated "in grand style" in Pyongyang, according to press reports, where it was—and still is—observed on August 15 and known as Liberation Day. Kim was said to have been greeted with "long, thunderous cheers" as he took to the stage and hailed as a "hero of the liberation of the Korean people."[4] It was a significant improvement from the jeers and confusion that had greeted his first appearance two years earlier and testament to the efforts of the Soviet public relations campaign.

But Kim was not content to rule just the northern half of the Korean peninsula. He had watched Mao sweep to victory across the border in the Chinese civil war in 1949, and he wanted the same glory for himself. He pressed Stalin for permission to invade the South and seize control of the entire peninsula. He was confident that he could win the war in a matter of days, and he predicted the United States would stay out of it.

Perhaps if Kim had fought a large-scale war before or experienced as much conflict as the propaganda claimed, he might have hesitated. But as it was, he believed there was no time to waste. Clashes along the border with South Korean troops were intensifying, and he feared that if he waited, Syngman Rhee would strike first.

Stalin eventually agreed to the plan, but he told Kim he would have to ask Mao for any help. "If you should get kicked in the teeth, I shall not lift a finger," he warned. Mao told Kim not to expect a quick victory, pointing out that his own conflict with the Kuomintang (KMT) had lasted more than a decade. But the younger man shrugged off his advice, insisting he could "solve the Korean problem" on his own.[5]

Apparently convinced that he could win the war and keep the corresponding credit for himself, Kim didn't even bother to inform the Chinese leader of his final plans until two days after he had launched his attack.

With the war underway, Kim sought to rally support at home by framing the conflict as a new battle against imperialist aggression, substituting their old enemy Japan for the United States. He continued to insist that North Korea had been invaded, but he explained the fact that there was no fighting taking place on their own territory in those early weeks by claiming that the Korean People's Army (KPA) had repelled the initial attack and their forces were now pursuing the enemy back south. To cover their tracks, the regime's internal planning documents referred to the offensive as a "counterattack."

"Even after Kim Il Sung dies, you won't be able to find any legal document about an attack," said Yu Song-ch'ol, one of his former officials, after defecting to the USSR. The plan was to claim "that South Korea was attacking us and that we should counterattack," Yu explained. "It was a fake, disinformation to cover ourselves."[6]

"Large spontaneous demonstrations appeared everywhere," reported the Soviet embassy in Pyongyang during the early days of the conflict, according to records in the Russian archives. "The population protested the provocative attack of the South Koreans and demanded that the enemies of the people be answered blow for blow." The Soviet diplomats said workers were rallying outside their factories and vowing to defend their country against the imperialist attack. "We should respond to this crime through combat and defend our Motherland," one man was quoted declaring. "Those who believe in the republic will rise together with all the people to fight."[7] Whether this account was a genuine reflection of public opinion is impossible to say, but it does at least give some sense of the official North Korean and Soviet narratives at the time.

The war started well for Kim, perhaps even better than he had dared imagine. On the second day of the conflict, June 26, the US ambassador to South Korea cabled Washington to report that he was evacuating the embassy in Seoul. "In view of rapid deterioration and disintegration, I am immediately starting evacuation of all females toward south," John J. Muccio said. "All indications are that situation is disintegrating so rapidly that we may not all be able to get out."[8] The following morning, the first North Korean troops entered the city. By June 28, the South Korean capital was under Kim's control.

The South Korean military was in full retreat. As the North Korean invasion force pushed south, Rhee's troops pulled back toward the southeasternmost tip of the peninsula and the port city of Busan. It was beginning to look like Kim's gamble might pay off and he would secure the swift victory he had promised. But his prediction that the United States would stay out of the conflict was wrong.

* * *

The Americans scrambled air, naval, and ground forces. The first troops were in action by July 5, 1950. Two days later, on July 7, the United Nations Security Council authorized the United States to lead a multinational force under the UN flag to repel the North Korean attack. Five-star general Douglas MacArthur, the US commander who had accepted the Japanese surrender in World War II, took charge of the United Nations Command force. In all, sixteen countries sent combat forces. Five more provided medical support.

Three months into the conflict, MacArthur pulled off a daring amphibious landing at Inchon, near Seoul, on September 15, cutting North Korean supply lines and forcing Kim's troops into a chaotic retreat north. The UN forces pursued them back into North Korea, crossing the thirty-eighth parallel on October 8 and taking control of Pyongyang in the following weeks.

MacArthur pushed farther north toward the Yalu River and the border with China, despite repeated warnings from Beijing. Mao deliberated. He didn't want to fight a full-scale war with the United States. The Communist Party had only been in power for a year, the country's economy was shattered, and he wanted to pursue his own offensive against the KMT in Taiwan. But with the US-led forces approaching the border, Mao decided he had no choice but to intervene.

Mao ordered the first Chinese divisions to begin crossing into North Korea on the evening of October 19. "To keep the operation absolutely secret, the troops should start crossing the river every day at dusk and stop at 4:00 A.M.," he instructed.[9] The Chinese troops were to be described as "volunteers" to try to avoid provoking a wider war with the United States. By the end of the month, hundreds of thousands of Chinese soldiers had crossed the border under the command of veteran People's Liberation Army (PLA) general Peng Dehuai.

The massive Chinese intervention turned the tide of the conflict again, driving the UN troops back south where the front line eventually stabilized around the thirty-eighth parallel, almost exactly where the fighting had started. After another two years of grinding, attritional trench warfare, North Korea, China, and the United Nations Command agreed to an armistice on July 27, 1953. But South Korea did not sign the agreement and without a formal peace treaty in place, the conflict was technically only on hold, as it remains at the time of this writing almost seventy years later.[10]

But just as Kim lied about the start of the war, so too he lied about its end. In reality, he had launched an audacious attack to try to seize the entire Korean peninsula and he would have lost the war decisively, likely within the first six months, had it not been for Mao's troops. But the story he told the North Korean public was that it was their country that had been attacked and that they had secured a great victory by repelling the "imperialist aggressors" and forcing the US military to its knees.[11] Photographs of American negotiators looking weary during the armistice negotiations were presented as evidence of how the world's most powerful military had been humbled. In North Korea, the battle to control the narrative of the war was second only to the fighting itself.

As an official North Korean history of the conflict published in 1961 told readers, the "attainment of an armistice in Korea marked a great historical victory for the Korean people and the Korean People's Army over the armed invaders of 16 nations headed by the U.S. imperialists and their hirelings." The work was titled *History of the Just Fatherland Liberation War of the Korean People* and compiled by historians at the Academy of Sciences. "The U.S. imperialists fostering a wild design of world domination mobilized large military forces equipped with modern weapons and used every conceivable, diabolical method to reduce the Korean people to slavery," the text claimed. But instead they had been dealt a "staggering blow," suffering "the most shameful crushing defeat in their history of war."[12]

Through heroic struggle, Kim Il Sung was quoted declaring, they had defended their country from the "invasion of the imperialist armed aggressors."[13]

The early versions of this story credited Chinese troops with contributing to the "victory," although their role receded in later accounts and the regime's historians always stressed the importance of Kim's earlier guerrilla experience. "On the basis of the rich experience and diverse tactics he had accumulated and created in the days of the arduous anti-Japanese armed struggle, he commanded operations and battles in each period and at each stage of the war," another official publication, *Outstanding Leadership and Brilliant Victory*, explained. Thus, "he defeated the US imperialists who had been making a show of their power, believing in their numerical and technical superiority."[14]

It was the second time in a decade that he had supposedly defeated a great power.

"Thanks to the outstanding and seasoned leadership of Kim Il Sung," North Korean readers were told, "our revolutionary armed forces won a great victory in revolutionary wars against two imperialisms—Japan and the United States—in a single generation and demonstrated the heroic mettle of the Korean people to the whole world."[15]

The myth of Kim's heroism in the guerrilla struggle against Japan was embroidered with this new triumph, as his fictional accomplishments were combined and the course of the war reimagined to make it seem as though the outcome was never in doubt. Subsequent generations were told that Kim had led fearlessly from the front and that his leadership had been the decisive factor. This wasn't true. But the devastation the country suffered during the war was all too real and the regime drew on those memories to try to convince the population that they were threatened by a monstrous enemy.

For the millions of North Koreans who lived through the conflict, their only contact with the United States was through the regime's propaganda and the US war planes that rained down death and destruction from the skies. The United States dropped more bombs on the country than in the entire Pacific theater during World War II, including more than thirty-two thousand tons of napalm.[16] The air war was so one-sided that US pilots complained they had run out of targets.

"We were bombing every brick that was standing on top of another, everything that moved," former US secretary of state Dean Rusk, who was a state department official during the war, later acknowledged. "We had complete air superiority. We were just bombing the heck out of North Korea."[17]

"Nowhere in the village have they buried the dead, because there is nobody left to do so," *New York Times* correspondent George Barrett reported from the scene of one bombardment in North Korea in February 1951. "The inhabitants throughout the village and in the fields were caught and killed and kept the exact postures they had held when the napalm struck—a man about to get on his bicycle, 50 boys and girls playing in an orphanage, a housewife strangely unmarked, holding in her hand a page torn from a Sears-Roebuck catalogue crayoned at Mail Order No. 3,811,294 for a $2.98 'bewitching bed jacket—coral.' "[18]

The situation in the capital was desperate. "There are very few houses left in Pyongyang," Polish diplomats in Pyongyang reported in a cable to Warsaw in September 1951. "We saw scenes of despair, for example, children who were pushing aside the rubble with their little hands in search of their mothers." They urged the foreign ministry to send emergency shipments of clothes, medicine, and food. "Half-naked people and naked, haggard children are nesting in caves in the hills," the cable said.[19]

Perhaps if the regime had confined itself to the genuine suffering the conflict wrought, it would still have been able to make its case as to the severity of the threats the country faced. But instead, North Korean historians added a litany of imaginary atrocities they claimed US forces had carried out against civilians.[20]

"The beasts stripped the people naked, bound them together by fours or fives, drove them into a pit at the point of the bayonet, and set fire after pouring gasoline over them," the 1961 history claimed. "The air was filled with the shrieks of the women and children and an offensive smell of burning human flesh." The Americans soldiers were depicted reveling in their victims' suffering. "They clapped their hands gleefully watching the people burning," the text said. "They shot those who crawled out of the pit and eventually closed the pit, burying alive those who were still breathing." One officer was said to have walked away, "whistling a jolly tune."[21]

The most infamous incident in North Korea's history of the war is a massacre the regime claims US forces carried out in Sinchon County, around sixty miles south of Pyongyang. There are indications that a gruesome attack took place in Sinchon, but there is no evidence it was as the regime describes, or that American soldiers were involved or even in the area at the time. Scholars point to inter-Korean violence as the more likely explanation.[22] But that didn't stop the North Korean authorities from retelling the story to future generations and erecting a museum at the site, known as the Museum of American War Atrocities, which would later be rebuilt at great expense by Kim Jong Un.

According to the official narrative, the Americans rounded up hundreds of women and children and locked them in separate warehouses, starving and torturing them for days. When the babies cried from hunger, they were supposed to have fed them gasoline and laughed as they writhed in agony from the toxic poison. Then they were said to have set fire to both buildings, making sure to burn the warehouse that contained the children first so that their mothers could hear their terrified screams as they were burned alive.

"When I first opened the door of the warehouse I found heaps of children's bodies piled up," one purported witness recalled. "The finger nails of most of the children were smeared with blood or torn off. It was obvious that the children had desperately tried to escape from the murderous flames."[23] This account is from the 1961 publication, but it has been reproduced, almost word for word, and falsely presented as fact in the decades since.

"They used all kinds of beastly ways to kill their captives," claimed another official text of the American soldiers, "such as shooting them, stabbing them, crushing them with tanks, boiling them in hot water, making savage dogs tear them apart, beating them, starving them, and freezing them to death."[24] The authors said the violence in North Korea "far surpassed the acts carried out by Hitler."[25]

The point of this almost cartoonish level of violence was to dehumanize the American troops and instill in the population a visceral sense of the barbaric nature of the enemy they were up against. The accompanying images often depicted the US soldiers as evil-eyed, hook-nosed caricatures. Whether or not people really believed these claims, this was the version of history children learned at school as they were taught about the threats Kim Il Sung—and later his direct descendants—were defending them from. As one publication summed it up: "The war clearly revealed the savagery of the U.S. imperialists, beasts in human skins and the man-eaters of the 20th century."[26]

Kim Jong Un would repeat the same story as he toured the site of the purported Sinchon massacre more than half a century later, insisting that the Americans had committed "bestial brutalities." The US forces, he said, were "cannibals seeking pleasure in slaughter."[27]

"North Korea needs the Korean War narrative extremely badly," Balázs Szalontai, professor of North Korean Studies at Korea University and author of *Kim Il Sung in the Khrushchev Era*, told me. The problem the Kim regime has faced through the decades, he explained, is how to maintain the sense that North Korea is under imminent threat of attack from the US despite no such attacks taking place in recent history. "Since 1953, the US has never killed any North Korean soldiers in a deliberate strike," he said. "So they need the war narrative to prove that the Americans are really dangerous and aggressive and destructive and all that, because most of the population has no direct experience of fighting the Americans. There is only the memory."

Stories of the US bombing raids had been passed down through the generations, Szalontai explained, and they were the foundation on which the dynasty built its other claims about the Americans.

"When the war started, only an extreme minority of people knew that it was a decision by their top leadership to start the war," he said. "The overwhelming majority of the population suddenly found himself or herself in a war, and very soon the Americans started bombing all over. If your parents or your grandparents lived during the war, they remember that everything was destroyed and that the US bombed the country to ruins. They bombed it down to the ground."[28]

The regime has worked hard in the years since to keep those memories alive.

* * *

Thae Yong-ho planned his escape from the Kim regime among the tennis courts and suburban family homes of Ealing in West London, where he was posted as North Korea's deputy ambassador to the United Kingdom. He still won't talk about the details and whether British or South Korean intelligence agencies were involved, but one day in the summer of 2016, Thae and his family disappeared. They reappeared six months later in Seoul, surrounded by bodyguards and security officials—such were the threats to Thae's life from his former employer.

When I met Thae three years later on a gray October day in Washington, DC, in 2019, he was still traveling with a bodyguard. Information and voices like his are what the regime fears most, he said, as they undermine the lies it tells its citizens.

"In North Korea, the whole system and society is based on this fabrication and mythology," Thae told me. From their early childhood, he said, they were taught that the Kim family leaders were defending the country and protecting their peaceful republic from its foreign enemies. "All North Koreans are educated and trained that the Kim family are not just ordinary—they are chosen, heaven-sent, and the 'sun' of the nation," he explained. They were said to have sacred "Paektu blood," invoking the fictional battles Kim Il Sung claimed to have fought on Mount Paektu during the guerrilla war, and the supposed birthplace of Kim Jong Il. "It is really, really important to carry on this mythology," he said emphatically.

Thae had grown up hearing the same stories. A charismatic man in his late fifties with a receding hairline and the impeccable manners of a veteran diplomat, he had been raised as a loyal supporter of the Kim regime, like his father and grandfather before him. He had risen through the ranks to become a senior official, with all the status and privilege that conferred, and was considered so trustworthy he was once tasked with escorting Kim Jong Un's brother on a visit to London. But the longer Thae spent outside the country, the more he found himself questioning the system and struggling to reconcile his doubts, until finally he decided to defect in search of a better future for his children. His own trajectory appeared to confirm that if the regime wanted to maintain the myth of the Kim family's heroism, it needed to keep the country isolated and its citizens' access to outside information strictly controlled.

"It is the same pattern with all dictatorships," Thae said. "First, they create an outside threat, which can really threaten the existence of the nation. When you create this kind of threat, then you need a savior. Then, all of a sudden, the Kim family becomes the savior of the Korean nation. That is the way they always do it."

I asked him if he thought the propaganda was effective, whether people really believed it. "I think so, yes," he replied, half-chuckling to himself as though the answer was surely obvious. "That's why they go on for generations."

Thae said he had visited the United States Holocaust Memorial Museum in Washington the day before and been struck by the simi-larities. "I think Hitler also applied the same pattern, you know. He created the external threat and enemies, and then all of a sudden approached the German public as though he was the only savior of the German nation from this outside threat. So it is all the same."[29]

* * *

It was not just the North Korean regime that exploited the history of the Korean War. In China too, the conflict became a crucial element of the revolutionary mythology that helped keep the Communist Party in power. Known there as the "War to Resist US Aggression and Aid Korea," Beijing similarly blamed the conflict on the United States and presented the outcome as a humiliating defeat for the US military.[30] Where World War II would later be depicted as the final act in China's century of humiliation, the Korean War was the first proof of what the country could achieve under Communist rule.

Winning the civil war against the KMT was only the start of the battle for Mao. After declaring the foundation of the new People's Republic of China on October 1, 1949, he still needed to consolidate his authority and convince the broader Chinese public of the necessity of the Chinese Communist Party's (CCP's) leadership. "The majority of Chinese have not rebelled against the [KMT]; they simply have not supported them," reported A. Doak Barnett, a journalist and scholar who was based in China at the time and watched the PLA march into Beijing. "Few Chinese outside of the ranks of the Communist movement itself know what Communism really means," he said, and a "wait-and-see attitude" was widespread.[31]

Internal party reports soon indicated that some of those people were not happy with what they saw. The economy was in ruins, and the responsibility for rebuilding the war-shattered country had transferred to the new government from the KMT. There were troubling accounts of resistance to the Communist Party. In the fall of 1950, anti-party graffiti and pamphlets were found at multiple locations in Shanghai. A new Mao statue in the city was defaced and daubed with the slogan "Defeat Mao Zedong!"[32] Party members in the port city of Dalian reported graffiti denouncing the CCP as "Traitors" appearing in public bathrooms at the central market and on the wall of the Dalian Transportation Company. They cleaned it up, but the slogans soon reappeared.[33]

"We now see reactionary slogans everywhere," complained an official in the northeastern city of Shenyang in November 1950. He said there were reports of sabotage, unrest, and workers walking off jobs. They had found anti-CCP messages "on blackboards in schools, street walls, and telephone poles, and even on the surface of a water pot."[34]

But with the entry of Chinese troops into the Korean War, the party launched an intensive propaganda campaign to rally anti-American sentiment and promote the Great Movement to Resist America and Aid Korea. Large crowds turned out in response, surrounding Western embassies in Beijing and chanting, "Defeat imperialism!" Students at the elite Peking University smeared slogans in support of the war on the walls in their own blood. "The tide of neo-patriotism has swept high, especially in the minds of young people," remarked H. Y. Hsu, the director of an engineering corporation in Hong Kong, after traveling to Guangdong in southern China that fall. "Everywhere in China one hears young people singing anti-American songs, and notices them rush for military training, as they feel that they are fighting for a righteous cause and in order to defend their nation."[35]

Schools and universities were urged to educate their students about US imperialism. Scholars convened study groups. High school teachers taught classes about the history of "U.S. 'invasions' of China since the mid-nineteenth century." Children drew anti-American cartoons in their classrooms. The alliance that had endured through the Second

World War was soon replaced on both sides with Cold War vitriol. "Many very fine students are actually volunteering to leave their middle schools and colleges to respond to 'the call of the fatherland,'" one British visitor to China reported. "Frequently one reads that it is a 'sacred task to resist the U.S.A.' When I asked one student what he was joining, he replied immediately, 'The Air Force to bomb Americans.'"[36]

* * *

Stapleton Roy had just turned fifteen when the Korean War started. As the son of American missionaries in China, he had already lived through his fair share of the country's history. He was in Chengdu as a young child during the Second World War and remembers running to the dugout air raid shelter with his family during Japanese bombing raids. As a teenager studying at the Shanghai American School, he would go up onto the roof with his older brother David and watch the arcs of tracer fire lighting up the sky at night during the final months of the Chinese civil war. He once calmly recounted to me how he had to run for cover when a fighter plane strafed the school courtyard as though this was a perfectly ordinary childhood experience. And he watched the first Communist troops march into Shanghai in the spring of 1949. They set up machine-gun emplacements in the street and loudspeakers on the rooftops that blared out revolutionary songs and propaganda, but at first he felt safe enough as an American and he quite liked some of the music. He and his brother were able to get permission to join their parents in Nanjing soon afterward, where his father taught at the university. "Then the Korean War broke out and everything changed," he told me.

"On June 25, 1950, everything went bad," said Roy, who would go on to play a key role in establishing relations between Washington and Beijing and later serve as US ambassador to China. He remembers how the Chinese authorities blamed the war on South Korea and the United States, claiming that it was North Korea that had been invaded, but that "the North had repulsed the attack and was moving into South Korea to teach the reactionaries a lesson."

His parents understood that the attitude toward Americans was shifting and decided Stapleton and David should leave for the relative safety of Hong Kong as soon as possible. Within two weeks, the children were on a train south, but they weren't out of danger yet.

"On the trip down, suspicious Communist guards came in and started interrogating us," Roy said. He remembered he had a set of Chinese drums in his suitcase and launched into a performance of CCP songs, complete with dance moves, to try to win over the guards and convince them he wasn't an American spy. "I took them out and went ta, ta, ta, ta, da, ta, ta," he said, miming how he had played the drum. "The guy closed up the suitcase and left, no problems whatsoever."[37]

Their parents did not fare so well. With the anti-American campaign intensifying, Andrew Tod Roy and his wife, Margaret, were accused of being imperialist spies and placed under house arrest. A number of their students and former colleagues denounced them and there were calls for them to be put to death. The Roys had devoted their lives to service in China, but now they were reclassified as enemies. After a public show trial, they were forced to sign confessions and expelled from the country in the spring of 1951.[38]

As in North Korea and the Soviet Union, the United States was now designated the main foreign enemy in China, and the fact that they had fought on the same side in World War II no longer mattered. The CCP leadership didn't go as far as Pyongyang in rewriting the history of the Korean War, but they left Kim's initial offensive out of the narrative and cast the conflict as a heroic struggle against US imperialism instead. Beijing, too, accused the Americans of carrying out terrible atrocities against civilians, falsely claiming that the United States had dropped bombs containing insects infested with plague and cholera on North Korea and that they had used biological warfare.[39]

In all three countries, the ruling regimes understood the importance of keeping a tight hold on the wartime past and cultivating a powerful sense of the enemies they claimed to be up against. That history would play a crucial role in the years to come as they found themselves facing serious threats to their survival.

4

Memory

No one is forgotten, nothing is forgotten.
—GREAT PATRIOTIC WAR MEMORIAL, St. Petersburg[1]

Moscow, USSR

Stalin was dead and his memory was under attack. The new Soviet leader, Nikita Khrushchev, denounced the dictator's cult of personality and his reign of terror at the Communist Party's Twentieth Congress in 1956, three years after his death. Khrushchev even criticized his handling of the war. But condemning Stalin was a dangerous gamble for the party. Many of the same officials who had served under him over the past three decades were still in place. Plenty had been complicit in his crimes. The problem the leadership now confronted was how to reckon with the Stalinist past without discrediting the party's continuing rule. There was a serious risk the whole Communist edifice would come crashing down. The answer they came up with in part was to dust off the memory of Lenin, and later the victory in the Great Patriotic War.

Unlike China and North Korea, the Soviet Communist Party had two founding fathers it could call upon. As Khrushchev prepared to attack Stalin, he resurrected the dormant cult of Lenin to help fill the void. In January 1955, a year before he delivered his critical speech to the party congress, Khrushchev signed a resolution moving the annual commemoration of Lenin from the date of his death to that of his birth. It marked the beginning of a new approach to remembering the former leader. Instead of a sorrowful event marking his demise, they would focus on the achievements of Lenin's life and the continuing inspiration he could provide. "Making this date a holiday," Khrushchev said, would reflect "the whole spirit of Leninism as an eternally alive, life-affirming teaching."[2] That spirit would be repeatedly invoked to provide political cover in the years ahead.

Khrushchev's 1956 speech unleashed a campaign of "de-Stalinization." Statues, busts, and the ubiquitous portraits of the dictator were taken down. Stalin was painted out of works of art. Even the "Hero City" of Stalingrad, the emblem of Soviet courage and resistance during the war, was renamed Volgograd after the Volga River. "The name Stalingrad is a glorious name," commented one factory worker at a meeting in the city to discuss the change, according to records in the regional archives. "But we must be governed by reason, not emotion, and we must honestly and directly state that the city cannot bear Stalin's name."[3]

Where once Stalin's cult had eclipsed that of Lenin, now it was the other way around.

The publishing houses churned out new books and collections of Lenin's speeches and essays. There were new paintings and statues. Vast quantities of Lenin badges materialized. Lenin's quotes were held up to attack Stalin's policies and advance Khrushchev's agenda. Lenin's ghost even made an appearance to resolve the issue of what to do with Stalin's physical remains. A diminutive older woman named Dora Lazurkina addressed delegates at the Twenty-Second Party Congress in October 1961 to demand that Stalin's body be removed from the Lenin-Stalin Mausoleum in Red Square. She had consulted Lenin, she said, and he was uncomfortable sharing his resting place with the man who had "brought so much misfortune to the party."[4] The congress ended on October 31, Halloween in many countries, although not traditionally celebrated in Russia, and perhaps a fitting date to reckon with the ghosts of the Soviet past. Late that night two trucks pulled up outside the mausoleum and a team of workers hurried inside. They descended the black granite steps into the crypt and removed Stalin's embalmed corpse from its crystal display case. Working quickly to complete the operation before dawn, they buried him in an unmarked grave beside the Kremlin wall. When the sun came up, Stalin was gone and a temporary sign over the entrance to the mausoleum now read only "Lenin."[5]

Even as Khrushchev revived and reimagined the old cult of Lenin, he claimed to be leading the Soviet Union into a bright new future. The economy was growing rapidly and in May 1957 he predicted they would catch up and overtake the United States in the production of meat and dairy products within a few years.[6] They would soon boast superior technology and living standards too, he said. The successful launch of the Sputnik satellite in October 1957 appeared to demonstrate real progress toward that aim. It shocked Americans and galvanized US officials to intensify their own efforts in the space and arms race, fearing they were falling dangerously far behind. Those fears and Soviet pride surged again when Soviet cosmonaut Yuri Gagarin became the first person to travel into space, successfully orbiting the earth in April 1961. Spontaneous demonstrations broke out in Moscow and Leningrad as triumphant crowds poured out onto the streets to celebrate the Soviet victory.

Repression and official censorship were also eased, during what became known as the Thaw. Khrushchev approved the release of hundreds of thousands of political prisoners and the publication of Aleksandr Solzhenitsyn's novel about life in a Soviet labor camp, *One Day in the Life of Ivan Denisovich*. Based on the author's personal experience, the work was a sensation when it was published in November 1962. But the Thaw and the project of de-Stalinization were never straightforward processes. There was resistance from inside the party and out, and progress was faltering and contested. Even as he boasted that it was his support that had led to the publication of *One Day*, Khrushchev was wary of liberal writers and artists, and at times outright antagonistic toward them.[7]

But Khrushchev's confidence in the Soviet project was such that after decades of being effectively closed to foreigners, he began to allow foreign tourists into the country and Soviet citizens to travel abroad.[8] He agreed to cultural exchanges with the United States and authorized a World Youth Festival in Moscow in the summer of 1957. Tens of thousands of young tourists duly descended on the Soviet capital and the event was soon out of the authorities' control. The streets of Moscow became "impromptu discussion clubs," as scholar Vladislav Zubok put it, with Muscovites engaging the visitors in enthusiastic and wide-ranging debates.[9]

Another surreal encounter took place at the opening of an exhibition of US consumer goods in Moscow in July 1959. Khrushchev toured the exhibits, which included a model American suburban kitchen, with Vice President Richard Nixon and the traveling press pack, pronouncing himself unimpressed with the various gadgets on display. The Soviet leader then launched into a lively exchange with Nixon on the merits of communism and capitalism in what would later be remembered as "the kitchen debate." Khrushchev assured Nixon that the USSR would shortly overtake the United States and then, performing the gesture for the cameras, "wave bye-bye."

But that confidence was soon proved wrong. Not only was the Soviet Union nowhere close to catching up with living standards in the West, but also the experiment with opening up enabled domestic audiences to see how far they had fallen behind. The popularity of shortwave radios had exploded and there were thought to be at least twenty million sets in Soviet homes by 1958, despite Stalin's earlier attempts to ban their production.[10] Now growing numbers of listeners could tune in to popular stations such as Voice of America. They could read novels by Ernest Hemingway and J. D. Salinger in translation through their public libraries. And they could watch major Hollywood movies at the cinema, where the lure of box office receipts increasingly trumped local officials' concerns about ideological purity. "The Tarzan series alone, I daresay, did more for de-Stalinization than all Khrushchev's speeches at the 20th party congress and after," remarked Nobel Prize–winning poet Joseph Brodsky.[11] Writer Vasily Aksenov remembers the experience of watching the films as a "window onto the outside world from the Stalinist stinking lair."[12]

The improved access to information and entertainment from beyond the Soviet borders undermined the party's messaging and its ability to control depictions of the outside world.

There was no letup in the official propaganda, which still bombarded citizens with stories about crime, unemployment, and racial injustice in the United States, as well as the inherent flaws of capitalism. But it was becoming harder to maintain the illusion of communism's superiority, and with it to explain the necessity of the party's rule.

Crucially, for the country's future trajectory, the Thaw also permitted the first concerted efforts to reexamine the heroic myth of the Great

Patriotic War—although, as it turned out, only fleetingly. As long as Stalin was alive, his role as the "greatest commander of all ages," and therefore the inevitability of the victory, had been unquestionable. But Khrushchev's denunciation of the former leader enabled some of those questions to be asked. As well as Stalin's cult of personality, Khrushchev had condemned his purge of the officer corps ahead of the conflict and his failure to prepare for the German invasion. These attacks provided cover for Soviet authors to explore the chaotic retreats and terrible losses that had characterized the early months of the fighting and the harrowing reality behind the glorious victory. The most notable example was the renowned war correspondent Konstantin Simonov, who published *The Living and the Dead* to great acclaim in 1959. It was the first in a trilogy of novels based on his own wartime diaries and interviews with former front-line soldiers, and where such a work would have been unthinkable under Stalin a decade earlier, now Simonov was inundated with letters from veterans commending his lifelike depiction of the fighting. Even Vladimir Putin later recommended the novel as part of a reading list for Americans seeking to understand the Soviet experience of the war.[13]

For the hardliners, who had never approved of Khrushchev's denunciation of Stalin in the first place, however, he had gone too far. "No one enemy brought us so much harm as Khrushchev did in his policy towards the past of our party and our state, and towards Stalin," Dmitry Ustinov, the official in charge of the Soviet defense industry, subsequently complained. General Petr Grigorenko, a decorated veteran of the Great Patriotic War who had been wounded in combat, accused Khrushchev of "dancing the cancan on the tomb of the great man."[14]

After a decade in power, Khrushchev was unpopular. He had brought the Soviet Union to the brink of nuclear war with the United States during the Cuban Missile Crisis, resulting in what was widely seen in Moscow as a humiliating defeat. He had lurched through crises over the Suez Canal and Berlin and presided over the breakdown of relations with the Communist Party in China. At home, he had divided the party into industrial and agricultural wings against the wishes of provincial party bosses and, far from overtaking the United States, Soviet citizens were standing in breadlines again. But it was

Khrushchev's domestic political maneuvering that sealed his downfall. Fearing for their own positions, Leonid Brezhnev led a group of plotters that included the head of the KGB and leading members of the ruling Presidium to remove Khrushchev from power on October 13, 1964.

Confronting the leader with their superior numbers and their complaints, which included accusations that he was building his own personality cult, Khrushchev's colleagues warned him not to put up a fight. "It's over," he told his son when he returned home that night.[15] At least, unlike previous eras, this meant that he was being pensioned off rather than a more serious fate.

Khrushchev's departure signaled the end of the Thaw and the ebbing tide of de-Stalinization. It also meant the end of the experiment in reexamining the history of the Great Patriotic War for the next quarter century. The memory of the conflict would play a critical role in the years that followed, but in a very different way than it had under Khrushchev, as his successors made a decision whose effects would be felt for decades to come.

On a bright spring morning in May 1967, a solitary armored personnel carrier rumbled through the streets of central Moscow. It was guarded by a phalanx of motorcycle escorts in military uniform, their expressions solemn, eyes fixed firmly ahead, as they formed a protective ring around the dark green hull. Large crowds gathered by the side of the road to watch them pass. In front of the Kremlin, a cluster of men in dark suits stood waiting, arrayed in order of importance around the stocky figure of the new general secretary, Leonid Brezhnev.

The armored car contained the most sacred of cargoes. Inside was a portion of the eternal flame from the revolutionary martyrs' cemetery in Leningrad, where the heroes of the October revolution that brought Lenin to power in 1917—along with the subsequent civil war—were buried. The symbolic fire had burned in their memory for the last five decades, but now it was being transported more than four hundred miles to light a new flame at a new monument in the heart of the capital, which the party leadership hoped would kindle a new source of public support for its rule.

The destination was the new Tomb of the Unknown Soldier commemorating the fallen from the Great Patriotic War. The remains of a Soviet soldier had been exhumed from the site of the Battle of Moscow, where the Red Army fought Hitler's troops in the winter of 1941–1942, and reburied with full military honors at the new memorial the previous year. All that was needed to complete it was to light the new eternal flame.

That the Soviet Union had built a memorial like this was not unusual. Many countries had their own similar ceremonial tombs and cenotaphs. What was strange was that it had taken them so long to do it, that this was all happening two decades after the end of the war, long after the fallen were supposed to have been laid to rest. But this was a reflection of how official attitudes toward the war were shifting. Stalin had canceled the Victory Day holiday and claimed the credit for himself. Khrushchev's tenure had allowed a more critical examination of the conflict's history. Now Brezhnev was embarking on a new approach as he set about building what would become known as the cult of the Great Patriotic War and rise to the status of a national religion under Putin in the following century. This new memorial would function as its central shrine.

The famous fighter pilot and Hero of the Soviet Union Aleksey Maresyev carried the torch with the eternal flame the final few yards and presented it to the waiting Brezhnev, who turned and mounted the steps of the monument alone. He lowered the torch to a gleaming bronze star at its center, lighting a new flame that has burned there ever since.

It was both a symbolic and an actual passing of the torch as the Communist Party turned to the memory of the conflict to bolster its appeal. In case anyone had missed the symbolism, Moscow party boss Nikolai Yegorychev spelled it out. "This fire," he said, "transfers across an entire half-century the undimmed flame of [the] October [revolution]. . . . It is as if the soldiers of the Revolution and the soldiers of the Great Patriotic War have closed ranks into one immortal rank."[16]

The leadership hoped these combined forces would now defend the party's position in power.

By the mid-1960s, the revolution was almost half a century old and the promised socialist utopia no closer to reality. Lenin's portrait and his quotes were all around. But that ubiquity was not the same as genuine enthusiasm. Even as they ordered up new busts and tributes to the former leader, the party was searching for new ideas to cement its popular support. Brezhnev's stolid personality made him a poor candidate for a new charismatic leadership cult. And as future leaders would similarly find, other than the early achievements of the space race, there was little in recent decades to celebrate. The economy was growing and living standards had improved, but they still lagged far behind the West. So it was perhaps not surprising that the new administration invested so heavily in the memory of the war.

Lenin had long provided an important source of legitimacy for the party, explained historian Nina Tumarkin, who researched the cults of Lenin and the Great Patriotic War for her books *Lenin Lives!* and *The Living and the Dead*. When Brezhnev took over, there was "really a very full-blown cult" of Lenin, she told me. "I wouldn't say that people were enthusiastic about it, but it was virtually everywhere." The idea was to reinvigorate popular support by combining the memory of the war, which stirred strong emotions, with that of Lenin. "The centennial of Lenin's birth was coming up in 1970," Tumarkin said. "So in a sense it was supposed to bring together symbolically the martyrs and the people who had died in the revolution, and by implication perhaps the Red Army during the civil war, with the people who had died in the Great Patriotic War."[17]

Six months after ousting Khrushchev, the new collective leadership headed by Brezhnev reinstated the Victory Day holiday to celebrate the end of the conflict.[18] The twentieth anniversary was approaching on May 9, 1965, and with just over two weeks to go, the ruling Presidium announced that there would be a massive parade through Red Square to mark the occasion. This was not quite as formidable an undertaking as it might sound. Instead of staging a completely new event from a standing start, the plan was to move the traditional parade celebrating Workers' Day on May 1 to May 9 for Victory Day, which was itself an indication of the symbolic shift taking place. As well as covering the May Day holiday on May 1 that year, the television news bulletins noted that it was also the date of the storming of the Reichstag.[19] But from the outset there was an improvised quality to the arrangements that suggested the Kremlin was piecing together the plan as it went along.

The order to move the parade was issued on April 15, giving officials a mere twenty-four days to organize the logistics, with the final details still being worked out in the hours beforehand.[20] But while the planning was necessarily last minute, it was also incredibly ambitious. As Russian cultural historian Jeremy Hicks explains in *The Victory Banner over the Reichstag*, the party "aimed to engage every possible level of society in some dimension of the commemorations." There was an extensive press campaign, plans to publish new books and articles, and a film festival screening movies and documentaries about the war that was meant to involve "every cinema and film club in the land."[21] Television coverage was an essential part of the spectacle, as it allowed viewers to tune in across the country. The authorities experimented with a new program called *Minute of Silence*, which was actually more like fifteen minutes long, on the evening of Victory Day, featuring somber music and footage of the eternal flame flickering in honor of the fallen. It was reportedly so effective that normally stern-faced officials openly wept as they watched and approving letters flooded into the Soviet broadcast agency.[22]

"You can see that they are trying out these ideas and formats for communication," Hicks told me of the 1965 event. "This idea for the *Minute of Silence*, for instance, was something they tried and then they went and interviewed people and examined how it had gone down. And in this case, it was so popular that it then became an absolute staple of Russian memory culture." His research in the Russian archives found indications of both genuine grassroots support for the idea of commemorating the war and a degree of trial and error on the part of senior officials in figuring out the precise approach. "Again and again," Hicks said, "I found that these things were a little bit more chaotic than you might think."[23] What is clear is that the memory of the war resonated with ordinary citizens in a way that, increasingly, Lenin and the endless paeans to his great teachings and glorious revolution did not. The strategy, Hicks explained, was to create a "comfort blanket of memory" around an event the whole country could agree on.[24]

Despite Stalin's decision to cancel the Victory Day holiday, veterans had continued to meet and hold their own commemorations. And while the renewed focus on the war was engineered from above, it was tapping into authentic enthusiasm and widespread support from below. The party needed something to rally public support behind and the war was the best available option at the time.

Brezhnev was not the first to come up with this idea. From the Peloponnesian War in Ancient Greece to the revolutionary wars in the United States and France and the world wars of the twentieth century, leaders have invoked the memory of the fallen to appeal to the living. And there has long been a political component to memorial ceremonies. In the United Kingdom after the First World War, for instance, in addition to acknowledging the genuine grief and the scale of the losses, "the country was seething with unrest, and the government feared that bolshevism might gain a foothold in Britain," explains George Mosse in *Fallen Soldiers: Reshaping the Memory of the World Wars.* Therefore, "It was felt that everything possible should be done to use the victory to work up patriotic feeling."[25] A cenotaph, or empty tomb, was unveiled in London in 1920 to honor the war dead, and King George V demonstrated his personal respect by walking behind the gun carriage bearing the remains of a British soldier to be laid to rest at the new grave of the Unknown Warrior in Westminster Abbey. Sacrificing your life for your country was held to be such a noble and venerable deed that the soldier was buried among the kings and queens of centuries past. Mosse described a "cult of the fallen" in Britain and France at the end of the war, which had its roots in the same impulse that drove the later commemoration of conflicts in the Soviet Union, China, and North Korea—the need to cultivate a shared sense of patriotism and support for those in power in an attempt to keep them there.[26]

Two decades after the end of World War II, the Soviet leadership began constructing its own cult of the fallen, or in this case, a cult of victory. And if they were later than some in beginning the task, Brezhnev's officials set about it with a sense of urgency. They minted new medals for veterans and built a series of new war memorials across the country, which was how the senior ranks of the Communist Party came to be waiting to at the new Tomb of the Unknown Soldier in Moscow on that bright May morning in 1967.

From Magnitogorsk in the Ural Mountains to Murmansk in the Russian arctic, colossal new monuments went up featuring heroic Soviet soldiers in the socialist realist style (which in practice was more propagandistic than realistic), all chiseled hulk and resolute jaws. The most famous was *Rodina Mat*, or "The Motherland Calls," in Volgograd, which was completed in October 1967. Depicting the Motherland as a ferocious female warrior with her sword raised, beckoning her countrymen to follow her into battle, she towers over the city at close to a hundred meters tall, the tallest statue in the world at the time.[27] Many of the new memorials were inscribed with the words of the poet and Leningrad siege survivor Olga Berggolts: "No one is forgotten, nothing is forgotten"[28]—although in fact this wasn't true. The version of the war the party now wanted to remember involved forgetting plenty.

"Those of us who had fought in the war thought, at first, that at last the war was getting the attention it merited," literary critic Lazar Lazarev, who had served in the Red Army, wrote. "But in fact that attention was purely an official attempt to turn the war into a show made up of concocted legends."[29] Like the towering new monuments with their idealized warriors, the focus was meant to be on the glorious victory and the stories that provided a shining vindication of the Soviet political system, not the suffering and the reality.

In general, the Twenty-Third Party Congress decided in 1966, there should be "less gloom" in depictions of the Stalinist past and discussion of the war.[30] In practice, this meant that what scope there had been to research the darker aspects of the war and Stalin's culpability shut down. Where Konstantin Simonov's previous novels, *The Living and the Dead* and *People Are Not Born Soldiers*, published in 1959 and 1962, had been praised for their realistic portrayal of the conflict, the third in his trilogy, *One Hundred Days of War*, was banned by the censors in 1966. The very quality that won him acclaim in the past—his firsthand experience and his extensive interviews with veterans—was now criticized. Glavlit, the official censorship body, called the work "catastrophic" and complained that he "relied on personal impressions" to inform his narrative.[31] At a meeting of the Politburo, senior officials attacked Simonov and others for producing "slanderous" accounts that "debunked the history of our party and people."[32] It had taken just a few years for official attitudes to the wartime past to shift and the policies of the Thaw years to be reversed.

"The truth must be founded on some kind of ideological line," insisted an official from the military archives during a meeting to discuss Simonov's work. Research on the war should focus primarily on heroism and "feats," he said.[33] His comments foreshadowed similar remarks by Vladimir Putin's minister of culture, Vladimir Medinsky, fifty years later, who claimed that protecting the image of Soviet heroism during the war was more important than the truth. "Even if this story were made up from start to finish," Medinsky said in 2016 over a famous story involving a tank battle on the outskirts of Moscow that turned out to be fabricated, "even if there had been nothing at all, this is a sacred legend, which simply cannot be touched." He later added that it would be "amoral" to conduct any further research.³⁴ Like Brezhnev, Putin would decide that maintaining the glorious myth of the Soviet victory mattered more than the facts.

As it was, portrayals of the war under Brezhnev were becoming increasingly fanciful. "We were supposed to paint a pretend reality consisting of champions and exemplars," painter Nikolai Solomin told historian Nina Tumarkin. "Soldiers had to look like perfect heroes. I remember once I painted some soldiers at rest, with their sub-machine guns pointing down. My superiors ordered me to repaint the scene with those guns pointing up." Even in art, Tumarkin wrote, "the men were to appear ready for battle."³⁵

The Military Publishing House took charge of censoring all memoirs about the war and stripped out all traces of the disastrous early months and Stalin's failure to prepare for the attack. "Not a word could be published about the catastrophic defeats of 1941 or the real reasons they occurred," Lazar Lazarev, the literary critic and veteran, recalled, "nor was a whisper permitted about the astonishing fact that three times as many officers in the Soviet army and navy high commands died in the Stalinist purges of 1937–38 as were killed by Nazi bullets and bombs throughout the war."³⁶ Even the most celebrated military commanders, he explained, soon found that their memoirs had "as much hope of surviving the savage ministrations of this special commission as a camel of passing through the eye of a needle."³⁷

The permitted narrative of the war also excluded the fact that Jewish citizens had been specifically targeted by the Nazis. Rather than focusing on the horrors of the Holocaust that were revealed with the end of the war, Stalin had stoked a new campaign of anti-Semitism and the official Soviet account insisted that Hitler attacked the USSR in general, rather than any one group in particular. As Stanford University historian Amir Weiner recounts in *Making Sense of War*, when Yad Vashem, the Holocaust archival center in Jerusalem, wrote to the Soviet government in 1965 to request documents on the fate of Soviet Jews, they were told that the archives "relating to the crimes of German fascism in World War II are not organized according to the nationality of the victims."[38]

Stalin's own role in the conflict was still a sensitive subject. There was no getting around the fact that the war was won under his leadership, but then he had also decimated the senior ranks of the military beforehand, refused to believe that Hitler would attack, and left his troops to suffer heavy losses when he did. Brezhnev halted the de-Stalinization campaign, but he also held off on a full-scale revival, continuing to refer to his "serious mistakes" as well as his "revolutionary merits."[39] This was not unlike the formula future Chinese leader Deng Xiaoping would arrive at for Mao Zedong, stressing that his contributions were "primary" and his mistakes "secondary."[40]

There were rumors during the early Brezhnev years that Stalin's corpse was about to be restored to the Lenin mausoleum in Red Square. This didn't happen—and perhaps was never a real possibility after he had already been buried for so many years—but a large gray stone bust was installed above his grave in the summer of 1970. It was a compromise that reflected his place in this revised version of history. Stalin would not be ignored. His memory would be treated with respect. But there would be no new Stalinist cult. Although his image would be further rehabilitated under Putin in the years to come.

The new cult of victory under Brezhnev was meant to inspire patriotism and, more important, loyalty to the party and faith in the Soviet system. Past efforts to commemorate the conflict had been led by the older generation who had lived through it and the former front-line soldiers who still wore their uniforms and medals on the major anniversaries. But now the authorities made a concerted effort to appeal to younger citizens and to instill the desired lessons from the war in the country's youth.

The government introduced a program of "military-patriotic indoctrination" for schoolchildren in 1967, the same year the eternal flame was transported to Moscow and the new Tomb of the Unknown Soldier was unveiled. Schools set up rooms of "combat glory" that displayed artifacts from the conflict, such as uniforms and photographs of past students who had served in the war. Medal-wearing veterans toured classrooms to talk about their heroic exploits. It was essential to instill in students the "readiness to defend the great socialist country" and the "willingness to die for it if it becomes necessary," instructed one school teaching guide published in the education journal *Sovetskaia Pedagogika* in 1967. Teachers, it said, should also strive to cultivate "hate towards the enemies of the country."[41] This process was meant to start on the first day of school, with every subject expected to contribute to the student's patriotic education.

"Soviet schools taught what may be described as the 'patriotism of everything,'" explained sociologist Anna Sanina in *Patriotic Education in Contemporary Russia*. "Geography lessons highlighted the battles that took place in different Soviet territories during the Great Patriotic War. Math classes provided a variety of examples of applied problems related to the 'extensive building of communist society.' Music lessons were based on classic Soviet compositions, mostly on military themes."[42] Students were asked to write essays on topics such as "The Glory of Those Days (World War II) Will Never Die" and "The Enthusiasm of Draft-Age Youth."[43]

It was an attempt to use the past to inoculate students against the contemporary threats to the Communist Party's rule, such as the appeal of Western living standards and greater personal freedoms, and the continuing failure of socialism to catch up. As it would be in China and North Korea over the coming decades, the victory in the Second World War (or what North Korea claimed as a victory) was presented as a singular achievement that should stir pride in the country and mobilize support for its leadership.

Soviet youth organizations worked hard to bring the subject to life and inspire the required sense of patriotism. Groups such as the Young Pioneers and the Komsomol staged large-scale war games and took part in weapons training with the Soviet military. "Armed with mock rifles, machineguns, hand grenades and artillery, the youngsters battled to a 'decisive victory,'" the report of one such exercise recorded. Elite paratroopers staged "mock air attacks," parachuting into the battlefield to add to the spectacle, and in the summer of 1971 the Soviet Navy helped participants replicate a series of amphibious landings. Millions of teenage volunteers marched off to the countryside every summer to search for war graves with active-duty and retired military personnel as part of the Red Pathfinders movement.[44]

Brezhnev also seized on the history of the war to boost his own image, although he took this idea to ludicrous extremes. With each new anniversary, the glittering array of medals on his chest increased, and the stories of his heroism grew more improbable. He published a trilogy of memoirs, which were highly embellished and almost certainly ghost-written. Brezhnev had served as a political commissar during the war (the officer responsible for ideological discipline among the troops), and the closest he came to any real action was during an obscure battle at Malaya Zemlya in southern Russia in 1943. But to read his memoirs, commented *The Guardian*'s literary critic, you would think he was the hero of Steven Spielberg's *Saving Private Ryan*.[45] The young Brezhnev is thrown into the air by an explosion, holds off the advancing Germans all but singlehandedly with his machine gun, and displays extraordinary courage under fire. It was so over the top that one popular joke from the 1970s, recounted Moscow-based scholar Sergei Medvedev, was to ask: "Where were you during the war? Did you fight at Malaya Zemlya, or were you just sitting around in the trenches at Stalingrad?"[46]

As the profile of the war soared, the Soviet economy was heading in the opposite direction. Growth stalled in the early 1970s as the combined effects of massive military spending and the limits of the command economy became clear. The promise of the early Brezhnev years gave way to the long years of stagnation that would become synonymous with his rule. But the less assured the future looked, the more the party turned to the memory of the sacred victory in 1945.

One of those who went through the Soviet patriotic education system—and later pronounced himself a "pure and utterly successful product" of it—was Vladimir Putin.[47] Born five months before Stalin died, he completed his early schooling during the Khrushchev years, and high school under Brezhnev. He would have been twelve when the Soviet Union brought back Victory Day. Little could he have known how much he would come to depend on the mythology of the war when he got his own chance at power thirty-five years later. Brezhnev could at least still claim to be the leader of one of the world's great superpowers, whereas the USSR would be long gone by the time Putin entered the Kremlin.

5

Victims

Chinese modern history is a history of humiliation.

—CCP CENTRAL COMMITTEE, 1994[1]

Beijing, China

Just before midnight on June 3, 1989, nineteen-year-old Wang Nan slipped out of his apartment on the outskirts of Beijing and set off toward Tiananmen Square. As his mother later told journalist Louisa Lim, a neighbor saw him leaving with his schoolbag over one shoulder and his red motorcycle helmet in his hand. He left behind a note that said, "Mom, I've gone to find my classmates."[2]

It was a dark night, which was not a coincidence. The People's Liberation Army (PLA) had deliberately selected the darkest night of the lunar month to carry out this operation and Deng Xiaoping had given them the final go-ahead that afternoon to "do whatever was necessary" to restore order and clear the square.[3] Tens of thousands of student protesters had been demonstrating in the capital for weeks calling for democratic reforms, free speech, and a free press. Only strength, Deng believed, would end the crisis and restore the Communist Party's authority.

That evening state television and radio stations began broadcasting emergency bulletins. They ordered people in Beijing to stay inside their homes to "safeguard their lives."[4] Government loudspeakers around Tiananmen Square instructed the protesters to leave immediately, warning that the safety of those who remained "could not be guaranteed."[5]

Inside the Great Hall of the People, the cavernous building on the western side of the square where the Communist Party held its congresses, a concealed force of PLA soldiers waited for the order to move out. Most were young recruits who had never fired their weapons outside the training grounds, let alone at their fellow citizens. They were told that counterrevolutionary riots had broken out and it was their job to end the disturbances and enforce martial law. Their commanding officers passed out live ammunition. Waiting behind the heavy ceremonial doors that led to the square, one of the soldiers later recalled, he gripped his gun so tightly that his hands started to shake.[6]

The protesters held an emergency vote and decided to leave Tiananmen Square in the early hours of the morning, but it was already too late. PLA units converged on the square from all directions. Tanks and armored personnel carriers rumbled toward them along the Avenue of Eternal Peace and the soldiers inside the Great Hall of the People streamed out into their midst. "The troops surrounding the Square began firing indiscriminately," one witness told scholar Timothy Brook. "Stray shots flew around the Square. A girl who was about three meters away from me suddenly went down with a bullet in her head."[7] The precise figure might never be known, but the most reliable estimates put the number of people killed that night between 300 and 2,600.[8] Thousands more were said to have been wounded. Most died not in the square itself but in the surrounding streets.

A taxi driver near the northwest corner of Tiananmen Square saw a young man in a red motorcycle helmet taking photographs of the advancing troops. A slender teenager with thick, plastic-rimmed glasses and a ready smile, Wang Nan had decided he wanted to be a photographer and he had started riding the bus into the city center between classes to document the protests, saving up his money to buy more film. The taxi driver told his mother, Zhang Xianling, that he saw the young man step forward to take a picture and then crumple to the ground as the soldiers opened fire. As she later recounted to Lim, who documented the case in *The People's Republic of Amnesia*, Zhang managed to track down more witnesses and discovered that several people had tried to help her son. He was bleeding badly from a head wound and an old lady had pleaded with the soldiers to let them save him. But the soldiers said they would shoot anyone who came any closer. Ten days later, after searching more than twenty different hospitals, Zhang heard that a body matching her son's description had been found in a shallow grave outside the entrance to a school. It was Wang Nan.[9]

Five days after the crackdown, while Zhang was still searching desperately through hospitals for her son, Deng addressed the PLA. He congratulated his commanders on accomplishing their mission and offered his condolences for their losses. "They went to their death unflinchingly, worthy of the title of heroes," he told senior officers in a speech on June 9, 1989. He said their actions showed "that the people's army is truly a great wall of steel guarding the Party and the country."

Deng didn't mention the unarmed civilians they had killed, the tens of thousands of students who had marched peacefully, or the ordinary workers, including government workers, who had joined them. Instead, he blamed the unrest on "rebels," the "dregs of society," and a "handful of bad people" who wanted to overthrow the Communist Party and establish a "bourgeois republic, an out-and-out vassal of the West."[10] He was already manipulating the history of the protests and reframing the decision to crush them as a necessary and patriotic act to protect the country's development and security.

The party's propagandists focused on the soldiers who died instead of the students. The protesters were reimagined as a bloodthirsty, violent mob, the troops as selfless patriots. They illustrated those claims with footage of wounded soldiers and one image in particular of a soldier who had been killed, strung up, and set on fire. The photo was as ubiquitous in official media outlets for a time as that of "Tank Man" in the West, the unidentified man seen facing down a line of tanks. But the whole event soon faded from the headlines in China as the party began to play down its significance.

What was initially described as a counterrevolutionary rebellion was downgraded to "turmoil" in Chinese publications and eventually just the "June 4th incident" when it was mentioned at all.[11] "Westerners would forget," Deng had assured officials before the crackdown, and the lure of the Chinese market was such that foreign business owners would soon persuade their governments to ease sanctions.[12] One year later, General Secretary Jiang Zemin dismissed the violence as "much ado about nothing."[13]

But the Communist Party would not forget the lesson it had learned. "Deng faced a public that had expressed more open opposition to the top leadership of the party than at any time since Communist rule began," historian Ezra Vogel wrote in his biography of Deng Xiaoping. "The use of force on June 4 intimidated the public into compliance, but it had only deepened the chasm between the party and the people. The morale of the military was also low; soldiers felt anything but heroic for having killed innocent civilians to help the party retain power and recruitment was down."[14]

There were deep divisions among the top ranks of the party, meanwhile, about the direction economic reform should take.

Deng was fighting on multiple fronts: to keep the party together, to keep the economy growing, and to persuade the Chinese people that they needed the party's leadership at all. The use of force had bought them time, but force alone would not keep them in power.

"During the last ten years our biggest mistake was made in the field of education," Deng told his commanders in his first speech after the crackdown, "not just of students but of the people in general." Memories of the bad old days were fading, he explained, among a population that now demanded better living standards and more of a say in their future and how the country was run. "We didn't tell them enough about the need for hard struggle, about what China was like in the old days and what kind of country it was to become," Deng said. "That was a serious error on our part."[15]

If the party wanted to stay in power, it would have to overhaul its political and ideological work and make the past better serve the regime. The party needed to convince the Chinese people how much the country had suffered before 1949 and how far they had come under its rule. The result was one of the most audacious attempts at mass reeducation in Chinese history.

* * *

The Tiananmen protests were the most visible sign of trouble, but by the late 1980s, the Communist Party confronted a broad crisis of faith. The old ideology was bankrupt and the revolutionary slogans had long since lost their effect. After Mao's death in 1976, Deng and the party elders declined to denounce him as Khrushchev had done Stalin. In China, there was only one founding father and no Lenin figure to fall back upon after all. Instead, they attempted to draw a line under his leadership with a resolution in 1981 declaring that Mao was a "great Marxist and a great proletarian revolutionary, strategist and theorist," whose "merits are primary and his errors secondary."[16]

But his legacy was complicated. Much of the population had lived through his decades in power, and while he still drew crowds of devoted followers, recent history was strewn with examples of the terror and chaos he had presided over. At least thirty-six million people had died in the Great Famine of the late 1950s and early 1960s, according to historian Yang Jisheng, following Mao's disastrous attempt to crash industrialize the Chinese economy known as the Great Leap Forward.[17] His final campaign—the Great Proletarian Cultural Revolution— unleashed ten years of violence, social upheaval, and economic chaos starting in 1966 that only came to an end with his death. The party didn't want to distance itself from Mao, but neither could it rely solely on appeals to his memory.

The economy was growing, but so was income inequality, inflation, and dissatisfaction with the authorities, particularly among the younger generation. Student protests during the winter of 1986–1987 had called for political reforms and there were signs of increasing resistance to the party's messaging.

When researchers from Beijing's municipal party committee asked university students in 1988 what they thought were the most important ideals to cultivate, only 6 percent answered "Communism" and 5 percent "Socialism." That was down from an already troubling 38 percent and 15 percent in 1986. The vast majority—79 percent of respondents in 1988—said that the values that mattered most to them were patriotism and the ability to "rely on one's own skills to survive."[18] Peking University, the country's most prestigious institution, announced in 1986 that it was cutting the study time devoted to Marxism-Maoism theory by as much as 40 percent to make room for other subjects.[19] And it was not just young people who were losing interest in Communist ideology.

Communism was "now of interest to hardly anyone in China outside the political elite," said Suisheng Zhao, professor of international studies at the University of Denver and author of *A Nation-State by Construction: Dynamics of Modern Chinese Nationalism*. In fact, he said, it was seen as "self-destructive and guilty of miring the Chinese in socioeconomic wretchedness and as having kept China poor and backward."[20]

Even party-run outlets reported doubts among the public as to whether "socialism can really save China" and complaints that "socialism cannot match capitalism."[21] These sentiments had been building for the better part of a decade since the start of the reform period under Deng. "Many people feel that there is more or less nothing to believe in," said an article in the *Workers' Daily* newspaper as early as 1979, foreshadowing similar complaints that would follow in the Soviet Union under Mikhail Gorbachev. "They don't believe in Marxism-Leninism and Mao Zedong Thought, the leadership of the Chinese Communist Party (CCP), the superiority of socialism, or the brilliant prospect of Communism."[22]

By the time the first students marched into Tiananmen Square in the spring of 1989, the international outlook for Communism was increasingly ominous too. Opposition to Communist rule in Eastern Europe was gathering strength and Mikhail Gorbachev said the Soviet Union would not intervene. On June 4, 1989, the same day as the crackdown in Beijing, the Solidarity movement swept to victory in elections in Poland, marking the beginning of the end of more than four decades of Communist leadership there.

Within twelve months, the Berlin Wall had come down, and Communist rulers had fallen in Poland, East Germany, Czechoslovakia, Hungary, Romania, and Bulgaria. If the CCP wanted to avoid the same fate, it needed to act quickly to shore up public support.

The United States and other Western countries were "waging a world war without gunsmoke," Deng warned in September 1989. He said they were trying to stir up domestic discontent and infiltrate China with bourgeois liberal ideas to bring the party down from within. It was all part of an effort to overthrow Communism around the world, he claimed, through a strategy of "peaceful evolution." Issues like inflation would be simple to resolve, Deng said, but addressing these ideological threats and the party's failures in education would be much more challenging. "For many of those who participated in the demonstrations and hunger strikes," he warned, "it will take years, not just a couple of months, of education to change their thinking."[23]

The party's new general secretary agreed. Jiang Zemin had replaced Zhao Ziyang after the Tiananmen protests. Zhao was deemed to have treated the students too leniently and was placed under de facto house arrest for the rest of his life. Deng nominally stepped down later that year, resigning the last of his formal titles as chairman of the Central Military Commission in November 1989, although he didn't cede power or influence, remaining the most important figure in Chinese politics until his death in 1997. Now the two most powerful men in the country, Deng and Jiang, surveyed the challenges ahead and concurred on the urgent need to ramp up ideological education. The previous approach, Jiang complained, had been "hard on the economy, soft on politics."[24]

The patriotic education campaign that followed was intended to reach the entire population. They would target children from their earliest days in kindergarten to pensioners in neighborhood committees. Students, civil servants, soldiers, engineers—every section of society was supposed to be involved. The aim was to instill in them the Communist Party's version of history and with it the need for its continued rule.

Jiang set out the main points for the new campaign to cover in a letter published in the *People's Daily* in June 1991. Above all, he said, they should focus on how China had been bullied and victimized by foreign powers before the party took control in what was known as the "century of humiliation." Beginning with the First Opium War in 1839 and culminating with the Japanese invasion at the start of World War II, China was said to have been carved up and torn apart during this long century due to the weakness and corruption of its "feudal rulers." It was only with the Chinese Communist revolution and the founding of the People's Republic of China in 1949—"new China," as officials often called it—that the Chinese people had finally been able to stand up and fight back.[25]

The main slogan of the new campaign was "Never Forget National Humiliation." But the subtext was: never forget the importance of the Communist Party.

* * *

This emphasis on the country's past humiliation and foreign enemies represented an important shift. The main focus in recent decades had been the great revolution Mao claimed to be leading, and the fight to build socialism at home and around the world.[26] Enemies were determined by class, not solely national boundaries. But the idea that China had endured previous humiliation was not new. Leading CCP figures had been influenced by the self-strengthening movement of the late nineteenth century and the efforts to halt what was viewed as China's humiliating decline and restore "wealth and power."[27] Mao himself had framed the founding of the People's Republic in 1949 as an end to the country's "bullying and humiliation."[28] In fact, the notion of rejuvenating China that would later feature so prominently in Xi Jinping's "China dream" dated back at least as far as Sun Yat-sen, the first Kuomintang (KMT) leader, and National Humiliation Day had long been an official holiday in China under KMT rule.[29]

Beginning in 1928 after a clash with the Japanese army, KMT leader Chiang Kai-shek had started a daily practice of reflecting on the country's past humiliation. Every day he made a solemn vow in his diary to "wipe clean humiliation" and listed different methods for doing so. "From this day on," he wrote in the first entry, "I will rise out of bed at six o'clock. I will remind myself of this humiliation and continue to do so until the national humiliation is wiped away."[30] He kept it up until China's victory over Japan in 1945.

There was no shortage of humiliations to choose from. An official calendar recorded twenty-six National Humiliation Days to be observed at one point, with at least one every month except December.[31]

The original holiday commemorated China's acquiescence to a set of demands from the Japanese government—known as the "Twenty-One Demands"—in May 1915, which granted Tokyo economic and territorial concessions. The agreement was widely seen to have brought "terrible shame" to China, and on the anniversary of the agreement, citizens were urged to stop work, lower flags to half-mast, and remember that humiliation. As one newspaper advised readers in 1922, "On National Humiliation Day you should shut yourself up in sadness and draw a lesson from bitter experience."[32]

But if the concept had been around for a while, it had been neglected in recent years. When political scientist William Callahan searched the records of the National Library of China, he found that not a single book had been published on the topic of national humiliation between 1947 and 1990.[33] That was about to change.

As the patriotic education campaign rolled out nationwide in 1994, the party called for the whole country to study China's history of humiliation. Every part of the propaganda apparatus and every government department and agency was expected to do its part.

"It is the sacred duty for the press and publishing, radio, film and television departments of all levels to use advanced media technology to conduct patriotic education to the masses," the party's central committee decreed. They should create a "very strong patriotic atmosphere," the committee said, so that people would be influenced and nurtured by patriotic thoughts "at all times and everywhere in their daily life."[34]

The CCP was attempting to redefine the concept of patriotism so that love of country now equated to love for the party. Under this formulation, the party was the only force that had been capable of ending China's century of humiliation and could deliver on developing its economy and ensuring its security, so if you were a patriot you should support CCP rule. And by the same logic, if you were against the party, you must be against the country too.

"Our Party," explained Jiang, ". . . has made the biggest sacrifice and the biggest contribution in the struggle of national independence and safeguarding of national sovereignty." Therefore, he argued, the party was "the firmest, most thoroughgoing patriot" and the "highest model of conduct for the Chinese nation and the Chinese people." As he drew the dividing line, there were "ardent patriots," who by inference were on the party's side, and then there was "the scum of a nation who [turned] traitor for their personal gain."[35]

* * *

The country's classrooms were designated as crucial battlegrounds, a sentiment that Xi would later echo. Senior officials declared the new campaign a matter of "strategic significance" and "the most important mission for all schools."[36] What was needed, concluded one education journal, was "to build an ideological Great Wall."[37]

Kindergartens held storytelling sessions to introduce children to the idea of patriotism and love of the party. Newspapers devoted special columns to writing about patriotic figures from history, including plenty of party members, and their exemplary deeds. The state broadcaster CCTV turned its prime-time programming over to dramas, movies, and documentaries with stirring patriotic themes that were meant to inspire pride in the nation and support for the party's leadership. Projection teams were dispatched to remote mountainous regions to hold screenings for those without access to television, and village committees held discussions on the importance of cultivating patriotic views. The PLA started conducting weekly patriotic sing-alongs. The State Education Commission scoured the country for old battle sites and significant locations that could be turned into "patriotic education bases."[38]

These new bases included the ruins of the Old Summer Palace or Yuanmingyuan (Garden of Perfect Brightness) in northwest Beijing— a magnificent imperial palace complex that had been looted and burned by British and French troops in the nineteenth century during the Second Opium War. The site had been abandoned and the remains of the white marble columns and intricate carvings left strewn on the ground where they fell. But now the ruins were held up as a monument to the country's past humiliation and a powerful reminder of what was at stake. Groups of students and workers were bused in to see the devastation the foreign powers had wrought and the shame they had suffered under corrupt, imperial rule.

By May 1994, the Xinhua news agency reported that 95 percent of elementary and middle school students in Beijing had watched the prescribed patriotic films and written more than 1.5 million essays in response. "I will learn from his spirit," vowed one boy after watching a child hero give up all his belongings and devote himself to the anti-Japanese resistance during the war.[39] Of course, whether he really felt this way or not is impossible to say, but at a minimum the students were learning how to supply the required answers. Local PLA units began holding military training courses for schoolchildren of all ages and officers were dispatched to classrooms to give talks and organize annual boot camps.[40]

There were also new rituals to perform. The National People's Congress passed a National Flag Law in June 1990, upgrading the daily flag-raising ceremony in Tiananmen Square to a much more elaborate procedure involving thirty-six goose-stepping guards (instead of the previous three) and becoming a must-see tourist attraction for visitors from out of town. Daily flag-raising ceremonies were mandated for schools, and all children from third grade and above—and all adult citizens—were meant to be able to sing the national anthem and understand the symbolism of the national flag.[41]

These practices were not unique to China—plenty of children in American schools pledge allegiance to the flag and the republic it represents every day—but this was a new direction for the Communist Party as it sought to tap into these patriotic ideals for popular support. "Patriotism," the central committee declared, should be the "main melody of our society, and we must make unremitting efforts and work tirelessly on this project for the long-term."[42] By going through the motions of patriotic devotion, they hoped the real thing would follow.

"A large country such as China needs something to keep the country together," remarked Xiao Gongqin, a history professor at Shanghai Normal University, to a visiting reporter. "So nationalism is taking the place of the previous ideology as the coalescing force."[43]

University students were singled out as particular priorities for reeducation after their role in the recent unrest. Freshmen at the country's top universities, which had supplied many of the protest leaders, were required to undergo military training and political indoctrination classes before they could begin their studies, with the entire incoming class at Peking University in 1990 dispatched to a military academy for a full year.[44]

Party newspapers reported impressive results. One study claimed 87 percent of students who went through the training made "substantial progress" in their political consciousness and that the proportion of students who agreed that "it is necessary to take the socialist road with Chinese characteristics" increased from 54 to 80 percent after the intervention.[45] But there were also clear signs of discontent.

A survey of third-year students who went through the reeducation program at the Hangzhou Electronics Industry Institute in the 1989–1990 academic year found that almost none said it had changed their minds. Eighty-one percent of respondents declared themselves either "completely unaffected" or only "grudgingly" affected by the process. Only 3 percent chose the response "Accept it in my heart and deeply believe it."[46]

Parents of students at Peking University, meanwhile, complained that their children were "wasting" a year on military training instead of embarking on the education they had worked so hard to secure and presumably getting into paid employment at the other side. Eighty percent of those surveyed were said to be "indignant" or to have "grumbled" about the decision. More worryingly for senior officials, given that university campuses were where the previous protests had started out, internal reports recorded students setting fire to their military uniforms and putting up posters calling for the training to be scrapped.[47]

In short, the party had its work cut out. Popular support could not simply be mandated from the top down. But the leadership had been clear from the start that changing minds and attitudes would take years, not months, to achieve, and it intended to use all leverage at its disposal, including the memory of the Second World War.

* * *

It took World War II longer to return to prominence in China than it did in the Soviet Union. When Leonid Brezhnev was reinstating the Victory Day holiday in Moscow in 1965, Mao was consumed with rooting out his domestic enemies and preparing to plunge the country into his disastrous Cultural Revolution. But as the party cast around for new methods of boosting public support in the 1980s, it began to reexamine the potential rallying power of the war.

It was not so much that the memory of the conflict had been deliberately erased in China, but that it was just not central to the party's messaging, which was focused on class struggle and the Communist revolution.[48] Plus, there was the fact that most of the fighting had been done by the KMT, the Communist Party's domestic rivals. But after Mao's death, with the appeal of the old ideology waning, the party needed something more. The new era demanded a "new ideological thrust," as University of Oxford historian Rana Mitter put it in *China's Good War*. "And now, everything that had made China's experience during the Second World War unsuitable for political discussion under Mao suddenly made it a potent source of ideological ballast."[49]

By the mid-1980s the international outlook had changed too. Mao downplayed the World War II alliance with the United States during his early decades in power, preferring to focus on the Korean War instead, where the Americans were the enemy. But as relations with the United States improved during the 1970s and formal diplomatic ties were established, there was no reason to hide the wartime relationship and in fact it could be held up as an example of past cooperation.

Relations with Japan, meanwhile, were heading in the opposite direction. With a growing trade deficit and outrage in China over new Japanese history textbooks in 1982, which downplayed Japanese atrocities during the war, nationalist protests had broken out in Beijing. The situation had been exacerbated by Prime Minister Yasuhiro Nakasone's visit to the Yasukuni Shrine in 1985—where the souls of Japanese war criminals were said to be interred—and there were calls for the Chinese government to take a stronger stance against Tokyo. Revisiting the war and the crimes Japanese soldiers had committed in China, therefore, made good political sense.[50]

Then there was the prospect of outreach to Taiwan in pursuit of the party's long-held goal of "reunification." As long as KMT leader Chiang Kai-shek was alive and a potential threat, Mao had been reluctant to credit his forces with their part in the fighting, lest any of the praise rub off on him. But now both leaders were gone and the shared experience of the conflict offered a useful source of common ground.

Finally, the war helped burnish China's international credentials as it sought greater access to the global economy. Beijing could point to the country's role in the Allied effort and its status as one of the original founders of the United Nations, in fact the first signatory of the UN Charter in 1945. This was a point Chinese leaders, including Xi Jinping, would make repeatedly in the years that followed, as they claimed to be defending the postwar international order rather than threatening it, a stance Vladimir Putin shared.

In any case, as Putin would similarly find, there was not a great deal of useful history for the regime to draw from. "If you eliminate the events in modern Chinese history which are problematic for one reason or another, you're not left with very much else," Rana Mitter told me. "There are the Opium Wars of course, which are useful for stoking memories of victimization and the century of humiliation, but the problem is that China loses all those wars. The civil war involves Chinese fighting other Chinese, so that's also not great." Then there was all the history the party didn't want to talk about. "You have the Great Leap Forward, the Cultural Revolution, perhaps 1989, even the reform era, which are all very difficult," Mitter explained. By contrast, the Second World War could be presented as a great victory. "During that conflict, China was part of a world anti-fascist alliance, which gives it significant moral standing in terms of something the rest of the world recognizes as a moral good—the Allied victory in World War II—combined with the idea that it is a founding member of the current world order."[51]

Historians and scholars in China had been pressing for greater access to the archives and more research on the war since the early 1980s. Serious scholarship had been all but impossible during the Cultural Revolution, when academics were regarded with suspicion and frequently "sent down" to the countryside for reeducation, but with the new era of reform and opening underway and the fortieth anniversary of the end of the war approaching in 1985, there was a concerted push to revisit the history of the conflict. Hu Qiaomu, an influential party theorist who had once served as Mao's private secretary, agreed that the time was right to return to the topic and lent his support. He had lived through the war and believed it was an important aspect of the party's history. Rising tensions with Japan at the time over the textbook controversy were said to have strengthened his resolve.[52]

The result was a dramatic shift in the way the war was remembered, as the official story of the war was revised to suit the politics of the day.

Before 1985, the KMT had generally been depicted as corrupt, unwilling to fight, or actively thwarting the struggle against Japan. Plus, they were blamed for allowing the invasion to happen in the first place. But from that year on, the conflict was reimagined as an "all-nation war of resistance," in which the whole country fought together—CCP and KMT forces alike—although still with the Communists in the leading role.[53]

Where previously the story of the war had been structured around class struggle, with the KMT leadership cast as class enemies, now the focus was on national identity and the KMT assumed the role of brotherly warriors, fighting on the same side as Mao's forces against the foreign aggressors. This new narrative was laid out at a grand exhibition at the Military Museum of the Chinese People's Revolution in the summer of 1985, which detailed for the first time how the KMT had contributed to the war effort.[54] Huge displays documented the battles they had fought and the heroic sacrifices they were said to have made.

The profile of the conflict in general was amplified. New museums and memorials were built, and there was a surge of new scholarship. In 1987, Deng opened the new War of Resistance Museum on the outskirts of Beijing, at the site of what was then deemed to be the start of the war in July 1937, although this date would be revised forty years later when the length of the war almost doubled under Xi.[55]

The new focus on the KMT's efforts—and the growing antagonism with Tokyo—enabled much greater scrutiny of the atrocities Japanese forces had carried out against civilians in areas under KMT control. This included the Nanjing massacre, a horrific attack that took place in December 1937, during which the Chinese government claims more than three hundred thousand people were killed. A vast memorial hall was erected in the city in 1987 to commemorate the victims of what has been called "China's Holocaust."[56]

A new film in 1986 called *The Battle of Taierzhuang* focused on KMT troops and depicted them fighting courageously.[57] Biographies of KMT commanders also began to appear in bookstores as they were written back into the history of the war, with titles such as *Kuomintang Generals Who Died for Their Country* published in 1987 and *Biographies of High-Ranking Military Leaders of the Republic* in 1988.[58] Where previously they had been pushed to the margins of the conflict or denounced as counterrevolutionaries, now they were celebrated as heroes. Individual figures were transformed from villains into patriots almost overnight.

General Zhang Zizhong, for instance, whose role in the fighting had been reduced to a single perfunctory line in a 1972 history—"Chiang's 33rd Army Group commander Zhang Zizhong was shot dead by the Japanese"—was now rediscovered and hailed as a revolutionary martyr. Several roads and a school were named after him in 1985, and two years later the National People's Consultative Conference sponsored a book about his heroic exploits titled *The Renowned General in the Anti-Japanese War Zhang Zizhong*. His grave was designated as a cultural site and martyr's shrine and an elaborate exhibition hall materialized to accommodate visitors.[59]

As the story of the war changed, so too did real lives. Peng Shiliang, the young KMT general whose family was persecuted during the Cultural Revolution, was posthumously rehabilitated in 1985. This meant he was officially recognized as a martyr and the black mark against his family's name was removed. It couldn't undo all the suffering they had endured over the past four decades, but it meant they no longer had to pretend he didn't exist. They could reclaim his memory at least. Peng's granddaughter told me it was a great comfort to her grandmother, Peng's widow, to receive his martyr's certificate and feel he could finally rest in peace. She died the following year, but she had at least lived long enough to see her husband's reputation restored.[60]

Most importantly for the party and its attempts to shore up support, the memory of the war resonated with the public in a way that renewed appeals to Communist ideology did not. As in Russia, the extent of the losses and the destruction during the conflict had been devastating. As many as twenty million people had been killed and up to one hundred million were forced to flee their homes. It was also true that the extent of China's suffering and its contribution to the Allied effort had been largely forgotten in the West. There was a rich seam of grievance, heroism, and tragedy to exploit. So it was not surprising that the party leadership seized on the history of the conflict to bolster its legitimacy, just as Brezhnev had done in Moscow, and Putin and Xi would do similarly in the decades to come.

The renewed focus on the war and the revision of its history in the mid-1980s was cemented by the events of 1989. The conflict—or at least the official narrative of that conflict—slotted perfectly into the new patriotic education campaign. It formed the final act of the country's century of humiliation. It showed the Chinese people coming together from across political backgrounds, and supposedly under the leadership of the Communist Party. And it culminated in a great victory against an imperialist foreign enemy. It would later be cast as the beginning of the road to national rejuvenation and what Xi called the China Dream.

The party would continue to play down the significance of the Tiananmen protests in public. But privately the leadership understood that it could never afford to take ideological and political work for granted again. The party's survival was at stake. If they needed evidence of how Communist rule could end, they only had to look to the Soviet Union.

6

Truth

The main problem today is that most people really don't believe in anything.

—SOVIET OPINION SURVEY, 1990[1]

Moscow, USSR

Mikhail Gorbachev was a true believer. He took power in 1985 determined to save the Soviet Union with a series of ambitious reforms, most notably *Perestroika* (reconstruction) and *Glasnost* (openness). He resolved to pull Soviet troops out of the unwinnable conflict in Afghanistan and end the financially crippling arms race with the United States. But while he was celebrated abroad—named *Time* magazine's "Man of the Decade" in 1989 and awarded the Nobel Peace Prize the following year—it was a different picture at home. In trying to keep conservative hardliners and liberals onside, he alienated both. Food shortages and ever-lengthening bread lines, meanwhile, provided daily evidence for ordinary citizens that the system wasn't working. And in the new era of openness, with an increasingly robust press, there was nowhere to hide those failures.

"Queuing for everything—from sausages to razor blades—has become a necessary part of Soviet life," reported *Moscow News* in the spring of 1989. "For citizens of a country which built atomic power stations and space shuttles, queuing for a bar of soap is humiliating."[2] "For decades we were striving to translate into life the idea of universal equality," wrote economist Anatoly Deryabin in the *Molodoi Kommunist* (Young Communist) journal later that year. "So what have we achieved after all these years? . . . What we have is equality in poverty."[3]

Not only were the Soviet Union's domestic difficulties now on full display, but also so were living standards in the West, and even the party's own newspapers admitted the disparity. "If we compare the quality of life in the developed countries with our own," said *Komsomolskaya Pravda* in April 1990, "we have to admit that from the viewpoint of civilized, developed society the overwhelming majority of the population of our country lives below the poverty line."[4]

This refusal to cover up the country's problems was part of a deliberate strategy by Gorbachev and his senior officials intended to root out corruption and lay bare the barriers to economic development.[5] They took the same approach to Soviet history, including Stalin's murderous purges and the sacred victory in the Great Patriotic War. Nothing was off-limits in the search for obstacles to progress. But after more than half a century of relentless propaganda, the shift was jarring, and as Gorbachev was about to find out, it was a lot harder to rally public support and pride in the Soviet system behind the truth than the glorious lies that had previously been on offer.

As it was, on top of the shortages and the economic dysfunction, Gorbachev decided to embark on a campaign to tackle the worsening health crisis by cracking down on alcohol consumption, tanking his personal popularity still further. As a joke he was fond of repeating to foreign dignitaries went, one man asks another to hold his place in the line for vodka so that he can go to the Kremlin and punch Gorbachev in the face—he returns several hours later to say that he has given up, because the line there was even longer.

The speed of the Soviet collapse took many observers by surprise, but the system had been unraveling for some time. Popular movements swept Communist rulers from power across Eastern Europe in 1989, and as the empire disintegrated around him, Gorbachev pleaded with newspaper editors in Moscow not to speed up the process. "We're knee-deep in kerosene," he warned. "And some people are tossing matches."[6]

The fatal spark landed on a balmy afternoon in the summer of 1991. At 4.30 p.m. on August 18, the phone lines at Gorbachev's Black Sea vacation home in Crimea went dead. "I tried to contact Moscow," he later wrote, ". . . only to discover that all five telephone lines, including the strategic communications line, were dead. Even the city telephone did not work." Armed guards took up positions around the compound, sealing Gorbachev and his family inside. Navy warships cut off any possibility of escape by sea. He told his wife Raisa that they should "expect the worst."[7]

The coup leaders went public the following morning. At 6:00 a.m. on August 19, a visibly shaken state television anchor read a statement from the "Emergency Committee"—a group of senior military officials and civilian hardliners determined to end Gorbachev's reforms and reassert central control. The committee said that it was taking over to save the "great Motherland" from a "mortal danger" and that Gorbachev was incapacitated.[8] Then the feed cut to a recording of the ballet *Swan Lake*, which played on a loop. As Tchaikovsky's famous score blared into living rooms across the country, tanks and armored personnel carriers converged on the capital, surrounding the Kremlin and the Russian parliament, the White House. But from there the plan fell apart.

Russian president Boris Yeltsin (Russia was then still a republic of the USSR with its own president) managed to evade the security forces sent to arrest him and raced to the parliament to lead the resistance to the coup, wearing a bulletproof vest under his suit. As the news reverberated across the city, crowds of people streamed out into the streets of Moscow, crowding around the tanks and appealing to the soldiers inside not to shoot their own people. Some offered them food and placed flowers in the barrels of their guns. Others held up the Russian flag and demanded they turn against their officers. A group of women stood between the tanks and the parliament holding hand-painted signs that said, "Soviet Soldiers: Don't Shoot Your Mothers."[9]

At midday, Yeltsin climbed onto one of the tanks and denounced the coup. He said it was right wing, reactionary, and illegal. His vice president, Aleksandr Rutskoi, a former military officer who had been decorated as a Hero of the Soviet Union, appealed to the troops in a radio broadcast, calling on them as "brother officers, soldiers, and sailors" not to act against their countrymen.[10] There were cheers as the first tanks swung their barrels away from the White House and soldiers made a show of unloading their guns.

In Crimea, Mikhail Gorbachev and his family huddled around a small pocket radio they had managed to hide to try to find out what was happening. His security team fashioned an aerial from pieces of wire. As more troops reinforced the blockade outside, Gorbachev recorded a video statement to be released in the event of his death and his bodyguards took up firing positions inside the house, setting up machine guns on the staircase. They locked the Gorbachevs' two grandchildren inside a bedroom with the housekeeper.[11]

The stand-off lasted seventy-three hours before the coup attempt collapsed. A delegation of loyal officials arrived in Crimea on the evening of August 21 to escort Gorbachev and his family back to Moscow. They traveled in a decoy aircraft in case any surviving plotters tried to bring down his official plane.

Yeltsin convened parliament and suspended the activities of the Communist Party in Russia. Instead of securing the party's future, the hardliners behind the coup had only hastened its demise. Crowds rallied outside the central committee's headquarters calling for the arrest of those inside and pulled down the statue of Felix Dzerzhinsky, the former leader of the Cheka, the first Soviet secret police. "The Party is dead. Why can't you see that?" Aleksandr Yakovlev, one of Gorbachev's top advisers, demanded after he tried to defend it in a press conference. "It's like offering first aid to a corpse!"[12]

One by one the Soviet Union's constituent republics, including Russia, broke away until there was no union left to preside over. Once one of the world's most powerful men, Gorbachev was left with no choice but to resign. He was the leader of a state that had ceased to exist; all that was left was to admit it.

On December 25, 1991, he announced that he was stepping down and the USSR was no more. The red flag was lowered over the Kremlin for the last time and the blue, white, and red tricolor of the Russian Federation raised in its place. Gorbachev, remarked literary critic Natalya Ivanova, was like "the man who gave the orders to begin the fateful experiment at Chernobyl. He wanted to refine the machine, but the machine went out of control and exploded."[13]

* * *

There was no one single cause of the collapse. The decrepit economy, political liberalization, conservative resistance, nationalism, and the individual personalities involved all played their part in exploding the Soviet machine, and so too did the brief reckoning Gorbachev permitted with the darker aspects of Soviet history. Where his predecessors had declined to excavate the horrors of the Stalinist past, halting the Thaw that began under Khrushchev in the mid-1950s and early 1960s, Gorbachev called for the "blank spots" of history to be filled in. "History must be seen for what it is," Gorbachev declared in 1987 as he embarked on his reforms.[14] But what it was, was devastating.

As the archives were unlocked and the files gave up their secrets, those blank spots turned out to be hiding vast numbers of corpses and unimaginable tragedies. And the appetite for digging deeper into that past was insatiable.

In *The Invention of Russia*, the *Economist*'s Moscow bureau chief, Arkady Ostrovsky, estimates that three-quarters of all publications during the *Perestroika* years were devoted to history. "It was not just a small group of intellectuals," he explained. "The whole country seemed obsessed with history." As sociologists Boris Dubin and Lev Gudkov put it, "Soviet society resembled a man who was walking backwards into the future, fixated on his past."[15]

Carrying out research could still be challenging. Much of the old security apparatus was still in place, and when volunteers from the new Memorial society, which was founded by former dissidents including Nobel laureate Andrei Sakharov in 1989, tried to investigate Stalin-era repressions, they were frequently harassed and even detained by the security services—so much so that they took to carrying signs with Gorbachev's quotes with them to try to fend off the police. "The Memorial people usually went to the streets in groups of threes," recalled David Remnick in *Lenin's Tomb*. "One held a poster saying 'Sign this appeal,' another collected signatures, and the third held up a quotation from Gorbachev's speech saying there should be no 'blank spots' in history."[16] The intimidation tailed off and they were finally able to make progress, identifying the locations of mass graves and putting up plaques with the names of the dead. The idea was to document these atrocities for future generations and reclaim the memory of

Stalin's victims. As Arseny Roginsky, one of the cofounders, explained the principle behind their work, "History must be measured in human beings."[17]

But some senior officials thought Gorbachev's policy of openness and tolerance for dredging up the past had already gone far enough. The same Communist Party that had enacted Stalin's terror was still in power, and as they were all too well aware, the repression hadn't ended with his rule. Historians were acting "like beasts of prey," complained Yegor Ligachev, a high-ranking Gorbachev ally turned rival, "tearing our society to shreds." He condemned what he called a "cresting flood of denunciatory articles engulfing the mass media" that made it seem as though "there was nothing good in the past" and undermined "the feeling of pride in our Motherland."[18]

It was certainly true that feelings of pride were thin on the ground. The old boasts about Soviet strength and the superiority of the socialist system felt jarring in the new era of introspection and economic collapse. At the annual May Day parade in 1990, which was meant to rally the workers and celebrate the victories of socialism, thousands of protesters marched into Red Square carrying banners that read, "Socialism? No Thanks!," "Marxism-Leninism Is on the Rubbish Heap of History," and "Down with the Politburo! Resign!" Then they turned to face the leadership directly and chanted, "Down with the Party!" "Down with Gorbachev!"[19]

The Kremlin loudspeakers pumped out rousing revolutionary songs in an attempt to drown them out, but the crowds just shouted louder. After twenty-five excruciating minutes pretending not to notice, Gorbachev turned and walked silently off the rostrum, followed by the rest of the Politburo. It was as dignified a retreat as they could muster.

The intensifying focus on the shameful aspects of Soviet history had serious implications for the memory of the Great Patriotic War. The glorious myth Leonid Brezhnev had cultivated around the Soviet victory to bolster popular support in the mid-1960s was hard to sustain against the reality that was now coming to light. In 1989, for the first time, the government acknowledged the existence of the secret pact with Hitler on the eve of the war agreeing to divide control of Eastern Europe, known as the Molotov-Ribbentrop pact, and Gorbachev established a committee to investigate the true scale of Soviet war deaths. He revealed the results during the Victory Day commemorations in 1990, raising the estimate for the number of Soviet citizens who died during the conflict to twenty-seven million, up from twenty million as it had been assessed under Khrushchev and seven million under Stalin.[20]

In his speech that year Gorbachev asked all those present to stand in memory of the "colossal loss" and described the date as "one of the very brightest and most tragic of our holidays." The story of the war now included the purges and the punishment battalions, and the vast numbers of Chechen, Ingush, and Crimean Tatar citizens who were forcibly deported to central Asia, many of whom died along the way or in exile. There was still resistance from some in the military and the party's senior ranks who thought that digging up the past risked undermining their own foundations. But Gorbachev vowed that from now on they would live up to the inscription on the war memorials and remember the conflict in its entirety. "We repeat," he said, "no one is forgotten and nothing is forgotten."[21]

Historian Nina Tumarkin was in Moscow for the 1990 Victory Day celebrations. She told me she was struck by how much of the previous hype and triumphalism had disappeared. "Everything was just much more toned down, much more serious," she said. Where five years earlier you could buy all manner of commemorative art and souvenirs perpetuating the heroic tropes of the war cult, now there was barely anything on offer. What there was reflected the changing attitudes to the war. Instead of the idealized images of dashing young soldiers, she remembers a poster showing an old soldier with bandages wrapped around his head and "sad, weary eyes." When she visited a school to observe what was meant to be a solemn flower-laying ceremony, she saw that the children no longer even bothered to feign interest. "Not even the older ones could muster up a few moments of respectful silence," she later wrote. "When one boy made believe he was going to eat his flower instead of placing it at the foot of the monument, the teacher slapped him across the face." They told her that none of them planned to turn out to congratulate the veterans and present them with flowers as they had been instructed the following day. "We feel silly doing it," one boy said, "and besides, why should our parents have to pay for the flowers?"[22]

Watching the parade that year, Tumarkin felt she was witnessing the beginning of the end of the cult of the Great Patriotic War. The commemorations felt hollow and the myth of the great Soviet victory had been punctured by the return of the truth and the humiliation of the ongoing economic unraveling.[23] It was impossible to imagine the role the war would play in the coming decades in rebuilding that lost pride.

It was the last Victory parade in the Soviet Union. By the end of the following year, the USSR was gone and Gorbachev with it.

* * *

As Vladimir Putin tells the story, he watched the Soviet empire fall apart from Dresden in East Germany, where he was posted as a young KGB officer at the time. It was his first and last overseas assignment and that he was there at all was the culmination of a childhood dream.

Growing up in Leningrad in a crowded communal apartment with no hot water and a single gas burner they shared with another family, Putin proudly describes himself as a "hooligan" and a "bad boy."[24] In an early biography designed to boost his appeal to voters, he says he got into fights and got into trouble for sneaking out of school. But then he discovered Judo and a Soviet spy drama called *The Sword and the Shield* that set him on the right path. "I was a pure and utterly successful product of Soviet patriotic education," he said.[25] He decided he wanted to become a spy and serve his country by working for the KGB. Brezhnev was in power and the earlier Thaw that had allowed a closer examination of the Stalinist past was over. Putin said it didn't occur to him to think about the terror the security services had perpetrated under Stalin at all: "Not one bit."[26] Instead, as a teenager in high school he walked into the city's KGB headquarters and asked how he could get a job. Unfortunately, the officer who came out to speak to him said they didn't recruit people who showed up on their own initiative and they didn't recruit out of school. If he wanted to join the KGB he would have to serve in the army first or get a university degree. The officer recommended studying law.

Undeterred, and apparently uninspired to join the military, Putin set his sights on getting into Leningrad State University's law school. He knocked the hooliganism on the head and knuckled down, turning his previously mediocre academic record around and securing his place on the course. The KGB recruited him, as he had hoped, in his final year, and a decade later, aged thirty-three, he set off for his first posting over-seas. Dresden was not a glamorous assignment. There would be none of the drama and intrigue he had seen in *The Sword and the Shield*, where Soviet spies went undercover to infiltrate Hitler's ranks. East Germany was under Communist rule and the KGB's presence there was openly declared. But it was better than being stuck behind a desk in Moscow for the next few years, which was the alternative.

He arrived in East Germany in 1985, the same year Gorbachev came to power, with his wife, Lyudmila, and their young daughter, Masha, in tow. Their second daughter, Katya, was born the following year. They lived in a government apartment building shared with agents of the East German secret police, known as the Stasi, who, Lyudmila noted, were better paid and enjoyed a higher standard of living than they did. Still, the Putins had enough money to buy a car at the end of the posting, which was a big deal at the time, and it was better than the bread lines and the shortages at home. In fact, it was so much better that Putin gained twenty-five pounds during the assignment, which he put down to his fondness for German beer and his habit of buying a keg from the local brewery every week—and of course, he added, working so hard that there was no time left to work out. On weekends they drove out to the Saxony countryside for beer and hot dogs and toured around in their prized Zhiguli, or Lada as it was branded outside the Soviet Union. Putin was fascinated with Western consumer goods, ac-cording to a former colleague, and liked to spend hours leafing through mail-order catalogs and poring over the latest gadgets and appliances.[27]

But Soviet power was slipping away, and when the Berlin Wall came down in November 1989, Putin's world changed. Late one night in early December, protesters surrounded the Stasi headquarters in Dresden, across the road from where Putin worked. They demanded access to the files inside and threatened to storm the building. Then they turned their attention to the KGB offices, another detested symbol of the old regime.

The guards at the gate abandoned their posts as the numbers swelled and Putin claims to have armed himself with his service pistol and confronted the mob alone. One of the protesters remembers a "quite small, agitated" man coming to the gate and warning them not to try to force their way in. "My comrades are armed," he said, "and they're authorized to use their weapons in an emergency."[28] According to Putin, he called the nearest Soviet military facility for help, warning that the crowds were "in an aggressive mood" and they were about to be overrun. But the duty officer told him there was nothing he could do. "We cannot do anything without orders from Moscow," he said. "And Moscow is silent."[29]

Eventually, the military did show up and the crowds moved on. But Putin and his colleagues understood that the reprieve was temporary. They set about destroying their files and everything that could not be shipped back to Moscow. Putin said he personally burned so much material the furnace burst. He returned to Leningrad the following month, in January 1990, where he witnessed the final implosion of the USSR. But it was his experience that night in Dresden that he claimed always stuck with him as a lesson in the exercise of power. "That business of 'Moscow is silent,'" he said. "I got the feeling then that the country no longer existed. That it had disappeared." It was clear to him then, he said, that the Soviet Union was failing. "It had a terminal disease without a cure—paralysis of power."[30]

When he got his own chance to resurrect that power, he would not make the same mistake. There would be no more paralysis. Never again would Moscow be silent.

* * *

Ten years on from that chaotic night in Dresden, Boris Yeltsin summoned Putin, who was then prime minister, to his office. He told him he had decided to resign and make Putin acting president. It was December 14, 1999, one of the shortest, darkest days of the Russian winter, and there was snow falling outside. Yeltsin said he wanted to make the handover two weeks later on New Year's Eve, at the turn of the new millennium. "The new century must begin with a new political era," he said. "The era of Putin."[31]

Yeltsin had been a bulldozer of a politician, but his health and his popularity were fading. Where once his approval rating had been above 80 percent, now it was down to the single digits.[32] The abrupt shift from central control to a market economy after the collapse of the USSR had sent prices skyrocketing under what was known as "shock therapy." It was meant to jump-start the new economy, but it created hyperinflation and extreme inequality. While the first oligarchs accrued eye-watering fortunes in the fire sale of state assets, elderly pensioners were forced to sell their belongings in the streets. A financial crisis in 1998 wiped out life savings overnight as Russia defaulted on its debt and devalued the ruble. Striking miners blocked the railways as wages went unpaid for months at a time. Yeltsin had succeeded in demolishing the old Soviet order, but the experience of democracy that followed for many Russian citizens was characterized by chaos, violence, and poverty.

Businessmen who could afford it took to traveling with machine gun–toting bodyguards as violent crime and contract killings soared. The country was at war with separatist militants in Chechnya for the second time in a decade and soldiers in bulletproof vests patrolled bridges in the capital to guard against terrorist attacks. Life expectancy for men fell to fifty-seven. Yeltsin had only won reelection in 1996 by throwing in his lot with a group of powerful oligarchs, and after suffering several heart attacks he had shifted his focus to finding a successor he could trust. He wanted someone who would continue the work of building the new state, but more important, he needed to find someone who would agree not to come after him or his family's wealth.

In Vladimir Putin, Yeltsin and his advisers thought they had found the ideal candidate. He was the ultimate gray man, an unimpressive and virtually unknown bureaucrat with no independent power base of his own. And he had shown himself to be loyal to his previous boss, Anatoly Sobchak. On that front, at least, Yeltsin's judgment was correct. After taking office on December 31, 1999, Putin granted the outgoing president and his family immunity from prosecution and Yeltsin lived out a peaceful retirement.[33] But the new leader had very different plans for Russia's future than his predecessor.

When he took over from Gorbachev, Yeltsin had ordered the removal of all Soviet symbols, including the flag and the national anthem, but he had tried and failed to come up with a new national idea to fill the void. It was not for the want of trying. He had established a special committee dedicated to the task and announced a nationwide competition for suggestions. "The search for a national ideology has become the Kremlin's idée-fixe," reported the *Kommersant* newspaper in 1997. "This is understandable. In the election of 2000, you can't attract voters by saying 'vote, or things will get worse.' "[34] But the committee had come up empty-handed. As a headline in the *New York Times* summed up the failure: "Post-Communist Russia Plumbs Its Soul, in Vain, for New Vision."[35]

Putin had no intention of repeating the public handwringing. On the eve of the handover he published a five-thousand-word manifesto on the Russian government's website titled "Russia on the Threshold of the New Millennium" that became known as his "Millennium Message." In it he set out what he called the "Russian Idea," which he said consisted of traditional Russian values such as patriotism, the desire for a strong state over individual freedoms, and the belief that Russia was and always would be a great power. Crucially, he also warned that the country was in the midst of one of the most difficult periods in its history and that if they did not act fast, Russia was in danger of becoming a second- or even a third-tier state.[36]

According to Putin's then-wife Lyudmila (the couple divorced in 2013), she only found out that he was about to become president a few hours before it happened, when a friend called to congratulate her. She said she spent the rest of the day in tears.[37] "I flipped out when I heard that Papa was going to become acting president," their youngest daughter, Katya, said, who remembers being impressed when she saw him on television later that night. "At midnight we turned on the TV and saw Papa shaking people's hands. I liked that. He was so serious."[38] But the footage they were watching was prerecorded. By then the new leader was already in Chechnya.

Putin was filmed handing out medals and hunting knives to front-line soldiers in the first of many images designed to show him as a man of action and a resolute commander in chief. His message to the troops that night would set the tone for his presidency and his next two decades in power. Their mission was "not just about restoring the honor and dignity of the country," he told them. "It is about putting an end to the disintegration of Russia."[39] From the outset, he presented himself as the man who would stop the rot and restore the country's stability and its rightful status as a great and respected power.

Putin's Millennium Message had been drafted by his political strategists, and while it captured his own beliefs, it also played into what they thought the public wanted to hear.[40] The new president was not imposing his vision on an unwilling public. There was real support for the idea of a leader who could end the chaos and the dysfunction that had accompanied the demise of the USSR. An opinion poll carried out in January 2000 found that more than half of respondents expected Putin to reclaim Russia's standing as a global power.[41]

Fortunately for Putin, his first term coincided with a sharp rise in oil prices that fueled rapid economic growth and made it seem as though he was already delivering on his promises. His advisers also understood the power of television—where an estimated 90 percent of the population got their news at the time—in hammering home the message. The Kremlin seized control of the main TV channels and embarked on a formidable public relations campaign to shape the new president's image.[42]

The evening news showed Putin flying into Chechnya again in March 2000, this time in a fighter jet. Newspapers called him "Iron Putin" and carried stories of his love of Judo and his KGB past to signal his discipline and strength.[43] He was pictured getting tough on the oligarchs, too, which was popular with everyone who had not made vast fortunes in the transition from Communist rule. He summoned a group of the country's wealthiest men to a meeting at the Kremlin in July 2000 and dressed them down on television like naughty schoolboys, ordering them to pay their taxes and play by the rules. Then he invited them to a barbecue at Stalin's old residence on the outskirts of Moscow to remind them who was in charge,[44] although privately he made it clear that he had no problem with them continuing to get fabulously rich just as long as they kept out of politics and did as he asked. A new school textbook published that fall introduced Putin to students as a man who "helped good people and very much disliked bad people" and was "not afraid of anything." The new president, they were told, "flies in fighter planes, skis down mountains, and goes where there is fighting to stop wars. And all the other presidents of other countries meet him and respect him very much."[45]

That respect was a critical element. After the embarrassment of a leader who slurred his words and appeared drunk in public—during one official visit to Berlin, Yeltsin had grabbed a baton, clearly inebriated, and started enthusiastically conducting a military orchestra—Putin cut a much more dignified figure. Forty percent of those questioned in one poll during his first term said the quality they most admired in the new leader was that he was sober.[46]

Above all, Putin made clear that it was time to stop apologizing and being ashamed of the past. The country had walked backward examining the mistakes of Soviet history long enough. "Isn't there anything to remember from the Soviet period except Stalin's prison camps and repressions?" he demanded in a televised address from the Kremlin in December 2000. What about the achievements of Soviet science, space flight, and culture, he asked. "And what about the victory in the spring of 1945?"[47] He announced that he was reinstating the Soviet national anthem, although with updated lyrics, getting rid of the "Patriotic Song" Yeltsin had adopted, which had no words. And he restored the red flag as the banner of the Russian Armed Forces.

For Putin, even more so than for Brezhnev or the Chinese Communist Party, there was not a great deal of useful recent history to draw from. The Soviet victory over Nazi Germany was perhaps the only enduring achievement of a century where even the space race had ultimately been lost to the United States, along with the Cold War. And while China's leaders could trace their lineage back to Mao's revolution and the foundation of the People's Republic, the USSR was gone, and the memory of the Russian revolution had to be handled carefully. The example of the masses taking to the streets to overthrow a corrupt elite was not something the current regime wanted to linger on. Elements of their tsarist-era heritage, such as the growing prominence of the Russian Orthodox Church and the use of the double-headed eagle as the state emblem, had been reintroduced under Yeltsin and would form an important part of Putin's appeal to conservative values in the years to come. But it was the wartime victory that would become the new religion.

* * *

From the start of his presidency, Putin seized on the Great Patriotic War as a unifying symbol to rally the country behind. He delivered his

first Victory Day speech on May 9, 2000, two days after his inauguration, and with it a rousing reassessment of Russia's place in the world.
Where Gorbachev had insisted on a more nuanced commemoration,
stressing the horrors that had taken place under Stalin's leadership and
the tragic aspects of the conflict, from that first address Putin made
clear that he was shifting the focus back to the glorious victory.

"As the greatness of our motherland is immortal," he told the crowd,
"the pride of the nation and Russian patriotism are immortal." Russia
had always been a "victorious country," he said, "and so it will remain
forever."[48] It was a welcome change of pace for many in the audience
from the more recent experience of loss and decline. Instead of belonging to a second- or even a third-tier state, Putin invited Russians
to see themselves as citizens of an extraordinary nation. Theirs was the
country that had saved the world from Nazism. It was incontrovertible
proof of what he had set out in his Millennium Message: that Russia
was and always would be a great power.

Of course, that great power needed a great leader, and Putin posi-
tioned himself early on as the heir to that magnificent heritage. He
would take every opportunity in the years that followed to show that
he was defending their history against those who sought to deny it,
standing up to their contemporary enemies and restoring Russian dignity and national pride.[49]

Putin's imagemakers stressed his personal connections to the conflict. Because he was not born until after it ended, they focused on his
family's experiences instead. There were newspaper articles about how
Putin's father had been deployed behind the German lines and evaded
capture by hiding in a swamp and breathing through a hollow reed,
and how his mother had almost starved to death during the siege of
Leningrad. He was shown on television laying flowers at one of the sites
where his father fought and finding his name in the honor rolls. In later
years he took to carrying his father's portrait during marches to commemorate the fallen. The images seemed designed to prove that Putin's
credentials and his links to the war were unimpeachable.

But there was also plenty of politics. Putin established and personally chaired the *Pobeda* (Victory) committee, which was made up of
high-ranking officials, including the head of the FSB (federal security
service), and tasked with coordinating commemoration of the war

across the country and promoting patriotism in the younger generation.[50] He ordered a concerted push on patriotic education, almost trip-
ling government spending on patriotic programs during his first decade
in power and creating a vast network of patriotic youth clubs, where
children took part in military-style drills and weapons training.[51] And
he revived the Soviet practice of what were known as "memory lessons"
in Russian schools, where veterans came into classrooms to talk about
their experiences of the war in an attempt to bring the subject to life.
Learning about their history, Putin said, should make students "proud
of their motherland."[52] As in China, that pride and patriotism was
meant to translate into support for strong, central leadership, and that
message would become even more important in the following years as
a wave of popular uprisings took hold in other post-Soviet states.

The cult of the Great Patriotic War, it turned out, hadn't ended
with the USSR after all. With every year, the Victory Day celebrations
got bigger and more bombastic as Putin took the commemoration of
the war to ever-greater heights. He reintroduced vast columns of military hardware to the parades and presided over fearsome displays of
the latest tanks and missile launchers in Red Square. And the consequences of Russia's returning swagger would soon be felt beyond its
borders. "This is not sabre-rattling," Putin insisted ahead of the 2008
Victory parade, where he staged the country's biggest show of force
since the Soviet days. "We are not and have no intention of threatening
anyone."[53] Three months later, almost to the day, Russian tanks rolled
into Georgia.

1. Visitors bow before the statues of Kim Il Sung and Kim Jong Il in Pyongyang.
Credit: Katie Stallard

2. Children at a Pyongyang kindergarten ride a rocket-themed merry-go-round.
Credit: Katie Stallard

3. A North Korean painting depicts a young Kim Il Sung taking part in anti-Japanese protests. Credit: Kevin Sheppard/Sky News

4. The Arch of Triumph in Pyongyang commemorating Kim Il Sung's purported victory in 1945. Credit: Katie Stallard

5. A mosaic in Pyongyang depicting the founding leader's homecoming rally in 1945 according to North Korea's version of history. Credit: Katie Stallard

6. The first Victory Parade in Moscow's Red Square in June 1945. Credit: Alamy

7. The Tomb of the Unknown Soldier in Moscow. Credit: Katie Stallard

8. Rodina Mat—The Motherland Calls Monument in Volgograd. Credit: Katie Stallard

9. Zhao Yan displays the medal posthumously awarded to her grandfather, Peng Shiliang. Credit: Katie Stallard

10. A picture of Peng Shiliang displayed in his granddaughter's magazine store. Credit: Katie Stallard

11. North Korean mosaic depicting Kim Jong Il's purported birthplace at a secret guerilla camp on Mount Paektu. Credit: Alamy

12. A North Korean painting shows a young Kim Jong Il learning the art of war at his father's side. Credit: Alamy

13. A monument to the Five Heroes of Langya [Wolf's Teeth] Mountain. Credit: Katie Stallard

14. The ruins of Yuanmingyuan, also known as the Old Summer Palace, in Beijing, preserved as a monument to China's past humiliation under imperial rule. Credit: Katie Stallard

15. The September 18 Museum in Shenyang, commemorating the 1931 attack that is now deemed the start of China's World War II. Credit: Katie Stallard

16. Schoolchildren line up to enter the War of Resistance Museum in Beijing. Credit: Katie Stallard

17. Rebel fighters in Slavyansk in eastern Ukraine wear the St. George ribbon as an identifying symbol. Credit: Katie Stallard

18. Improvised armor and weaponry at the entrance to the headquarters of the self-proclaimed Donetsk People's Republic in eastern
Ukraine. Credit: Katie Stallard

19. Graffiti in rebel-controlled Slavyansk declares, "Russia Yes, NATO No".
Credit: Katie Stallard

20. Farmers rely on livestock to work the fields in the North Korean countryside.
Credit: Kevin Sheppard/Sky News

21. Many North Koreans suffer chronic food insecurity. Credit: Kevin Sheppard/ Sky News

22. A North Korean border guard monitors the border with China. Credit: Kevin Sheppard/Sky News

23. The Pyongyang skyline. Credit: Kevin Sheppard

24. The mandatory portraits of Kim Il Sung and Kim Jong Il displayed in school-teacher Ms. Han's living room. Credit: Katie Stallard

25. Pyongyang schoolteacher Ms. Han gestures proudly to the portraits of the former leaders. Credit: Kevin Sheppard/Sky News

26. Waiting for Kim Jong Un to appear in Kim Il Sung Square. Credit: Kevin Sheppard/Sky News

27. Kim Jong Un waves to the cheering crowd below. Credit: Kevin Sheppard/Sky News

28. Party officials and military officers applaud Kim Jong Un. Credit: Kevin Sheppard/Sky News

29. North Korean propaganda postcards depicting the fight against the United States. Credit: Katie Stallard

30. Commemorative stamps celebrating North Korea's intercontinental ballistic missile launch in 2017. Credit: Katie Stallard

31. Kim Jong Un leads his generals on horseback to the summit of Mount Paektu in 2019. Credit: Associated Press

32. Vladimir Putin and Xi Jinping observe the Victory Day military parade in Beijing in 2015. Credit: Associated Press

33. The Dong Feng-21D "carrier killer" missile on display in China's Victory Day military parade. Credit: Katie Stallard

34. Vladimir Putin marches in the Immortal Regiment procession in Moscow carrying a portrait of his father in 2016. Credit: Alamy

35. A young girl in Red Army uniform and St. George's ribbon during Victory Day celebrations in Moscow. Credit: Rory Challands

7

Lies

If a lie is only printed often enough, it becomes a quasi-truth, and if such a truth is repeated often enough, it becomes an article of belief, a dogma, and men will die for it.

—ISA BLAGDEN[1]

Pyongyang, North Korea

The television news reader could barely get his words out. As he tried to read the statement in front of him he fought back tears. Kim Il Sung, North Korea's founding leader, was dead. At the age of eighty-two, he had succumbed to a heart attack. The country had lost more than a head of state. His citizens had long been told that everything they had they owed to Kim—their food, clothes, housing, security—and that he worked tirelessly to improve their lives and keep them safe. After almost half a century in power, he was the only leader many of them had ever known, and they worshipped him, in public at least, like a god. And now he was gone.

"It felt like the world was coming to an end," said In-hua Kim, who wrote about the experience after escaping to South Korea. She remembers watching the announcement on television at her sister's house and running home to tell her mother the news. "She switched on the TV, hands shaking," Kim recalled. "The announcer was still delivering the same news, but in a hoarse voice from crying too much. 'How in the world could this happen,' my mother said. She began wailing as well."[2]

State television showed people weeping in the streets. They fell to their knees in front of the cameras and beat the ground with their fists.

Reporters burst into tears as they tried to describe the scene and sobbed through their interviews. Radio Pyongyang started reading aloud from Kim's memoirs to comfort listeners. "There is mass shock and hysteria," reported Polish news agency PAP when the death was announced on July 9, 1994. "In our embassy the gardeners and translators just sit and cry. People who tried to go shopping said they could not because shop assistants do nothing but cry."[3]

"To us, he was a peerless patriot and the Sun of the people who regained a lost nation from Japan [and] defeated the U.S. in the Fatherland Liberation War," said In-hua Kim, referring to the official name for the Korean War. A North Korea without Kim Il Sung was unthinkable, she said, "and so without him the Korean people felt that they no longer had any purpose in life."[4]

Not everyone felt that way. While Kim was genuinely revered by many of his citizens, others said they had been forced to feign their grief for fear of appearing disloyal. Neighborhood committees, which acted as local government informants, were said to be monitoring who was mourning and how fervently. Workers reported being assigned schedules to pay their respects. A former kindergarten teacher from the northern city of Chongjin told Barbara Demick, author of *Nothing to Envy: Ordinary Lives in North Korea*, that she was instructed to visit Kim's statue twice a day during the official mourning period with her class. During one visit she noticed one of the children spitting into her hand and wiping her eyes to make it look like she was crying. "My mother told me if I don't cry, I'm a bad person," the little girl, who was five years old, confessed. Another interviewee, who was a university student in Pyongyang at the time, explained how he had deliberately worked himself into a state of hysteria to fit in with his classmates, forcing himself to keep his eyes open until they began to tear up of their own accord. "It was like a staring contest," Demick wrote. "Stare. Cry. Stare. Cry. . . . The body took over where the mind left off and suddenly he was really crying. He felt himself falling to his knees, rocking back and forth, sobbing just like everyone else."[5]

The one feeling that almost everybody shared was uncertainty. North Korea scholar Hazel Smith traveled to the country three weeks after Kim died and remembers the situation on the ground as "very scary." She said people she knew from previous visits were stunned by the news. Even midlevel officials were unsure about what would happen next. The biggest question was whether Kim's son and designated heir, Kim Jong Il, would succeed in taking over power and pulling off the Communist world's first dynastic succession. But there was very little information to go on. The second Kim had a reputation as a recluse and he had barely been seen in public since his father's death. "Nobody knew whether he was really going to take over," Smith told me. "Nobody knew."[6]

Outside observers echoed those doubts. South Korea's president put the military on high alert and ordered his defense minister to prepare for all contingencies as rumors swirled about Kim Jong Il's health and his state of mind. The first international crisis over North Korea's nuclear program had been defused only weeks earlier. US military action had begun to look like a real possibility before Jimmy Carter flew to Pyongyang and secured the elder Kim's agreement to return to talks. It was unclear what his son would do. The speculation ranged from launching a war against South Korea to prove his bona fides with the military to embarking on dramatic economic reform, if he managed to take over at all. The *New York Times* described him as a "deeply mysterious man" who "may not be mentally stable," while US intelligence agencies received reports that he was seriously ill or facing a leadership challenge behind the scenes.[7] One former American ambassador to Seoul predicted that if Kim did succeed in taking control, he would "lead the country briefly and then be ejected by a general."[8]

The timing of the new leader's ascension in the summer of 1994 could not have been worse. The Soviet Union had collapsed three years earlier, taking with it a vital source of aid, trade, and crude oil. After tracking the South Korean economy for decades, and initially outpacing it, North Korea's economy was grinding to a halt. Food shortages were already evident and the government had launched a "Let's Eat Only Two Meals a Day" campaign as early as 1991.[9] While the full extent of the suffering would not be known for years, the country was on the brink of a devastating famine. The end of the Kim regime seemed to be just a matter of time.

But the Dear Leader, as he came to be known, would prove his doubters wrong. Along with a formidable domestic security apparatus and a fledgling nuclear weapons program, he had inherited the myth of his father's wartime heroism, and he would use all three to stay in power.

* * *

By the time the first Kim died in 1994, the story of his past as a guerrilla war hero—which was already exaggerated—had been embellished even further. Whereas in real life he had returned to the Korean peninsula after the end of World War II, when Japan had already surrendered to the Allied powers, by the 1990s, Kim Il Sung was depicted in the regime's propaganda almost single-handedly defeating Japan and freeing Korea from colonial rule. He was also now portrayed as "winning" the Korean War with very little help from China, relying solely on his own strategic acumen. There was at least an internal logic to the lies as Kim was said to have developed his martial prowess through his earlier experience fighting the Japanese, where he learned the skills needed to defeat the United States in the Korean War and bring a second great power to its knees.

This was the heroic legacy his son now claimed, along with his own invented role in those past wars. To understand how this happened, and the extent to which the Kims rewrote the country's history to suit themselves, we need to return briefly to the 1950s and the early years of the dynasty, when the Kims' version of the past first began to diverge from that of their patrons in Moscow and the work to build the first leader's cult of personality began in earnest.

The first edition of Kim Il Sung's biography was crafted with considerable input from the Soviet military officials who were in charge of the northern half of the Korean peninsula after the Second World War.[10] The Americans had backed the much higher-profile Syngman Rhee in South Korea and the Soviets needed a leader who could hold his own in Pyongyang. So it was in their interests to bolster Kim's credentials by playing up his past as a guerrilla fighter and presenting him as a major figure in the struggle for Korean independence—although within limits. The early versions of the story still credited the Soviet army with defeating Japan in 1945.

By 1952 and the celebrations to mark Kim's fortieth birthday, however, Seoul-based researcher Fyodor Tertitsky found that there was already evidence of efforts to give the North Korean leader a more prominent role in the liberation struggle. An official biography published that year in Pyongyang said Kim's forces had fought alongside the Soviet army in the final offensive against Japan, which wasn't true.[11]

Three years later, in 1955, the Soviet embassy in Pyongyang reported to Moscow that the North Koreans were also inflating their role in the Korean War and failing to acknowledge the extent of China's contribution. "The Korean comrades underrate the role and importance of Chinese aid to Korean [sic] and, in particular, downplay the role of the Chinese volunteers in the [Korean War]," the Soviet diplomats complained. As evidence, they described a recent exhibition on the war in the capital where only one of the twelve pavilions mentioned that Chinese troops had been involved in the conflict, with the rest dedicated to the valiant battles Kim's forces had purportedly fought.[12] The report warned that Kim was concentrating power in his own hands and cultivating a growing cult of personality.

The following year, future Soviet leader Leonid Brezhnev, then a candidate member of the Politburo, recorded his own concerns after visiting Pyongyang for the Korean Workers' Party Congress in April 1956. "The cult of Kim Il Sung continues to flourish in [North Korea]," Brezhnev reported disapprovingly. He was troubled by the "numerous portraits, busts, all possible exhibits, films, pictures, and books" he had seen, which were all "completely devoted to the glorification of Kim Il Sung." One new biography that was being distributed to party members referred to Kim as "the savior of the Korean people."[13] Cults of personality were by then officially frowned upon by the Soviet Communist Party leadership. Nikita Khrushchev had denounced Stalin in February 1956, and Stalin's statues, busts, and portraits were disappearing in the USSR. But clearly the North Korean comrades had not gotten the message.

Kim had begun to chart a course away from his dependence on Moscow, but he still needed Soviet money and support, so when Khrushchev admonished him that summer, the North Korean leader acknowledged the criticism and undertook to mend his ways. But his contrition was short-lived. Kim returned to Pyongyang to face a leadership challenge from rivals who based their complaints on his growing personality cult. He outmaneuvered and purged the challengers, and soon resumed his self-promotion.

From the relative safety of Moscow, North Korea's ambassador to the Soviet Union, Ri Sang-jo, warned that Kim had "set himself above the party, the government, and the people, and he himself has ended up as an untouchable personality." Streets, squares, and the country's most prestigious university had all been renamed after Kim, he said, and his image now dominated newspapers, magazines, school textbooks, and works of art. "The name of Kim Il Sung is raised higher than the names of kings in bourgeois countries," Ri complained. He accused Kim of rewriting the history of the liberation struggle against Japan to inflate his own role and claim all of the glory for himself. The story of the war as it was now being told in North Korea, Ri said, was "unceremoniously falsified."[14]

It was an extraordinary indictment from a man who had served alongside Kim at the highest levels of the regime and been entrusted with the Korean War armistice negotiations three years earlier. But it was already too late. Kim was not interested in listening to criticism. He recalled Ri, demanding that he immediately return to North Korea. Understanding the fate that awaited him there, Ri sought asylum in the Soviet Union instead.

The historical revisionism and the deification of Kim kicked into overdrive. The whole population was urged to learn from his revolutionary example and a new campaign promoted the extraordinary achievements of his guerrilla war against Japan, in which he was now said to have played an increasingly pivotal role. Between 1957 and 1960, more than ninety-five million copies of books about the guerrilla movement were printed, according to historian and North Korea analyst Andrei Lankov, who pointed out that if that figure was correct, it worked out to roughly nine books for every man, woman, and child in the country.[15]

Mysterious carvings were suddenly discovered that appeared to back up the regime's version of history. Purportedly carved by Kim's guerrillas between battles, these "slogan trees," as they were called, were located around the base of Mount Paektu, where Kim claimed to have operated from a secret camp, and featured inscriptions such as "General Kim Il Sung is the Sun of the Nation!" and "We'll make General Kim Il Sung the great leader of our nation after liberation!"[16]

The slogan trees were not particularly convincing. They looked like they had been recently carved, with no signs of weathering or fading, and they were found in places the guerrillas had never fought, such as Pyongyang. After the discovery of seven hundred slogan trees at a popular picnicking site overlooking the capital, Hwang Jang-yop, the former party ideology secretary and close aide to Kim Il Sung who defected to South Korea, asked another official whether this was not "going a bit too far." After all, he pointed out, he had often visited the site himself as a child and had never seen any sign of these carvings. But his colleague brushed off these concerns, assuring him that the guerrillas had used a special technique that he would not have been able to recognize and the find was perfectly credible.[17] Whether he actually believed that or just knew better than to voice his own doubts was not the point; the story of Kim's heroic guerrilla struggle had become an article of faith that was not to be questioned, no matter how implausible it seemed.

An East German foreign ministry report concluded in 1963 that this "exaggeration of the role of the anti-Japanese partisan struggle" had become the "foundation for the current policy of the KWP [Korean Workers' Party] and the DPRK [Democratic People's Republic of Korea] government." In other words, the regime was basing its claim to power on this false version of history.[18]

Kim took credit for other victories too. He promoted *Juche*, or self-reliance, as the official ideology of North Korea—although some scholars argue it was little more than a convenient slogan—and insisted that the country was achieving all progress and development through its own efforts. The guerrilla struggle was invoked here too as the inspiration behind so-called *Juche*-based economic development. "This is the shining embodiment of the revolutionary spirit of the anti-Japanese partisans," explained one official publication in 1963. "This spirit is based on the principle 'everything by our own force.'"[19]

But the exaggeration and the self-aggrandizement had yet to reach its peak. After facing down another leadership challenge in 1966, Kim declared that the country would adopt a Monolithic Ideological

System, effectively ending pluralism within the ruling Workers' Party and enshrining his own authority as absolute ruler. This was followed by a mass purge of books, with any publications that contradicted the official line on history removed from public libraries in what was euphemistically called an "arrangement of books."[20]

From then on, all new works would hew to the updated narrative, which credited Kim's leadership for the country's successes and elevated his role in the liberation struggle to even greater heights. As the party newspaper *Rodong Sinmun* told the story on the anniversary of the end of the war in August 1967, it was Kim's guerrillas who had "crushed the Japanese imperialists" along with the Soviet army and "achieved a historical victory."[21]

Where previous iterations depicted Kim's forces supporting the Soviets, now it was the other way around. An official biography published five years later, in 1972, described Kim leading a dramatic offensive against Japan in August 1945, with the Soviet forces firmly relegated to the supporting role, and returning home in triumph.[22] This was complete fantasy. In reality, Kim had been stranded in the forests of the Russian Far East at the time, far away from the action. But it made for a dramatic tale and a compelling claim to power, and it was this version of history that he handed down to his son and heir.

* * *

When a high-ranking North Korean security official fled across the border to South Korea in 1974, he brought with him some interesting news. Party members across the country were swearing loyalty to the Supreme Leader's oldest son, Kim Jong Il, he said, and large portraits of the young man were being installed in offices and factories.[23] Hereditary succession had been condemned in a North Korean political dictionary just four years earlier, in 1970, as a "reactionary custom of exploitative societies," but now the regime had reversed its position.[24] The offending paragraph was deleted from the 1972 edition of the same book and hereditary succession was presented to the public as the best possible course for North Korea, with Kim Jong Il styled as the obvious choice.

The East German ambassador to Pyongyang reported in April 1975 that the younger Kim had begun to feature prominently in North Korean propaganda. "For the first time, the chronology of Kim Il Sung's family strongly highlights his first wife and his oldest son," the ambassador said, noting that he was now frequently pictured meeting workers like his father. "This visual observation confirms in fact our assumption we have made earlier: Kim Il Sung's eldest son is systematically groomed to become his successor."[25]

The young Kim proved his worth to his father and his worthiness as heir through his propaganda work. After being installed as the head of the party's propaganda department in 1973, he took charge of protecting and promoting his father's image and, in particular, his heroic exploits as a great guerrilla warrior.[26] He began by recalling all memoirs from the period for careful review, presumably understanding, as Stalin had done after the Great Patriotic War, that truthful accounts of the fighting, however innocently intended, risked undermining the official version of events. He also set about shaking up the country's cultural industry, instructing writers, artists, and filmmakers to "create truly revolutionary works" that would contribute to "the transformation of the whole of society."[27]

He wrote a book titled *On the Art of the Cinema* (or put his name to it at least), in which he called for films to have more vivid, lifelike characters who demonstrated genuine emotions, rather than behaving like "marionettes," and more judicious editing. "If the film drags on tediously when it has finished telling the story and has nothing more to add, it will dissipate the emotional excitation which has cost so much effort to arouse," Kim said. "The stronger the long-term effect, the greater the real influence of the film on the audience."[28]

As an avid consumer of foreign films himself, an act that would have been considered a serious crime for an ordinary citizen, Kim reportedly maintained a private collection of more than twenty thousand titles, which he kept in a special climate-controlled vault. He was said to be a particular fan of the *James Bond* series, *Rambo*, and anything starring Elizabeth Taylor. It was clear to him that North Korea lagged far behind the standards in South Korea and the West and he came up with a bizarre and audacious plot to catch up. In 1978, Kim ordered the kidnapping of South Korean actress Choi Eun-hee and her estranged husband, the director Shin Sang-ok, holding them captive and forcing them to make movies in North Korea for the next eight years until they were able to escape during a shoot on location in Vienna in 1986, where they fled to the US embassy in a taxi. "We have to admit that we're falling behind," Kim told the couple in a secret recording they managed to smuggle out with them. "We should make films that stay with you and give you something to think about later, an ideology. . . . Why do we only make rubbish?"[29]

As well as abducting foreign talent, Kim invested in technical development, demanding that North Korean studios improve their production values so that their films—and the propaganda they disseminated—would resonate more convincingly with the masses. He was frequently listed as the executive producer on major titles. He was also credited with developing a series of new revolutionary operas, which told the stories of daring guerrillas and courageous ordinary citizens standing up to foreign aggressors and class enemies, and were staged in continuous rotation in North Korean theaters in the 1970s and '80s.

Such enemies were a constant presence in the regime's propaganda and throughout its education system, where children were taught about the never-ending schemes of hostile imperialists to attack and enslave their country and the Kim family's ceaseless efforts to protect them.

"As we enter one class the children with crayons are drawing pictures of a tank firing and running over two enemies," a delegation from the pro-Communist American-Korean Friendship and Information Center recounted of a visit to Pyongyang in 1972. In a kindergarten classroom, they described how the children were learning to count with the teacher holding up pictures of tanks. "The children, individually and collectively, add up the number of tanks and shout out the answers," their report said. They saw study groups learning about "the nature and history of imperialism, particularly Japanese and American," at the Pyongyang Children's and Students' Palace and watched combat drills, noting admiringly how they had seen "a team of girls mount an anti-aircraft weapon and fire it, and another group assemble rifles and fire them at moving targets." They were also taken to the Museum of American Atrocities in Sinchon to see evidence of "the crimes of

U.S. imperialism" that North Korea falsely tells its citizens the United States carried out during the Korean War. "Here we are told story after story of merciless massacres . . . drownings, violations, tortures, and other atrocities," the delegation reported. "There is no doubt in this country about who the enemy is."[30]

The younger Kim carved the regime's fiction into the capital's skyline. He commissioned enormous monuments to his father's accomplishments, where citizens were required to bow before his image to pay their respects. The new installations included a twenty-two-meter-high gold-covered statue of Kim Il Sung to mark his sixtieth birthday in 1972, which was later stripped back to bronze after it was deemed too extravagant, and an Arch of Triumph to commemorate his purported victory over Japan in 1945, which was unveiled to celebrate his seventieth birthday in 1982. It was exactly like the Arc De Triomphe in Paris, a North Korean official once told me proudly, only bigger. A vast mosaic next to the arch depicted Kim's triumphant return to Pyongyang at his homecoming rally in 1945, although in this version the Soviet officers who stood behind him and the Red Army medals on his chest had disappeared, and the crowds were cheering instead of heckling him.

From 1972 onward, every North Korean citizen over the age of twelve was required to wear a badge with Kim's likeness over their heart whenever they left home, and his portrait was installed in every home, office, and factory across the country. His birthday became the main national holiday in 1974, as it remains to this day, and he acquired an ever more elaborate array of accolades, including "Sun of the Nation," "Iron All-Victorious General," and "Marshal of the Mighty Republic."[31] As the party newspaper explained to readers in 1977, "All through the passage of time since men came into being and history began on this earth, no one has equaled Comrade Kim [Il Sung], an eminent hero revered by all people."[32]

* * *

Once Kim Jong Il was selected as the heir apparent in 1980, he got his own personality cult, although it would never be quite as impressive or as convincing as that of his father. "The propaganda focuses its efforts in order to convince the population that the son, a genius theorist and practitioner, is accepted worldwide as a leader of the Korean people," reported the Polish embassy in Pyongyang in 1982. Foreigners were being quoted in North Korean media outlets praising Kim, they said, and the regime seized "every opportunity to underline the son's qualities and care."[33] Hungarian diplomats described lectures taking place in colleges, universities, and workplaces around the country stressing that "only Comrade Kim Jong Il (the son of Kim Il Sung) can be the true successor and follower of the Great Leader."[34]

The propagandists did not have a great deal to work with. Unlike his father, the younger Kim had no experience of combat and a strong distaste for public speaking. As a young man he was rarely seen in public at all. When he did appear, he cut a distinctly underwhelming figure. He was a small man with large glasses and big hair, teased up in a bouffant style to make him look taller. He often wore platform shoes. "Small as a midget's turd, aren't I?" he reportedly remarked to one visitor, who knew better than to agree.[35] But they set about building a legend around him anyway, and his father lent his personal support to the campaign.

For a start, they altered the story of his birth. In real life Kim Jong Il was born in the Soviet Union, where his father was serving in a Red Army unit after abandoning his guerrilla struggle against Japan. But just as the older Kim's backstory was puffed up to strengthen his leadership credentials, so too his son's childhood was reimagined—or in this case wholly invented—to bolster his claim to the dynasty.

North Korean citizens were told that the young Kim was born at a secret camp on the slopes of Mount Paektu during his father's guerrilla campaign. A bright new star was said to have appeared in the sky to herald his birth, which took place in a humble wooden hut that was missing only an ox and a mule to complete the nativity scene. The guerrillas hailed his arrival as a portent of their victory, proclaiming him the "Bright Star of Mt. [Paektu]." Even their enemies were supposed to have been similarly awed. "It is predicted that the heaven-sent boy will become a general who will bring independence to Korea," warned a Japanese report that was quoted in an official biography of Kim Jong Il, which the authors almost certainly made up. "Korea will certainly become independent in the near future."[36] The year of his birth was also changed from 1941 to 1942 to better mirror that of his father in 1912.

As the fanfare around the younger Kim ramped up, his father summoned some of his old guerrilla comrades and ordered them to identify the site of the secret camp where they had fought together all those years ago and his son had been born. "Obviously they could not find something that did not exist," wrote Hwang Jang-yop, the former ideology secretary. "So Kim Il Sung said that he would have to do it himself. He looked around and picked a scenic spot and claimed that was where the secret encampment had been. He then named the mountain peak behind it 'Jongilbong' (Jong Il Peak)." Hwang said the Party History Center found a "huge granite rock" and inscribed the word "Jongilbong" on it, and then they built a hut and proclaimed it the "Home of the Mt. Baekdu [Paektu] secret encampment."[37] From then on, the regime claimed this was where Kim Il Sung had lived, and this was where Kim Jong Il had been born.

The later volumes of Kim Il Sung's memoirs, which were published after his death and under his son's supervision, reinforced the second Kim's revolutionary roots. "Born to guerrillas, he grew up in clothes impregnated with powder smoke, eating army rations and hearing shouts of military command," the text claimed. The women at the camp were pictured lovingly stitching together scraps of cloth and old uniforms to make a blanket for the future leader, while the men "carved pistols out of pieces of wood while working in the enemy area and gave them as presents to Kim Jong Il."[38] None of this was true. But to say so publicly was heresy. More slogan trees were duly discovered around the area of the secret base to support the official account. Supposedly carved by the guerrillas to celebrate the birth, they proclaimed, "Korea, Rejoice! The Great Sun has been born!"[39]

Kim Jong Il was written into the history of the Korean War too. Although he was only eight years old at the start of the conflict in 1950, he was said to have followed his father into his command bunker and studied the art of combat at his side. "I followed him and learned his pre-eminent art of leadership," Kim claimed in one biography. He was depicted learning to read maps and analyze the enemy's troop movements. "In the course of his stay at the Supreme Headquarters," readers were told, "Kim Jong Il developed the intelligence and resourcefulness of a brilliant commander."[40]

Kim Jong Il—and later his own son—would draw heavily on this revolutionary heritage in the years to come. But what his father did not leave him was a functioning economy.

* * *

Kim Il Sung had claimed to be devoting every waking moment to his citizens' welfare, but he was leading North Korea toward catastrophe. When he first took power, the northern half of the Korean peninsula was more prosperous than the south. It was where the vast majority of heavy industry was located and it had rich reserves of coal, iron ore, and other minerals. But decades of poor management and central planning, on top of the devastation wrought by the Korean War, had crippled the economy. By the time he died in 1994, the country was on the verge of a terrible famine that would kill at least half a million people and threaten the future of the Kim family's rule.[41]

There were many factors that contributed to the famine of the 1990s: the collapse of the Soviet trading bloc and with it the loss of foreign aid and subsidies, outdated farming practices and ill-conceived attempts to reclaim land for agriculture that stripped trees from the hillsides and left parts of the countryside prone to flooding, and the severe droughts that struck in rapid succession. But the reason so many people died was the political system. "The famine in North Korea was not inevitable," social anthropologist Sandra Fahy explained in her study of the period, *Marching through Suffering*. "However, avoiding it would have necessitated restructuring existing government priorities of international isolation and civilian control, which could have led to changes to ordinary ways of life and possibly the end of North Korea as we know it today."[42] In other words, the country's new leader, Kim Jong Il, chose to let his citizens die rather than risk eroding the regime's political control. "Kim let the people starve," Fahy told me. "He expected them to eat ideology."[43]

The food supplies that were available went to the elite in Pyongyang and the military first, cutting provisions to areas where those perceived to be less politically reliable were housed under the country's castelike classification system. With almost two-thirds of the North Korean population dependent on the central Public Distribution System at the time, those decisions could mean the difference between life and death.[44] When international aid agencies were finally allowed in, it was only under strict supervision and to limited parts of the country, as the government sought to maintain its monopoly on the distribution of rations and ensure that no unwanted outside information came with them.

North Korea told its citizens that the "downturn" was the result of a combination of natural disasters and the hostile policies of their imperialist enemies, chief among them the United States. The famine was presented as an "Arduous March" to endure, just as Kim Il Sung had suffered through the hardships of his guerrilla years. In the absence of other information, Fahy found many of the people she interviewed had accepted the official explanation at the time. "'America and the international community, along with the puppet South Korea,' that's the way they explained it," one survivor told her when she asked who they were told was to blame for the country's difficulties. "America, the international community, and the puppet South Korea are ceaselessly preparing for war. We have to tighten our belts to build up the national defense, to build up the economy."[45]

Even if you didn't believe the propaganda, it was prudent to keep those doubts to yourself. Those who criticized the leadership had a tendency to disappear, and people caught stealing food were put to death in public executions as an example to others, not of the consequences of theft, but for allowing the wrong sort of thoughts to enter their minds. "Dozens of interviewees reported that criminals had their heads completely shot off," Fahy said. "When I asked why the entire head was blown off, I was told it was because the criminal's thinking was wrong: the criminal was thinking like a capitalist."[46]

But a certain amount of thinking like a capitalist had become necessary to survive. "The regime had conditioned its citizens to depend on the state for food and other critical resources," scholar Patrick McEachern wrote. "When food did not come and regime instructions to work harder or plant patches of grass to eat did not solve the problem, many people died." The only solution was to look beyond the regime. Those who could, particularly among the younger generation, crossed the border into China illegally to find food or consumer goods to trade, and farmers began to sell some of their produce in "gray" markets that were technically against the law but frequently tolerated by the authorities. The result, McEachern said, was the emergence of a new class of entrepreneurs, and "those who made the greatest gains were those who defied the regime and pursued individual interests in markets."[47] This was a lesson that would shape the North Korean economy for decades to come as the gap between what the state could provide and what its citizens needed widened and they were forced to turn to informal markets to make up the difference—while still repeating the required slogans and condemning capitalist tendencies at political meetings.

Kim Jong Il codified his support for the military with his *Songun* or "military first" policy in 1998, which, like all great ideas, was said to have been inspired by his father's guerrilla struggle. The decision to prioritize the military was a calculated ploy to bind his own interests together with those of the generals and discourage any thoughts of a coup, but he sold it to the wider population as a necessary move to protect the country from its enemies. "Songun politics makes it possible to crush the imperialists' aggression and war moves by giving priority to arms and bolstering up the military strength," a North Korean pamphlet explaining the concept told readers. "It means defending national security and revolutionary gains at all costs by strengthening the army into an invincible revolutionary armed force."[48] In practice, this meant the military's needs came first, with the military economy estimated to account for 30 to 50 percent of all production by the late 1990s, according to former diplomat and scholar Adrian Buzo.[49]

Kim set out the same defensive logic for North Korea's nuclear program, which the regime prioritized over the basic needs of its citizens while insisting it was the only way to keep them safe.

The rationale for channeling the country's scarce resources into developing nuclear weapons and advanced military capabilities depended on maintaining the Kim regime's lies. The notion that North Korea was in constant and imminent danger of attack came from the claim that this had happened before—that the country had been invaded in a surprise attack by South Korea and the United States at the start of the Korean War. And the idea that only the Kim family's leadership could protect the country was based on the similarly spurious assertion that

Kim Il Sung had done so twice previously, defeating Japan in 1945 and then the United States in the Korean War in 1953. North Korean citizens were fed these stories from childhood, and regardless of whether they actually believed them, they were required to repeat them and behave as though they did.

The second-generation leader never did get over his distaste for public speaking, but the early predictions that his rule would be erratic and the regime would soon collapse were wrong. Kim Jong Il proved himself to be utterly ruthless and focused on retaining power at all costs. Even at the height of the famine, with his citizens starving to death in the hundreds of thousands, he refused to loosen his grip. He held fast to the false version of history his father had helped create and he had helped promote, and he wrapped himself in that revolutionary legacy, claiming to be battling the country's contemporary enemies and funneling money to the military and the nuclear weapons program under the auspices of self-defense.

Instead of ruling briefly and being ejected by a general, as those first projections foretold, Kim Jong Il led North Korea into old age and well beyond good health. When he passed the dynasty down to his own son, Kim Jong Un, the family myth was intact and the old lies would be used to fuel dangerous new ambitions.

8

Control

God himself has probably ordered us to legislate to protect the very recent past.

—VLADIMIR PUTIN[1]

Donetsk, Rebel-Controlled Eastern Ukraine

"Wait." Eleonora stopped in front of me. "We need to go back." She hurried toward the thick gray wall of the apartment block. "Quickly. Quickly," she urged. I heard the dull roar of rockets taking off. They sounded close. Eleonora pressed up against the wall and retreated farther back into the hood of her anorak, pale features knotted in concentration. I realized she was listening for the impact, working out whether they were firing toward us or not.

Eleonora was not a soldier. She was a thirty-six-year-old mother of two with unruly blond curls escaping from her ponytail and a no-nonsense approach to most aspects of life. She wore blue jeans and a heavy black parka zipped up to the neck, faux fur trim cinched tight around her face. It was a cold gray day in January 2015. The snow by the side of the road had frozen solid and the sun was a weak glow behind the clouds. This time a year ago Eleonora had lived in an unremarkable suburb of an unremarkable city in Ukraine's industrial heartland. But now that city was a war zone, and this was what life was like here now. You heard the roar of the rockets, you got into cover, and you listened for the impact. Coming in or going out? Close enough to make a run for the shelter or better to stay where you were? If they were going out, what would be the reply? Eleonora listened as another volley roared into the sky. "It's OK," she said. "They're far away. We can go."

We were on our way to see her apartment. The building had already been hit and it wasn't safe to stay there long, or really to be out here at all, but she couldn't help going back to check on her home, to reassure herself that some trace of her old life was still intact. If you had heard of Donetsk before all this happened, it was probably for its coal mines, as a host city for the Euro 2012 soccer tournament, or because it was the hometown of Ukrainian president Viktor Yanukovych. But after he was ousted in the 2014 Maidan revolution, Russian-backed rebels had seized control of the city and declared it the capital of the Donetsk People's Republic, one of two neighboring separatist enclaves in eastern Ukraine that refused to recognize the new government in Kyiv.

Now Eleonora was on the front lines of a conflict that would pit Russia against the West as Vladimir Putin redrew the borders of Europe by force, annexing Crimea and funneling troops and weapons into eastern Ukraine to fight an undeclared war. Then–US vice president Joe Biden condemned Russia's actions as a "brazen military incursion" and British foreign secretary William Hague called it an "outrageous land grab" and warned that Russia posed "the most serious risk to European security we have seen so far in the 21st century."[2] But that was not how the crisis was reported in Donetsk and Moscow.

Political loyalties in Ukraine had long been divided between the predominantly Russian-speaking regions in the East that traded heavily with Russia and the more European-leaning cities in the West.[3] Individual sympathies didn't break down along these neat geographical lines, and indeed polls before the conflict showed strong opposition in the East to the idea of Russian military intervention, but if you watched Russian television in cities like Donetsk, where much of the population got their news, you were told that the country's legitimately elected president had been overthrown in a violent, US-backed coup. To make matters worse, the new government was said to be made up of right-wing extremists and nationalists who were hostile to Russia and Russian speakers in eastern Ukraine.

People like Eleonora were caught in the middle. She had little love for either the separatists or the central government in Kyiv, and she had never been particularly interested in politics before. But now the war had come to her, and it was the Ukrainian military she could see bombarding the city.

"Look at this." She gestured to the gaping hole in the ceiling of her neighbor's apartment above the remains of what used to be a bed. The bedframe had been split clean in two by the impact and chunks of rubble and plaster littered the floor of the small Soviet-era flat. Electrical wires dangled down from where the roof should have been, but instead there was just a tangle of splintered rafters and pale gray sky. They had managed to salvage the headboard and a wooden card table. Everything else had been destroyed. It had happened four days earlier, Eleonora said, late at night. Fortunately, the family who lived there had already moved into the underground shelter so they were not at home at the time, but she wanted me to understand that this was what they were up against: a government that would shell its own people in their sleep.

The "shelter" was the unfinished basement of the local community center, where at least a dozen families had taken refuge when the shelling reached their neighborhood. It was dark down there and the power went on and off, but they had hung sheets and blankets between the beds to give at least the illusion of privacy, and the hot water pipes that ran across the ceiling provided heat. More important, they thought it was deep enough to withstand a direct hit.

"They started to shell us from the Ukrainian side," another mother, named Luba, told me as she showed me around. Wearing a thick woolen shawl over her bright green fleece and looking utterly exhausted, she described how she had wrapped her four-year-old son Anton in a blanket and carried him down into the shelter in the middle of the night. He was a small blond-haired boy in a striped, blue sweatshirt, with skin that was ghostly pale from the weeks of living underground. Luba called him over to illustrate her point. "Who is bombing us?" she asked him. "Is it fascists?" "Yes," he said, nodding emphatically. "Yes, yes."[4]

By "fascists" they meant the new Ukrainian government, which was being described as a "fascist junta" on the main Russian television networks, where the term was broadly applied to anyone who opposed Russia. The Ukrainian channels had been taken off the air at the start of the conflict (it was rumored with help from Russian special forces), but the Russian-language stations had long been popular in this region anyway, and now they were filled with stories about the fascists and extremists who had supposedly taken power in Kyiv.[5] The new authorities were portrayed as hell-bent on persecuting Russian-speaking citizens in the East, banning Russian language and culture, and pounding cities like Donetsk into submission.

This was a twenty-first-century conflict, fought online and on television through sophisticated influence operations and disinformation, as well as guns and bullets on the ground. From the outset, the Kremlin framed the crisis as part of the contest between Russia and the West, drawing heavily on memories of the previous century, when Ukraine was under Soviet rule, and the Great Patriotic War. The sacred memory of the Soviet victory in 1945 that Brezhnev had resurrected, and Putin had stoked to even greater heights, was a constant presence in the separatist-controlled territories from the start. The rebels wore the orange-and-black ribbon of St. George—the symbol of the Soviet victory—as an identifying marker, pinning it to their lapels and wrapping it around the barrel of their guns. It was the one surefire way to know which side somebody was on. Every year on Victory Day, the anniversary of the end of the war, they paraded through the streets of Donetsk and claimed to be fighting a new generation of Nazis and Banderovtsy—followers of the late Ukrainian nationalist fighter and Nazi collaborator Stepan Bandera. In one widely shared video posted to social media, they started up an old Soviet tank that was mounted on a plinth as part of a World War II memorial and boasted that they were bringing the weapons of the past war "back to life."[6]

In Russia, as in China and North Korea, the political leadership understood the power of the past war to rally public support and lay claim to the moral high ground. Even as he seized Crimea and stoked the conflict in Ukraine, Putin claimed that he was the one defending the peace and protecting Russian interests and the lives of their compatriots. According to this logic, Ukraine had been plunged into violence and chaos because of Western interference and expansionism, and now a new fascist threat was rising on Russia's border. But just as they had defeated Hitler in 1945 and saved the world from fascism then, so they would stand against the rise of this new fascist menace. Russian media outlets carried endless reports of the bloodshed in eastern Ukraine and the families like Eleonora's who were trapped by the fighting. Every shell the Ukrainian military fired into the city only strengthened their case.

* * *

The struggle in Ukraine fed into a vision Putin had been cultivating since his earliest days in office as he claimed to be resurrecting Russia's status as a great power, although in practice his actions often smacked more of opportunism and a leader who was making the most of his available resources than a great strategist executing a cunning master plan. From his first Victory Day speech on May 9, 2000, just two days into his first term as president, Putin held up the memory of World War II as evidence of Russia's greatness and deserved status as a major global player. He presented himself as the heir to that heroic legacy—the president who would reclaim the country's dignity and self-respect.

After the color revolutions in neighboring Georgia and Ukraine, both former Soviet republics, in 2003 and 2004, the Kremlin ramped up the idea of a "fascist threat" to marshal domestic support and founded patriotic youth movements that were meant to come out onto the streets to counter any similar unrest in Russia.[7] But it was in response to the mass protests in Moscow and other Russian cities in the winter of 2011–2012—following fraudulent parliamentary elections and the news that Putin planned to return to the presidency after four years as prime minister—that the volume on that supposed threat was really turned up. From the Kremlin's perspective, there was plenty to be worried about. During the past decade, the North Atlantic Treaty Organization (NATO) had expanded into Central and Eastern Europe and promised that Ukraine and Georgia would one day become members. In the last twelve months, the Arab Spring had swept a series of long-standing dictators from office across the Middle East, and now there were protesters marching through Moscow with placards that read, "Mubarak, Gaddafi, Putin."[8] The Russian leader was determined not to meet the same fate.

At the height of those protests in December 2011, the Kremlin launched its counterattack. As heavy snow fell in the capital, pro-Kremlin political scientist Sergey Kurginyan rallied a crowd of thousands of Putin supporters in a central Moscow square calling for an end to the "orange leprosy"—a reference to the earlier orange revolution in Ukraine—and to what he claimed was a US-led scheme to foment a color revolution in Russia.[9] White ribbons were the symbol of the anti-government protests, so the pro-Putin crowd wore orange-and-black St. George's ribbons and invoked the Great Patriotic War as they cast themselves as modern-day patriots coming to Russia's defense. "The Red Army's first counter-advance in 1941 came on the second day of the war," one of the speakers that day told the crowd. "Today is our counter-attack against the orange plague." The term deliberately conflated the orange revolution with the "brown plague," as Hitler's paramilitaries, who wore brown shirts, were known in Russia.[10]

A lawmaker from the ruling United Russia party threw a white ribbon onto the floor of the Russian parliament in front of the cameras and theatrically stamped on it. "I want to do with this ribbon the same thing that people who ordered provocations wanted to do with our country—I want to tread [on] it," Aleksandr Sidyakin declared. The white ribbon of the protesters was a "symbol of capitulation, of betrayal, the color of revolution for export, which foreign political technologists are trying to impose on us," he said. By contrast, the St. George's ribbon proudly pinned to his lapel was the symbol of "respect for one's history and one's values."[11]

In the following months, Putin's campaign to return to the presidency was framed in the same terms: as a battle to defend Russia from its enemies. He didn't need the message to appeal to everyone—and it didn't—he just needed to fire up his supporters and tarnish his opponents as traitors and foreign-backed provocateurs. At an enormous rally at the Luzhniki Stadium in Moscow in February 2012 under the slogan "Let's Defend the Country," Putin invoked the memory of the Great Patriotic War and claimed to be leading his own great struggle against their adversaries. "We are the victor-nation. This is in our genes. And we'll be victorious again now!" he told the crowd to resounding cheers. "It's symbolic that we have gathered here on the Day of the Defender of the Fatherland [the holiday to honor Russia's armed forces], because you and I are, today, during these days, the defenders of our Fatherland."[12]

He won the election, but there were claims of widespread vote-rigging and protests on the eve of his inauguration. The regime was sufficiently concerned about the reception he would receive that they cleared the streets of central Moscow for his return to the Kremlin. One man set the resulting footage of the presidential motorcade traveling through the deserted city to the soundtrack of the zombie apocalypse movie *28 Days Later*.[13]

Putin embarked on his third term in full grievance mode, insisting that Russia was both a great, victorious nation and surrounded by mortal threats, forced to defend itself against endless Western schemes to stir up trouble on its borders and mobilize a "fifth column" of domestic agents to destroy the country from within. So when protesters took to the streets of Kyiv in the winter of 2013–2014 against Ukrainian president Viktor Yanukovych—who had opted for closer ties with Russia over the European Union—the Kremlin turned to this increasingly well-worn playbook and launched into its familiar script as to who was to blame.

The unrest in Ukraine was another US-orchestrated plot to stoke trouble in Russia's near abroad and draw Kyiv into the Western sphere of influence, Russian state media told viewers. It was an attempt to finish what they had started two years earlier and bring about a color revolution in Moscow. The actions of senior American diplomats inadvertently played into this narrative. The US ambassador to Ukraine Geoffrey Pyatt and assistant secretary of state Victoria Nuland were pictured visiting the protesters' camp and handing out bread and cookies, although they pointed out they also met government officials and offered bread to the riot police. Then, in February 2014, part of a private phone call between the two discussing which of the opposition leaders should be part of the new Ukrainian government was intercepted and leaked online.[14] It wasn't difficult to make it look like a conspiracy. And perhaps the Russian leadership genuinely believed it. When I once asked a senior Kremlin adviser whether the president seriously believed that US intelligence agencies were orchestrating the protests, he replied without a moment's hesitation: "of course."

The same coalition that had rallied against the anti-Putin protests in Russia in 2011–2012 reinvented itself as an "anti-Maidan" movement in response to the protests in Kyiv. The "Maidan" was the central square in the Ukrainian capital—officially Maidan Nezalezhnosti, or Independence Square, but often shortened to Maidan—where the protesters set up camp and the revolution got its name. As the unrest intensified in Ukraine, the leaders of the anti-Maidan movement in Moscow drew on the same patriotic tropes and wartime imagery they had before and urged Russian "patriots" to fight for their country as their predecessors had done during the Great Patriotic War.

"In 1941–1945 we fought under a red banner, with a particular set of values, and so we fight today under the Saint George ribbon," anti-Maidan activist Anton Demidov told journalist Matthew Luxmoore. "We're also fighting ideologically, and physically, with fascism, twenty-first century fascism."[15]

"If we don't come out in support of Vladimir Putin," warned another man, who had wrapped himself in a giant orange-and-black St. George's ribbon–style flag, "we will die and rot in ditches, like people who didn't understand that the fascists are descending on them."[16]

The movement's emblem was a red flag with the ribbon of St. George running across it and an image of the Motherland Calls monument—the memorial to the heroes of the Battle of Stalingrad.

The Kremlin-controlled television networks were soon dominated by images of the violence in Kyiv and a relentless focus on the most radical protesters, accompanied by grave warnings that fascism was on the rise in Europe once again.[17] There were claims of pogroms and plots to kill everyone in eastern Ukraine, deport them, or lock them up—it wasn't clear. At one point there were reports that a "fascist concentration camp" was being built to house citizens from the country's predominantly Russian-speaking East.[18]

These were not fringe conspiracy theories. From the president down, Russian officials insisted Ukraine was gripped by violence and terror. There had been "an armed seizure of power," Vladimir Putin said after Yanukovych was ousted. "Reactionary forces" had taken over the Ukrainian capital and "people wearing armbands with something resembling swastikas" were patrolling the streets. He told the entirely false story of one man who had supposedly pleaded with the new authorities to help some women escape from a building that was surrounded by protesters. "He was shot right there in front of the crowd," Putin said. "Another employee was led to a cellar and then they threw Molotov cocktails at him and burned him alive."[19] Russia's ambassador to the United Nations told a Security Council meeting there was "open terror" in Ukraine, with "ongoing threats of violence by ultranationalists against the security, lives and legitimate interests of

Russians and all Russian-speaking people" in eastern and southern Ukraine.[20]

But the most infamous example to emerge from the subsequent conflict was a report on Russia's most popular television network, Channel One, claiming that Ukrainian forces had crucified a child. The channel's reporter interviewed a distraught woman who described how the soldiers had nailed the three-year-old boy's hands to a post in a public square and tortured him as he bled to death. People fainted at the sound of the little boy's screams, she claimed, and the men forced his mother to watch before tying her to the back of a tank and dragging her through the streets to her own death. It was all supposed to have taken place in the town of Slavyansk, around two hours' drive from Donetsk, in retaliation for the boy's father joining one of the separatist militias that was fighting against Ukrainian government forces there.[21] It was a grotesque lie that was quickly debunked by other journalists, but the damage was already done. Television was where the overwhelming majority of Russians got their news, and although Channel One later admitted that it "was not able to confirm or refute the information" in the report, viewers were never told that it wasn't true.[22] The magic box had a powerful hold on its audience. When we returned to Moscow from reporting trips to Ukraine, Russian friends sometimes struggled to convince their families of what they had seen with their own eyes over the version that was shown on the evening news.

Viewed through the lens of Russian television, the protests in Ukraine had been instigated by the West, unleashed fascists and violent extremists onto the streets, and plunged the country into civil war, although this didn't necessarily translate into public support for sending Russian troops to intervene, which remained broadly unpopular throughout the conflict.[23] The world beyond Russia's borders was depicted as chaotic, dangerous, and immoral. Only Putin and the patriots who supported him were said to be standing in the way of the same thing happening there. This played into the broader narrative Putin had been pushing since his return to the presidency as he claimed to be defending "traditional" Russian values against the moral degradation of the West. He spoke proudly about his Orthodox Christian faith and deliberately conflated gay rights and pedophilia, which he claimed some European countries were considering legalizing.[24] In this context, his decision to seize Crimea was presented as an act of self-defense against a hubristic West that had gone too far in testing the limits of Russia's patience.

"Our western partners, led by the United States of America, prefer not to be guided by international law in their practical policies, but by the rule of the gun," Putin said during the ceremony to mark the annexation on March 18, 2014. Beneath the glittering chandeliers of the St. George Hall in the Kremlin, he railed off a long list of grievances that included the North Atlantic Treaty Organization (NATO) bombing of Belgrade in 1999 (Serbia was a Russian ally), the eastward expansion of NATO (Russia insists the United States promised the alliance would not move farther east), and US missile defenses in Europe (which Russia considered a threat to its security).

"But there is a limit to everything," Putin declared. "And with Ukraine, our western partners have crossed the line, playing the bear and acting irresponsibly and unprofessionally." The lives of Russian citizens and Russian-speaking Ukrainians had been in danger, he insisted, and anyway, it was a historical accident that Crimea had ended up in Ukraine at all. The territory had been transferred from Russia to Ukraine in 1954 when both were republics of the Soviet Union and it was unthinkable they would end up as separate states, Putin explained, so taking back Crimea was simply righting a historical wrong. Besides, he said, if they had done nothing, the peninsula would have ended up under Western control with NATO troops in Sevastopol, the famous port city where the Russian Black Sea Fleet had long been based. "NATO's navy would be right there in this city of Russia's military glory," he warned. This was a reference to the Battle of Sevastopol during the Great Patriotic War, when the Crimean port city held out against the Axis powers for more than 250 days. "Russia found itself in a position it could not retreat from," Putin said. "If you compress the spring all the way to its limit, it will snap back hard."[25]

The "return" of Crimea, as the annexation was billed in Russia, was popular, and not just among Putin's traditional supporters. His approval rating, which had dropped to 61 percent in the preceding months—disappointing by his standards—shot up to 88 percent by the end of the year, according to the independent Levada Center, and remained above 80 percent for almost the next four years.[26] When political scientists Samuel Greene and Graeme Robertson conducted their own surveys, they found that whereas just over half—53 percent—of educated urban respondents said they approved of Putin before the annexation, by June 2014, three months later, that number was up to 80 percent. The proportion of people who said they felt pride in Russia's leadership more than doubled in the same period, as did the number who said the leadership inspired hope for the country's future.[27] "Collective euphoria over events in Ukraine, as portrayed on Russian state television," wrote Greene and Robertson, "led to a huge outpouring of pride, hope and trust in Russia's leaders."[28]

Russian opposition politician Leonid Volkov likened the decision to seize Crimea to a magic bean in a computer game that restores a player's powers. "Putin grabbed that magic bean and ate it," he said. "And then Putin galvanized his dead political system for another two to three years and gave his political corpse a little more life."[29]

As the Kremlin presented it, Putin was delivering on the promises he had made when he first came to power, when he vowed to stop the disintegration of Russia and restore the country's rightful status. Instead of the humiliation and defeat that had accompanied the Soviet collapse and the end of the Cold War, they were living up to the heroic legacy of the Great Patriotic War as a victorious nation and a major power once again.

That victory was a continual point of reference in the celebrations that accompanied the annexation of Crimea in Russia. In the run-up to Victory Day in the spring of 2014, the streets of Moscow were flooded with orange-and-black ribbons, flags flew from car windows and hung from balconies, and entire building facades were draped in orange and black. The slogan *"Krym Nash!"*—Crimea Is Ours!—was everywhere. The wartime past was the prism through which this contemporary "victory" was portrayed, although both aspects of that framing required considerable efforts from the propaganda apparatus and Putin's political technologists to maintain, as they sought to ensure the seizure was seen as a great achievement, not an illegal occupation, and the war with Hitler was remembered as an unadulterated and glorious success.

In his Victory Day speech on May 9, 2014, before the massed ranks of the Russian military in Red Square, Putin said it was a date when "we see the all-conquering power of patriotism and feel especially acutely what it means to be loyal to our homeland and how important it is to be capable of defending its interests."[30] Then he flew to Sevastopol in Crimea to preside over a triumphant parade of Russia's Black Sea Fleet and underline that point.

* * *

Putin drew heavily on the history of the Great Patriotic War to bolster his image and rally support for his actions, so it was important to keep the popular narrative of the conflict under tight control. Where Gorbachev had called for the blank spots of history to be filled in and the war to be remembered as both a tragic and a valiant endeavor, Putin shifted the primary focus back to the glory and the heroism. He insisted he was leading a great battle to defend the memory of the conflict from those who were trying to undermine their hard-won status as the country that had saved the world from fascism in 1945. It was not just Russia's contemporary interests that were under attack, he claimed; it was also their history.

As with all good propaganda, there was an element of truth in this. The preceding years had seen a series of what scholars termed "memory wars" between Russia and several European states over the Soviet occupation and Red Army atrocities during the conflict.[31] Where the Russian account focused on the bravery and the great sacrifices of the Red Army during the war, there was growing scrutiny beyond its borders of Stalin's secret pact with Hitler on the eve of the war, the Soviet massacre of Polish officers at Katyn, and the mass rape of women and girls by Soviet troops. This was not the side of the war the Kremlin wanted to focus on and it duly moved to protect its version of the conflict's history.

On May 5, 2014, just ahead of that year's Victory Day celebrations, Vladimir Putin signed a new law into effect making it a criminal offense to "deny facts" established by the international military tribunal at the end of the war or to spread "false information about the Soviet Union's activities during World War II."[32] Ostensibly, the law was meant to counter the "rehabilitation of Nazism"—which the state television coverage of the crisis in Ukraine insisted was a real and growing threat—but the real purpose was to silence discussion of Soviet conduct during the war and seal off the official account from scrutiny. The most serious offenses were punishable by up to five years in prison. The law was clearly intended, commented veteran broadcaster Vladimir Pozner, "to shut the mouths of journalists, historians and writers."[33]

Eight months later, on December 24, 2014, a young car mechanic named Vladimir Luzgin finished up a long day at work in the city of Perm in the Ural Mountains and scrolled through his social media accounts to unwind. He reposted an article he thought was interesting on VKontakte, Russia's equivalent of Facebook, and went to bed. The article was about the Ukrainian nationalist movement during World War II and, crucially for Luzgin's fate, it included a line that said: "The Communists and Germany together attacked Poland, unleashing the Second World War." A total of twenty people saw the original post, but it came to the attention of the local prosecutor and the system cranked into gear.

The Federal Security Service (FSB), one of the successor agencies of the Soviet-era KGB, raided Luzgin's apartment and seized his computer, and he was charged with knowingly spreading false information about the Soviet Union's wartime actions under the new law.[34] In its verdict, the court found that Luzgin's "B" grade in his high school history course should have equipped him with the facts to understand his mistake. He was convicted and fined 200,000 rubles (around $3,400 at the time, more than five times the average monthly wage in Russia).[35] Luzgin appealed and lost again in Russia's Supreme Court before fleeing abroad and seeking asylum in the Czech Republic.

The idea for the law had been around since 2009, when the first draft legislation was presented to the Russian parliament, but it had failed to get traction, reportedly because of pushback from senior officials.[36] Then-president Dmitri Medvedev had set up a "Commission to Prevent the Falsification of History to the Detriment of Russia's Interests," which was also quietly abandoned. The legislation had reappeared in the summer of 2013 after Putin's return to the presidency, but nothing happened for a further six months until February 2014—just as the protests in Ukraine were reaching their height—when a new draft of the bill was swiftly approved and signed into law.[37] It was not a major anniversary year, as the seventieth anniversary of the end of the war in 2015 would have been, providing a more logical opening, but clearly the Kremlin felt the situation was sufficiently urgent that it could not wait another twelve months. Historian Mark Edele, who has written extensively about the memory of World War II in Russia, commented that the decision to pass the law looked like an "ad hoc decision by a government that increasingly feels embattled and under threat from enemies within and without."[38] It was a clear signal that the leadership would no longer tolerate any challenges, however valid, to its sacred myth. The history of the war was not up for debate.

The early cases were few and far between, but the effect was chilling nonetheless. Historians who examined the darker aspects of the war now did so at their own risk. St. Petersburg–based scholar Kirill Aleksandrov found out the cost of pursuing such research when he defended his doctoral dissertation on Soviet general and Nazi collaborator Andrey Vlasov in 2016. PhD defenses have long been open to the public in Russia, but Aleksandrov was surprised to find a rowdy crowd of around a hundred people waiting for him at the St. Petersburg Institute of History, including Russian Orthodox priests and Red Army veterans. "Where would you be, had we not won?" shouted one elderly veteran as he tried to answer the committee's questions. Another complained that the dissertation "destroyed the memory of the great victory." The institute's director said he was called in to the prosecutor's office for what he described as a "prophylactic conversation" about Aleksandrov's research, where he was urged to "think about the fate of the institute" before approving the award.[39]

The committee held its nerve and passed the dissertation, but it was overruled by a higher body and Aleksandrov's doctorate was withheld. For good measure, the local prosecutor's office announced that it would investigate his work to see whether it violated the new law against the rehabilitation of Nazism.

"The situation changed in the last five to ten years," Aleksandrov told me in 2019. "The discussion of my master's thesis in 2002 [on the same topic] did not cause any political reaction." But now he found himself at the center of a political storm. "My [academic] board and I were under aggressive pressure," he said. "There were threats of criminal prosecution. I have no doubt that this decision was political." The doctorate that he had worked for so long to earn was denied, and he was told that his work was a "black spot" on his institution's history. But he was heartened by the support he received from other academics.

"Dozens of colleagues, irrespective of their views, gave me support," he said. "This proves that we can have hope for the future."[40]

Others were less optimistic. Nikolay Koposov and his wife, Dina Khapaeva, both well-regarded scholars of historical memory in Russia, concluded that the only way they could continue their research with Putin in power was to leave the country.

"I didn't want to leave," Koposov told me from their new home in Atlanta, Georgia, but Khapaeva convinced him that they had no other choice. "Her family was really decimated by Stalin's repressions, and this kind of genetic fear of the Soviet state very much directs her analysis of the situation," he said. "And she was right. Soon dozens of people were saying to us, now we understand that you were right. You saw it coming." Koposov published an influential book on the subject, *Memory Wars, Memory Laws*, which examined how the Kremlin had used legislation to enshrine its version of history in the country's laws. "The dark side of Stalinism has been selected for amnesia, and the dark side of the war," he said. "Remembering the dark side of the war is now a criminal offense in Russia."[41] He believed the situation would only get worse.

* * *

Unlike in China, where the famine and the violence of the Mao years and the Tiananmen massacre had all but disappeared from the official narrative, Vladimir Putin still acknowledged that atrocities did take place under Soviet rule. Perhaps it helped that the Communist Party was no longer in power in Moscow as it was in Beijing. The Russian government funded a new museum on the history of the Gulag that opened in 2015, and Putin unveiled a new memorial to the victims of Soviet repression two years later, although he was immediately accused of hypocrisy for presiding over his own simultaneous crackdown on civil society.[42] But the message seemed to be that while the horrors of the past would not be completely erased in Russia, neither should they be the main focus of attention. The selective amnesia Koposov described cast the terror of Stalin's rule as just one aspect of that period, which should not be allowed to overshadow the heroic victory in the war.

The same year the new Gulag museum opened in Moscow, Russia's last surviving Gulag site, known as Perm-36, was forced to close. It had been restored by a group of local historians in 1995 to serve as a memorial to the Soviet Gulag system and an educational site, where visitors could see the guard towers and punishment cells for themselves and learn about the suffering that had taken place there. The museum had been supported by successive regional governors, but when Putin returned to the presidency for his third term in 2012, he replaced the governor and the museum's funding stopped. As relations deteriorated over the next three years, the authorities cut off the water and electricity supply over claims of unpaid bills and began investigating whether the group that ran the site should be designated as a "foreign agent" under a new law targeting nongovernmental organizations (NGOs). The state-controlled television network NTV accused the museum of taking money from the US State Department and claimed it was depicting Nazi collaborators and Ukrainian nationalists as heroes, cutting between shots of the complex and the ongoing conflict in Ukraine in its coverage.[43]

Finally, in March 2015, the museum's director admitted defeat. "We cannot do anything anymore," Viktor Shmyrov told reporters in March 2015. "It's enough that they've seized the museum, seized the property. We don't even have a kopek [cent] in our account. They've weighed us down with a bunch of debts. . . . We just can't go on anymore." He said they had no choice but to close the museum. "There are very powerful forces at work in this confrontation," Shmyrov added. "The Kremlin has many towers."[44]

The Perm-36 Museum reopened four months later, in July 2015, under new management and with a new focus on the Gulag's "contribution" to the war effort as an important source of labor for the local logging industry. A few of the original displays about Stalin's repressions and the Gulag system were still in place, but they were no longer the focal point. "We don't want to take sides," the new director, Yelena Mamayeva, told reporters. "We're trying to talk more about the architectural complex, and not to get involved in assessing specific people who served sentences there, and assessing Stalin, and so on. Because right now this is not quite politically correct." The region's culture minister, Igor Gladnev, focused his remarks at the opening ceremony on the war. "Glory to the heroes," he said. "Glory to those who fought, who laid down their lives in the name of our great victory and the preservation of our country."[45]

Memorial, the organization founded during the *Glasnost* era to preserve the history of Soviet repression, was repeatedly targeted by police and tax inspectors after Putin's return to office. Memorial's international branch was declared a "foreign agent," along with dozens of other NGOs, a designation that was intended to undermine its integrity and public trust in its research. The days of volunteers going to the streets holding quotations from the leader to ward off overzealous policemen were long gone. The political leadership and the enforcers were now on the same side. Activists wearing St. George ribbons hurled eggs and green dye at teenagers taking part in Memorial's annual history competition in Moscow in the summer of 2016, hurling abuse at the students as "traitors" who were trying to "rewrite our history."[46] The police just stood and watched.

Then, in November 2016, the chairman of Memorial's branch in the far northwestern region of Karelia, on the border with Finland, was summoned to his local police station. Aged sixty at the time, with long gray hair and a long gray beard, Yuri Dmitriev was a well-known local figure—an amateur historian who had devoted his life to locating the mass graves where the victims of Stalin's purges were buried in the vast surrounding forests. He had helped identify the burial sites of more than six thousand people so far. But all that counted for nothing as official attitudes to history changed and Dmitriev found his research was suddenly unwelcome. He was charged with the possession of child pornography, which his supporters, along with human rights organizations and the European Union, denounced as absurd and blatantly politically motivated, noting that spurious claims had been used to discredit other Kremlin critics.[47] His real crime was digging into the wrong aspects of the country's history.

Dmitriev was denied bail and held in a detention center, while historians from the Kremlin-backed Russian Military Historical Society set about undermining his work. They carried out their own excavations at the sites he had found and argued that the remains buried there could belong to Red Army soldiers captured and executed by the Finnish military during World War II. The local culture minister latched onto the claim, arguing that Soviet-era atrocities in the area had been exaggerated by "anti-government forces" to "damage Russia's international image."[48] The story of brave Soviet soldiers being murdered by foreigners suited the regime much better than the idea that they had been shot by their own side. Dmitriev was initially acquitted in 2018, but the verdict was overturned, and he was tried again and convicted. In 2020, at the age of sixty-four, he was sentenced to serve thirteen years in a high-security prison, which was later increased to fifteen years.

History had become a loyalty test. It was now deemed unpatriotic to focus on Stalin's terror and his murderous purges because that undermined the sacred memory of the wartime victory, which was fought under his leadership. Putin didn't approve of ignoring the dictator's crimes altogether, but neither did he think he should only, or even mainly, be remembered for them. They had built a memorial and a museum to deal with Stalin's atrocities, and that was supposed to be enough. "The problem," as Putin once explained to a group of Polish journalists, "is that it was under his leadership that this country won World War II. . . . It would be stupid to ignore that."[49]

Public attitudes toward Stalin improved under Putin. When the Levada Center asked people about their perception of Stalin in 2003, just over half—53 percent—said he had played a positive role in Russian history. But when they asked the same question in 2019, 70 percent thought his role was either "mostly positive" or "entirely positive."[50] Every five years since 1989, the center had asked people to name the "Ten most outstanding people of all times and peoples," and while Stalin had fared poorly at first, he topped the two most recent polls in 2012 and 2017, with Putin tied for second place in the latter case.[51]

* * *

Just as it had been during the Brezhnev era, the increasing focus on the Great Patriotic War under Putin was broadly well received. Starting in 1999, the Levada Center had carried out an annual poll of the historical events people were most proud of, and every year the Soviet victory in 1945 came in first. It was not even close. In 2017, the wartime victory polled forty points ahead of the next most popular answer: "Returning Crimea to the Russian Federation."[52]

"You can't say that Putin forced the war cult on the people, but you also can't say that the people independently demanded it," far-right political theorist Alexander Dugin told Shaun Walker, author of *The Long Hangover: Putin's New Russia and the Ghosts of the Past.* "It was a natural process that flowed in both directions. It was organic," Dugin said.[53] It was true that there was real enthusiasm around the commemoration of the war. Every family had some connection to the conflict, and grassroots initiatives sprang up alongside the official ceremonies. But the Kremlin was careful to retain overall control.

Three friends in the Siberian city of Tomsk came up with the idea of holding their own march on Victory Day in 2012, hoping that perhaps a few hundred people might show up. The plan was to carry portraits of their grandfathers, who had fought during the war, and encourage others to do the same, shifting the focus back to the individual soldiers and their suffering and sacrifice, instead of the increasingly bombastic official parades. They called it the Immortal Regiment. Several thousand people turned out for the first event and the idea soon spread. The following year, in 2013, Immortal Regiment processions took place in at least 120 towns and cities across Russia.

But with that popularity came the attention of the authorities. Sergei Lapenkov, one of the original organizers, said their priority was to keep the movement "noncommercial, apolitical, and nongovernmental," so that it wouldn't become "a promotional tool for any force or personality."[54] They turned down an approach from the ruling United Russia party to join forces on the initiative. But soon afterward another politician set up an identical organization called "The Immortal Regiment of Russia," and Sergei Ivanov, then Putin's chief of staff, directed local officials across the country to support the new movement, which soon subsumed the original and turned into everything they had sought to avoid. Businesses handed out placards to marchers, complete with their logo; schools corralled their students to take part. There were reports of participants being given photographs of strangers to march with, which they dumped in the trash at the end.[55] Before long, there were millions of people taking part in Immortal Regiment marches across Russia and around the world, with events in New York, London, Sydney, and

Beijing. In 2015, Putin marched in the Immortal Regiment in Moscow holding a black-and-white portrait of his father. It was the opposite of what the founders had intended.

"Everything this is now turning into is not right," Igor Dmitriyev, one of the original organizers, complained in 2016. He appealed to those who had taken over the movement to let it return to its original form. "Guys, stop, just stop," Dmitriyev pleaded. "You're all people. You all have grandfathers who fought. Let's just remember them. Sometimes this turns into dancing on bones."[56] His words had absolutely no effect. The next year's march was even bigger and more bombastic.

The Kremlin had decided the war should be remembered as a great and glorious victory, which best suited its current needs, and the leadership went to extraordinary lengths to wall off that version of history. While it was becoming increasingly difficult to talk about some of the aspects of the war that did take place, such as Soviet collaboration, Stalin's pact with Hitler, and the atrocities, the government moved to protect the fiction of those that did not, such as the legend of Panfilov's men. The famous story had been taught to every Soviet schoolchild and passed down through the generations. In November 1941, during the Battle of Moscow, twenty-eight guardsmen from the Red Army's 316th Rifle Division under the command of Major General Ivan Panfilov were said to have faced down a fearsome German tank assault. Armed only with rifles, hand grenades, and Molotov cocktails, they vowed to halt the German advance. "Russia is vast, but there is nowhere to retreat," one of the men was supposed to have declared. "Moscow is behind us."[57] They fought to the last man to stop the tanks and succeeded in stalling the attack, but all twenty-eight of Panfilov's men died in the battle, the last of them managing to recount the details of their struggle with his dying breaths. Their story was reported in the Red Army newspaper *Krasnaya Zvezda* (Red Star) in late 1941, where it attracted Stalin's attention. He declared the men Heroes of the Soviet Union and they were feted as the epitome of the Soviet fighting spirit. Streets were named after them and colossal monuments erected in their honor. The only problem was that the story wasn't true.

When one of the men turned up alive, Stalin assigned a team of military prosecutors to investigate the story and in a top-secret report in 1948 they concluded that the account was "pure fantasy."[58] Panfilov's unit did take part in the fight on the outskirts of Moscow and many of his soldiers undoubtedly displayed great bravery and heroism, but the story of the last stand of the twenty-eight was the work of a newspaper reporter's imagination. *Krasnaya Zvezda* correspondent Vasiliy Koroteev had visited the unit on the hunt for stories from the front to boost morale during the Battle of Moscow in the fall of 1941. He took down the names of twenty-eight soldiers who had recently been killed or were missing in action and made up the rest himself, including the famous rallying cry that they could not retreat because Moscow was behind them. The Soviet Union needed heroes, Koroteev later insisted in his defense. In fact, at least five of the men he depicted dying had survived the war, the investigation found, concluding that "the deeds of the 28 Panfilov guardsmen reported in the press are the fiction of correspondent Koroteev."[59] But apparently Stalin agreed with Koroteev on the need to preserve that fiction and the report was kept classified for almost half a century, while the imaginary feats of Panfilov's men were enshrined in the country's history as fact. The details resurfaced with the opening of the archives in the early 1990s, but to little notice among the torrent of other revelations, and then again in 2015 with much more serious consequences.

With a new action movie based on the tale in production, titled *Panfilov's 28*, the director of Russia's State Archives published the report from the original 1948 investigation on their website. The story was based on a "falsification," Sergei Mironenko said, and it was his duty as a historian to make the authentic documents from the time available. "History—it's a science that seeks the truth," he told one reporter. "There can be as many theories and hypotheses as you like, but there is only one truth."[60] He suggested they remember the many thousands of Soviet soldiers who really did die defending the capital instead of the fictional account. But instead, the film's producer attacked Mironenko for "trying to debunk instances of national heroism" and Russia's culture minister, Vladimir Medinsky, said anyone who dared question the tale was "filthy scum."[61]

"It would be good if we had a time machine and could send you, poking your dirty, greasy fingers into the history of 1941, into a trench armed with just a grenade against a fascist tank," said Medinsky, whose ministry spent 30 million rubles (roughly $460,000 at the time) of public money on the film. "Even if this story were made up from start to finish," he declared, "even if there had been no Panfilov, even if there had been nothing at all, this is a sacred legend which simply cannot be touched."[62] And clearly those above him agreed. Mironenko was removed from his position as director of the archives and his boss was summoned to a meeting with Putin at the Kremlin where he was told that the Federal Archive Agency would be brought under the president's direct supervision. "The materials in your agency's possession are of particular value for the country," Putin said.[63]

Panfilov's 28 was a box office hit and received an award for "fidelity to historical truth" from the Russian Military Historical Society, which Putin founded and Medinsky, the culture minister, chaired.[64] The Russian president was photographed enjoying a private screening of the film and his ambassador to the United States screened it at the embassy in Washington, DC, on the anniversary of the battle. "In one form or another the story of the Panfilovtsy's heroism did take place," Putin's spokesman insisted.[65]

The country needed its myths and its heroes more than it needed the truth, Putin had decided. In this he agreed with the man he would soon call his "best, most intimate friend," Chinese leader Xi Jinping, and the latest member of the Kim dynasty to rule North Korea, Kim Jong Un.

9

Heroes

A dictator must instil fear in his people, but if he can compel them to acclaim him he will probably survive longer.

—FRANK DIKÖTTER, *How to Be a Dictator*[1]

Pyongyang, North Korea

The phone beside my bed rang just after midnight. It was the younger
of our two government minders. He said there was going to be a "special event" the next day and we should be ready to leave by 5.30 a.m. He
couldn't tell me anything more, only that it would be "very high security"
and we should leave our phones and most of our equipment behind. I took
that to mean there was a good chance Kim Jong Un would be there.

I was in Pyongyang to cover Kim's first Workers' Party Congress in
May 2016. It was an important event. The last one had been held thirty-
six years earlier by his grandfather, Kim Il Sung, when he named his
son, Kim Jong Il (Kim Jong Un's father), as his successor. This latest
party congress was a chance for the third-generation leader to set out
his vision for the country and introduce his first five-year economic
plan. But so far the closest we had managed to get to Kim or any of
the proceedings was the outside of the building where the congress was
being held—or, to be more accurate, the far side of a six-lane highway
from the outside of that building. I could see the enormous portraits of
the first two Kims smiling down from the high gray walls and the outer
cordon of security guards, but that was pretty much it. Our two-person
team—me and Sky News camera operator Kevin Sheppard—was accompanied at all times by our two assigned minders, or guides, as they

preferred to be called. They slept in our hotel, which was on an island in the middle of the Taedong River, and they came with us every time we left. We wore blue armbands to identify ourselves as journalists to everyone we met as we toured model factory after model factory, and model workers told us how happy they were. "We work eight hours a day and everything is perfect," one woman told me in a typical response as she operated machinery at a silk factory in the capital.

Inside the factories, enormous propaganda posters urged the workers on to ever-greater feats of production, and the signs on the wall recorded all quotas being met and exceeded. But it was impossible to know what anyone really thought, even as their eyes filled with tears of gratitude for the Kim family during interviews, because my constant companions were always next to me, writing down the names of everyone I spoke to and everything they said.

The roads were deserted as we drove through Pyongyang in the early dawn on the morning of the special event, but the sidewalks were filled with people on foot. They streamed out of the subways and over the bridges, all heading in the same direction, all in their finest clothes. The women wore beautiful silk traditional gowns and the men were dressed in crisp white shirts and dark pants. Many carried the bright pink and magenta flowers named after the first two leaders, Kimilsungia and Kimjongilia. They vanished again as we approached Kim Il Sung Square in the city center, where soldiers with machine guns patrolled the empty streets.

Named after Kim Jong Un's grandfather and North Korea's first leader, Kim Il Sung Square was the regime's preferred location for grand parades and showing off its latest military hardware, and when we arrived that morning, the vast ceremonial space was already full. It was also completely silent. The crowds in the square stood in neat lines in their finery, Kimilsungia and Kimjongilia flowers by their sides, looking straight ahead. The military band waited in their places, motionless apart from the occasional glimmer as the polished brass of their instruments caught the strengthening sun. The VIP viewing stands behind me were crammed with men in black suits, the senior ranks of the ruling Workers' Party, and military officers in khaki dress uniforms, their chests glittering with an improbable array of medals.

They were all straining to look up at the balcony above us where the leader would appear. No one said a word. I had never seen so many people make such little noise.

Then the band struck up and they began applauding furiously. The crowd burst into ecstatic cheers. Blank expressions switched to euphoria. Flowers waved wildly overhead. Finally, Kim Jong Un stepped out into view. The square around us erupted into deep roars of adulation and a booming artillery salute. From my vantage point, Kim was a stocky figure in a dark suit, strolling slowly along the balcony, periodically clapping his hands and waving to the crowd, apparently pleased with what he saw. And what was there not to like. Everyone within sight was cheering and chanting his name. University students marched by in lockstep, punching the air with bright red torches and shouting "Mansae!" or what loosely translates as "Long live!" Goose-stepping soldiers held a rigid salute. A replica missile launcher rolled by laden with models of the regime's latest intercontinental ballistic missiles (ICBMs) to celebrate Kim's signature policy of simultaneously developing North Korea's economy and its nuclear weapons capabilities. Then came the adoring crowds of teachers, scientists, engineers, and factory workers, waving frantically and breaking into delirious cries as they neared Kim on his balcony.

Everybody cheered. Some wept. I watched an elegant woman in a sunflower yellow dress who looked to be in her early thirties screaming at an ear-shattering pitch as she approached the leader, eyes wide, apparently overcome with emotion. An older man wearing a suit that was too big for him waved his flowers in wild, uncoordinated circles and stumbled along, almost tripping over himself with the effort. It was uncomfortable, watching grown adults essentially prostrate themselves in these displays of hysterical devotion. Presumably some amount of the regime's relentless indoctrination does work, and some proportion of the crowd was genuinely delighted to be there—to get the chance to see the leader with their own eyes—but there was no way to be sure. The state broadcaster's camera crews were out in force, running back and forth alongside the parade, not to mention all of the foreign journalists. With so many cameras trained on their faces and the top ranks of the regime watching, it wasn't like they had a choice.

Kim Jong Un clapped his hands one last time and disappeared back into his sanctum. The music stopped and the crowd turned and walked away. Just as suddenly as it had started, the mass delirium stopped. There was no excited hubbub, no murmur of friends comparing notes, just a sea of people heading quietly for the exits. It was like watching a tide going out. I remembered the words of one man I had met in Seoul, a former soldier who fled North Korea in the early years of Kim Jong Un's rule. Everyone understood what was expected of them at these events, he told me, and how important it was to signal your loyalty. "If you don't clap, or if you nod off, you're marked as not following Kim Jong Un's doctrine," he said. "You have to do it because you don't want to die." He paused and clapped his hands for effect. "You chant 'long live' and clap because you don't want to die."[2]

* * *

It was once claimed that Kim Jong Un's father had nightmares about being stoned to death by his own people. "The first stones are thrown by Americans, followed by South Koreans, and the third by North Koreans," he reportedly told Hyundai founder Chung Ju-yung, according to an interview with Chung's son.[3] While there is no independent evidence that Kim Jong Il actually said this, and indeed there are reasons to be skeptical that he did, the current North Korean leader didn't have to look far to see much more gruesome examples of what happened to dictators who lost power in real life.

Saddam Hussein was captured cowering in a hole in the ground in Iraq and hanged on television. Libya's Muammar Gaddafi was dragged from a drainage ditch, brutalized, and shot. Both had presided over their own mass rallies of devoted citizens. Vast crowds had chanted, "Saddam is Iraq! Iraq is Saddam!" Gaddafi had been worshipped as the "Leader Who Lived in all Libyans' Hearts."[4] Just as I couldn't tell how much of the emotion in Kim Il Sung Square that day was genuine, neither could Kim Jong Un. When the penalties for disloyalty were so severe, how could he possibly know who was truly loyal and who was just acting the part?

But then the same went for everyone else, and that was part of the point of these performances. For some, the proximity to the leader and the collective fervor affirmed their faith, but for everybody else it demonstrated the leader's power and that unless they could be sure that many others felt the same way they did, it was safer to shout the slogans and clap along. Maintaining the Kims' cult of personality was as much about maintaining control as it was about inspiring genuine devotion, although that was clearly desirable if it could be achieved.

"The paradox of the modern dictator," writes Frank Dikötter in *How to Be a Dictator*, "is that he must create the illusion of popular support."[5] Repression alone was not enough. If a leader wanted to hold on to power, it was important to maintain the impression that they were genuinely popular, to manufacture at least the impression of consent. This meant the newspapers and television channels should always be brimming with praise and the leader should be met by adulation wherever they went. "The point was not so much that few subjects adored their dictators, but that no one knew quite who believed what," Dikötter explained. "The purpose of the cult was not to convince or persuade, but to sow confusion, to destroy common sense, to enforce obedience, to isolate individuals and crush their dignity. People had to self-censor, and in turn they monitored others, denouncing those who failed to appear sufficiently sincere in their professions of devotion to the leader."[6]

When Hafez al-Assad—father of the current president, Bashar al-Assad—ruled Syria, for example, he cultivated an elaborate personality cult, giving the impression that he enjoyed widespread public support, not unlike the Kim family in North Korea. But after extensive research into Assad's cult of personality, scholar Lisa Wedeen argued that it should be understood instead as a "strategy of domination," where citizens were required to act "*as if* they revere the leader," regardless of how they really felt, reinforcing the extent of his control. Assad was powerful, Wedeen said, "because people treat him as powerful," and the bigger the spectacle and "the greater the absurdity of the required performance, the more clearly it demonstrates that the regime can make most people obey most of the time."[7]

But the opposite was also true. The illusion of that power could be abruptly dispelled if the cheering crowds refused to perform. In December 1989, at the end of a tumultuous year for the Soviet bloc that had seen successive Communist regimes toppled across Eastern

Europe and the Berlin Wall brought down, Romanian leader Nicolae Ceausescu delivered a public speech to a vast crowd in Bucharest's Palace Square. During almost a quarter of a century of autocratic rule, he had built up his own pervasive cult of personality and presided over countless mass rallies cheering his name. But a few minutes into his speech that day, the crowd started to boo and jeer. Ceausescu stumbled to a halt, clearly confused. The state television cameras cut away and the network began playing patriotic songs, but the damage was already done. The protests that had been gathering strength in the country erupted into a full-blown revolution and the army turned against the regime. Four days after that speech, the dictator and his wife were convicted by a special military tribunal and shot by some of the paratroopers who had previously sworn to protect them.

Writing a decade before Ceausescu's downfall, Czech dissident and writer Václav Havel—who would go on to become president—described how the ruling Communist regime there coerced its citizens to go along with the charade of popular support. Using the example of a greengrocer who put a sign in his window with the slogan "Workers of the World, Unite!" he said that this behavior should be understood as a display of obedience and conformity rather than any indication of the man's real beliefs. The greengrocer put the party's slogans in the window, Havel explained, "because everyone does it, and because that is the way it has to be. If he were to refuse, there could be trouble." It was simply one of those things that "must be done if one is to get along in life."[8] Regardless of whether people really supported the regime, Havel said, if they wanted to be left in peace they were required to "behave as though they did" and "live within a lie."[9]

The lie Kim Jong Un required his citizens to live within was that he was following in his grandfather's footsteps and defending North Korea from its enemies. He blamed hostile foreign forces for the country's problems and claimed they needed to build up their military strength and nuclear capabilities to protect themselves. As his father and his grandfather had before him, Kim drew on a heavily distorted, in parts wholly fabricated version of history to support his claims, insisting that it was Kim Il Sung who had freed the country from Japanese colonial rule and then defended North Korea against an invasion by South Korea and the United States in the Korean

War, and that he was the next great leader in this heroic lineage. If he wanted to avoid ending up like Gaddafi, Saddam, or Ceausescu, the third Kim understood that he had to double down on that myth and maintain at least the appearance of public support—perhaps even the real thing.[10]

* * *

When Kim Jong Un took over after the death of his father in December 2011, there were the familiar predictions that he would fail to consolidate power and the regime would soon collapse. There was also a brief flurry of optimism among some outside observers that he might lead the country in a new direction. He was young, thought to be in his late twenties, although his precise age wasn't clear. He had been educated in the West at an elite private school in Switzerland, so he had seen what life was like outside North Korea and what a market-based economy could achieve. He was obsessed with basketball, the Chicago Bulls in particular. He had even flown to Paris once to watch them play in an NBA exhibition game. And he liked to play video games. He showed his school friends his new Sony PlayStation, his MiniDisc player (a popular music-storage device at the time), and pictures of him jet-skiing during vacations back home.[11] In an early speech, Kim called for officials to adopt a "creative and enterprising attitude" and "resolutely do away with the outdated ideological viewpoint and backward method and style of work."[12] There were hopes that perhaps this new, tech-savvy, basketball-loving young leader would follow the neighboring Chinese model of reform and opening and chart a course out of the country's isolation. But a decade later, North Korea would be under even stricter control.

The regime apparatus had been preparing for a third-generation leader from as early as 2005, when an official biography claimed Kim Il Sung had declared that if neither he nor his son was able to complete the work of building socialism, then "his grandson would carry it out."[13] After Kim Jong Il suffered a stroke in 2008, that preparation intensified. He told his top officials in January 2009 that he had chosen his youngest son, Kim Jong Un, as his successor, and the work of promoting him as the next great leader began in earnest.[14]

It had been hard enough to connect Kim Jong Il to his father's military exploits, but the regime had invented the story of his birth at the secret guerrilla base on Mount Paektu and portrayed him learning at Kim Il Sung's side during the Korean War. But Kim Jong Un's image makers had even less to work with. He had been born long after the mythologized conflicts ended and his own childhood of luxury palaces, elite private schooling abroad, and video games was hardly befitting of a revolutionary hero, especially when much of the country had been suffering through a catastrophic famine at the time.

But once Kim became the designated heir to the dynasty, the propaganda outlets began referring to him as the "Young General" and stressing his military credentials. In 2009, North Koreans began to hear a new song on the radio praising "General Kim." It played over and over again in continuous rotation, and they were instructed to memorize the words during compulsory political study sessions. The lyrics were printed in soldiers' notebooks. But they were not hard to remember: "Tramp, tramp, tramp, the footsteps of our General Kim . . . Bringing us closer to a brilliant future. Tramp, tramp, tramp, ah, footsteps."[15]

At first, there was very little public information about Kim Jong Un. "We knew nothing about him," one man later recalled to Anna Fifield, author of *The Great Successor: The Divinely Perfect Destiny of Brilliant Comrade Kim Jong Un*. "We had no idea what he looked like; we had no idea how old he was. We knew only how great he was."[16] But the details were soon filled in.

Kim had graduated from the Kim Il Sung Military University, as a top student, of course. His instructors lauded his instinctive grasp of military strategy, his prodigious intelligence, and his extraordinary work ethic. He would work until the early hours of the morning, they said, just like his grandfather, and he had a clear affinity with the famous guerrilla struggle. According to one account, instead of going to sleep one night, he stayed up sketching a detailed image of Mount Paektu, where the guerrillas had supposedly fought, and declared that it should be the cover for a new book about their great battles. The officials who were with him were said to have been "filled with deep emotion" at this pronouncement as they "realized he would carry forward the bloodline of Mount Paektu in its purest form."[17] The young leader-in-waiting was promoted to the rank of four-star general in the Korean People's Army in 2010.[18]

Once Kim Jong Un was in power, he drilled down on this martial theme. From his first public speech—at a military parade in April 2012 to mark the centenary of his grandfather's birth—he described how their country had been subjugated and forced to suffer before the rise of the Kim dynasty, echoing the Chinese Communist Party's (CCP's) argument, "because it did not have a proper leader and did not have the strength to defend itself." But just as Mao Zedong was said to have united the Chinese people and enabled them to stand up for themselves under the CCP's leadership, so Kim Il Sung was portrayed leading the Korean people to liberation with the "invincible might" of his "powerful revolutionary army of Mount Paektu." Kim Jong Il had "ushered in the golden age of the development of our revolutionary armed forces by dint of his uncommon wisdom, outstanding military leadership and matchless courage," his son claimed. And now he would lead the next phase of that valiant struggle. "Let us all fight vigorously, united firmly in one mind and one will as befits the descendants of President Kim Il Sung and the soldiers and devoted followers of Kim Jong Il," the young leader urged. "Forward towards final victory!"[19]

Kim Jong Un cut a very different figure from his father. Unlike Kim Jong Il, who rarely spoke in public and looked distinctly awkward during public appearances, his son gave televised speeches and waded into crowds of admirers during official visits, hugging his citizens and on one memorable occasion appearing to give a soldier a piggyback ride.[20] The new leader looked and acted much more like his grandfather, Kim Il Sung, who was often pictured smiling broadly and interacting warmly with the crowds during his own public appearances. At times he even dressed like the beloved founder, mirroring his penchant for wide-brimmed fedoras and great coats. But the third Kim also differed from his father in his approach to the economy. Where Kim Jong Il had introduced his *Songun* or "military first" policy, his son announced a new strategic line in March 2013 known as *Byungjin*, or "parallel advance," which called for a simultaneous push on developing the economy and nuclear weapons.[21] He promised an end to the days when citizens had to "tighten their belts" and allowed a degree of experimentation with the economy, including allowing farmers to keep and sell a proportion of their crops. The North Korean economy appeared to grow during Kim's first five years in power and he reiterated his commitment to developing the economy at regular intervals.[22] But it was clear that domestic political stability would always come first.

In a speech to propaganda workers in 2014, Kim warned against the "imperialists" he claimed were trying to "infiltrate corrupt reactionary ideology and culture into our country," and called for them to erect a "mosquito net" against the "viruses of capitalist ideology."[23] This was a long way from Deng Xiaoping's comment at the start of China's reform period in the early 1980s, when he said that "if you open the window for fresh air, you have to expect some flies to blow in."[24] And instead of embracing Chinese-style reform and opening, at the Korean Workers' Party Congress in May 2016 Kim denounced the "filthy wind of bourgeois liberty and 'reform' and 'openness' blowing in our neighborhood," and vowed to "let the spirit of *Songun* [military first] rifles fly."[25] Economist and North Korea analyst Ruediger Frank commented that it was hard not to see his remarks as "giving the bird to Beijing in the most undisguised way I have seen in official North Korean media for a long time."[26]

Kim stepped up the nuclear aspect of his "parallel advance," conducting four nuclear tests in his first five years in power. By the end of 2017, he claimed to have developed a hydrogen bomb and the long-range missiles needed to deliver it anywhere in the world, including the United States. He tested his first ICBM on the eve of the July 4 holiday and described it as a "gift" for the "American bastards," before declaring victory the following year in his *Byungjin* line and calling for all efforts to be focused on "socialist economic construction."[27] But he kept up the weapons development and stoked memories of the country's wartime past, reminding the population how much they had suffered during the Korean War and what the Kim family claimed to be defending them against. From the beginning of his rule, Kim commemorated the conflict with what historian Adam Cathcart called a "new urgency," channeling vast sums of money into rebuilding and significantly expanding the Korean War museum in Pyongyang.[28]

North Korea did not have the money to spare. In 2013, the same year Kim ordered the museum rebuilt, the United Nations warned that an estimated sixteen million people—almost two-thirds of the population—regularly lacked enough food to meet their daily needs, and children were dying from preventable illnesses because they didn't have access to clean water and basic sanitation facilities.[29] But preserving the regime's version of history had clearly been identified as a priority that was worth spending money on.

Like his father and his grandfather, Kim Jong Un perpetuated the fiction that the Korean War—or Fatherland Liberation War, as it was called there—was started by the United States and South Korea and that it had ended in a great victory for Pyongyang. The anniversary of the armistice on July 27, 1953, was celebrated every year as Victory Day, and the memory of that victory was hard-wired into daily life. Children learned about the Great Victory at school, and it was referenced in books, in newspaper articles, on television, and in films. Kim Jong Un's top officials were chauffeured around the capital in a fleet of gleaming black Mercedes with the prefix "727" on their license plates in honor of Victory Day, and one of the chain-smoking young leader's favorite cigarettes was said to be the luxury 7.27 brand.[30]

So it was perhaps not surprising that Kim demanded a complete overhaul of the conflict's main memorial site—the Victorious Fatherland Liberation War Museum in Pyongyang. According to state media reports, he took personal control of the project, approving plans, supervising the construction, and making at least a dozen visits to the site.[31] The scale and extravagance of the new museum was extraordinary. There was a palatial new entrance hall stretching three stories high and an ornate domed ceiling with a crystal chandelier in the shape of a five-pointed star, along with a colossal statue of Kim's grandfather, Kim Il Sung, which looked so much like Kim Jong Un that visitors sometimes struggled to tell them apart.

The new complex spanned more than a million square feet, according to the guidebook, and included more than 120,000 "war relics" such as captured enemy weapons, ammunition, and Kim Il Sung's uniforms, along with a replica battle scene that rotated through 360 degrees, complete with sound effects of explosions and gunfire. There was a heavy focus on the American "defeat," as it was characterized in North Korea. An entire hall had been made to look like a cemetery, with life-sized waxworks of US soldiers in various states of despair. One man stood near the front of the display with his head bowed and his cap in his hands before the visitors. Another sat on the ground among the ruins of their weaponry, his shoulders slumped and his head in his hands. Ravens picked over the remains of their comrades. One of the birds perched on a dead soldier's chest, its beak bloodied as it pecked at his heart. Row after row of ghostly white headstones stretched into the distance beyond in a literal rendering of the graveyard of imperialist ambition the conflict was held to be.[32]

But the museum was not just about the Korean War. It also featured exhibits about Kim Il Sung's guerrilla struggle against Japan, including his "secret camp" on Mount Paektu and a picture of the wooden cabin where Kim Jong Il was supposed to have been born. There were paintings, black-and-white photographs, and piles of old rifles that were supposed to be from Kim Il Sung's final offensive against Japan in August 1945, when he was actually in the Soviet Union. A large, colorized photograph showed his homecoming rally in Pyongyang, which if it was real had been airbrushed to remove the Soviet medal from his chest. The final displays brought the timeline up to the present, depicting incidents such as the capture of the USS *Pueblo*—a US naval intelligence ship that was seized by North Korea in 1968 and was now moored outside the museum and open to visitors—the murder of two US Army officers in the Demilitarized Zone (DMZ) in 1976 (which North Korea claimed was self-defense), and the shelling of Yeonpyeong Island in South Korea in 2010 (which the display said was "in response to the enemy's military provocation"). The exhibition ended with a celebration of North Korea's advances in developing nuclear weapons and long-range missiles, including photographs of the road-mobile ICBMs displayed during Kim Jong Un's first military parade in 2012. The accompanying caption informed visitors that North Korea had "achieved victory in the nuclear confrontation with the US on the strength of *Songun* [military first] politics."[33]

The underlying message was that it was all one endless conflict. From the first Kim's guerrilla struggle through the Korean War and the second and third generation of the family's rule, the Kims were depicted leading a tireless, heroic battle against the country's enemies. They were fighting on all fronts—to keep the country safe, to guard against ideological threats, and to develop the socialist economy—right up to the current leader, Kim Jong Un, and his ongoing showdown with the United States. It was all meant to remind citizens why they needed the Kims' leadership and why they needed to keep building up their military strength and their nuclear capabilities. Kim Jong Un called for the new museum to serve as a "base for anti-U.S. education" and inspire visitors in "carrying forward the fighting spirit displayed by the former generation."[34]

But that wasn't the end of Kim's museum-building projects. In 2014, he turned his attention to the Sinchon Museum of American War Atrocities commemorating the infamous massacre the regime falsely claims the United States carried out during the Korean War.[35] Around an hour's drive south of the capital, there had long been a memorial at the site, but the new leader decided it needed to be replaced with a new, much bigger museum and dramatic exhibits that would capture the imagination of younger visitors and bring the story to life for a new generation.

Where once there had been a modest building with displays of photographs and descriptions of the atrocities that were said to have been carried out at the site, now there was an enormous new museum filled with waxwork models reenacting the massacre. Jean Lee, who founded the Associated Press bureau in Pyongyang and reported extensively from across North Korea, described the rebuilt museum as a "veritable house of horrors, with room after room graphically bringing to life the gruesome atrocities attributed to the Americans." Visiting the museum, she said, was like "walking through the set of a horror movie; visitors can walk right up to the tableaus and can practically smell the blood and hear the screams."[36] In one room, a life-sized model of a beautiful young Korean woman was bound to a tree by two American soldiers, one of the men grabbing her by the hair while another drove a knife through her heart. "In another room," Lee recalled, "suffused in red light as though drenched with blood, American soldiers drive nails into a Korean woman's head. Rabid glee distorts their faces."[37]

Sinchon had been turned into a "mecca of anti-Americanism" under Kim Jong Un, Lee told me, where it functioned as a visceral reminder of the type of enemy they were up against and the regime's broader narrative that it was "continually fighting off American aggression." The museum went to great lengths to drive that message home. She remembers being taken into one building where she was told that hundreds of children had been burned alive. The walls were covered with scratch marks, she said, and the dimly lit space felt haunting and claustrophobic. Two purported survivors told the story of how they had been trapped inside the building and desperately tried to claw their way out, but when she tried to interview them afterward, she found they couldn't answer her questions or provide any details that convinced her the story was true.[38]

The experience was meant to be shocking. Like the Korean War museum in Pyongyang, Kim Jong Un declared that the Sinchon museum should be preserved as an educational site that would reveal "the bestial brutalities of the imperialist United States" and serve as the "provenance of thirst for revenge." The younger generation must never be allowed to forget "even for one second," he said, that their American enemies were "cannibals seeking pleasure in slaughter."[39]

As they left the museum, visitors were directed to the "revenge-pledging place" where they lined up in a concrete amphitheater and vowed to avenge these atrocities and smash the imperialists. "I will deeply ingrain in my students the brutal nature of the US imperialists, and that it will never change," Jang Yun Chang, a vice director at an elementary school, told journalists from Agence France-Press after visiting the museum in the summer of 2018. "My spirit for revenge is growing stronger."[40]

* * *

According to the Kim regime's logic, there is no contradiction between commemorating these past atrocities and sitting down with the current US president. In fact, the series of high-profile summits between Kim Jong Un and Donald Trump in 2018 and 2019 were portrayed in North Korea as testament to how far the country had come under the Kim family's rule. Where once they had been victimized and preyed upon by their imperialist enemies, the story went, now their leader was able to sit down as an equal with the president of the United States and demand respect and an end to that country's hostile policy against them. State media outlets aired carefully selected images from the summits that showed Trump looking contrite and listening attentively to Kim, and the meetings were presented as a great victory for the North

Korean leader. Footage of cheering crowds and banks of photographers greeting Kim's motorcade was used to bolster his image as the respected global statesman the regime had always insisted he was.

Throughout it all, the ideological study sessions continued as usual at home. Some of the more prominent anti-American propaganda disappeared from the streets of the capital, where foreigners were likely to see it, but the buses of schoolchildren, students, and workers still pulled up outside the war museums every day, and the lessons on US atrocities and vows of vengeance went on as before.[41]

But then Kim had stressed the connection between building up North Korea's military capabilities and developing the country and its economy from the start, ignoring the fact that his weapons programs brought sanctions that stifled economic development. Strength—and Kim's strong leadership—was presented as the foundation on which everything else depended.

As he explained it, they were in a perpetual battle for survival, with their enemies seeking to thwart them at every turn. They had experienced "grim struggle and glorious victory" in recent years, he said at that first party congress in 2016, after the Soviet Union collapsed and the "allied imperialist forces" focused their offensive on North Korea, plunging their socialist republic into "unprecedentedly hard times." From then on, he said, the "imperialists strained the situation constantly for decades to keep our people from living at peace even for a moment and blocked all the pathways to economic development and existence through all manner of blockade, pressure and sanctions."[42] Unlike his predecessors, however, Kim would later acknowledge and even tearfully apologize for his own failure to deliver more.[43]

When he celebrated what he claimed was the successful completion of his nuclear arsenal at the start of 2018, he described it as a "mighty sword" for "thwarting and countering any nuclear threats from the United States" and preventing their enemies from "starting an adventurous war."[44] Even the opening of a new ski resort and hot springs spa in 2019 was characterized as a victory over "the enemies who adamantly attempt to halt our advance."[45]

In this context, there was no disconnect between Kim Jong Un supervising artillery drills or the testing of a new long-range missile one day and inspecting cosmetic factories or a new waterpark the next. The message this juxtaposition was intended to send, explained Jung Pak, a former Central Intelligence Agency (CIA) analyst and author of *Becoming Kim Jong Un*, was that "they have this prosperity *because* of the nuclear weapons program that keeps them safe from the hostile outside world and provides them with status."[46] One could not exist without the other, the argument went, just as North Korea could not exist without the Kims.

Maintaining control of this narrative meant keeping a tight grip over access to information, which was even more challenging for Kim Jong Un than it had been for his predecessors as the world beyond North Korea became increasingly connected and technologically advanced.

It was increasingly common to see smartphones being wielded by the elite in Pyongyang, but the authorities enforced strict controls over which sites could be accessed, allowing citizens to connect to what was effectively an intranet, instead of the World Wide Web. Kim stepped up security along the border with China too and cracked down on the illicit but thriving trade in foreign media, such as popular South Korean dramas and films. There were reports of people being put to death by firing squad in public executions as an example to others after being caught distributing large quantities of foreign media.[47]

In late 2020, the government introduced a new law against "reactionary thought," which included punishment of up to two years in a labor camp for those caught using South Korean slang terms or speaking with a South Korean accent.[48] The idea was to keep citizens living within the regime's lie, where the leader was always fighting to defend them and the threat from their enemies was never far away. It was one of the reasons Kim was unlikely to be tempted by overtures to open North Korea up to the outside world, and the trade and investment that would follow, as he sought to maintain strict control over the ideological environment. Far from leading the country out of its isolation and loosening his hold, Kim ordered ideological education to be stepped up, which was no small task given the extent of the efforts at indoctrination that were already taking place.

* * *

Children were immersed in the regime's mythology from their first days at school. The idea that the country was fighting to defend itself against its enemies ran through their cartoons, schoolbooks, and playground games. When I visited a kindergarten in Pyongyang, there were soothing lullabies drifting across the schoolyard and smiling teachers in cotton candy pink uniforms and starched white caps tending lovingly to their charges. It was bucolic—apart from the rocket launchers. The pastel yellow walls of the playground were decorated with cartoon animals manning tanks, aircraft, and what appeared to be multiple launch rocket systems. The children played on a merry-go-round made up of miniature fighter jets circling a replica long-range rocket, waving happily as they sped around.

This was not unusual. Visiting another kindergarten in 2012, Jean Lee, the Associated Press bureau chief, remembers seeing children taking turns to pummel a dummy dressed like an American soldier in what she was told was "a favorite schoolyard game." The principal proudly explained that "our children learn from an early age about the American bastards."[49]

"There were usually two rooms in the kindergartens, one that was devoted to anti-American education and another devoted to anti-Japanese education," Lee told me. "The walls would be covered with very graphic imagery and there were shelves with props that they could use in games designed to teach them how to attack the Japanese or Americans." She remembered being shocked to see toy bayonets among the props, but the teachers were never embarrassed to show them to her. "They were very proud," Lee recalled. "They found it fascinating that I took such an interest. They were perfectly happy for me to learn and convey that this was part of their education."

In the afternoons, state television showed cartoons that were clearly meant for young children with violent, frequently anti-American plots. One long-running classic was *Squirrel and Hedgehog*, whose main characters I had seen on the walls of the kindergarten, who work together to defend their peaceful territory, known as Flower Hill (meant to represent North Korea), from invading weasels (Japan) and wolves (the United States), defeating their enemies' greater strength with courage, ingenuity, and teamwork. It was not a subtle allegory.

Even when they were not at school, they were learning about the threats their country faced, and children were expected to do their part to protect the nation too. From the age of seven, they joined the Korean Children's Union where they pledged to "turn out as human bullets and bombs" to defend the country "like the heroes of the Anti-Japanese Children's Corps and juvenile guerrillas" were supposed to have done during Kim Il Sung's guerrilla struggle and the Korean War.[50]

"Young people should be a death-defying corps defending their socialist country," Kim Jong Un told a meeting of the Youth League, which children join at the age of fourteen, in 2014. "All young people, their hearts burning with the will to annihilate the enemy, should participate in military training with all sincerity and make full preparations for combat mobilization, thereby staunchly defending their streets, villages, factories, farms and schools."[51]

The other main priority of the education system was to instill in students the importance of the Kim family's leadership. In 2015, high school students had to complete a 160-hour course on the life and work of Kim Il Sung, 148 hours on Kim Jong Il, and a new 81-hour course on Kim Jong Un.[52] But in fact the Kim-related content went far beyond this. As one former teacher told a UN inquiry into human rights in North Korea in 2014, studying the sacred teachings and the examples of the leaders made up "most of the education" in the country's schools.[53]

An elementary school teacher in Pyongyang told me the same thing, although she clearly meant it as a positive. Our minders had taken us to a new apartment building in the capital to see "how the average citizen lives" and Ms. Han, a soft-spoken woman with neat rectangular glasses, short dark hair, and pink floral throws on every item of furniture, was our designated "average citizen." She graciously showed me around her home, stressing how grateful she was to the socialist system and the hard work of the Kim family leaders for providing for all of her needs. "At the school we teach about the great president Kim Il Sung and great leader Kim Jong Il, as well as the respected marshal Kim Jong Un," Ms. Han (she didn't give her first name) explained when

I asked her about her work. "There is a special section at the school that specializes in teaching their greatness and what they are all about. For all of us, giving priority to the education about all the great leaders comes first of everything, before they have real knowledge about the other science fields."[54] And then she turned and gestured up at the smiling portraits of Kim Il Sung and Kim Jong Il on the wall above her with a smiling flourish as though their greatness was clearly evident and what more was there to say.

"The people of the DPRK [Democratic People's Republic of Korea] are taught from young to revere the Kim family and to internalize the state ideology as their own thoughts and conscience," the UN inquiry found, with children expected to respect and cherish the leaders more than their own parents. The aim of the education system was two-fold, it concluded: "to instill utmost loyalty and commitment toward the Supreme Leader" and "to instill hostility and deep hatred towards Japan, the Unites States of America (USA), and the Republic of Korea (ROK)."[55]

In this respect, Kim Jong Un was simply following in his father's and his grandfather's footsteps, packaging up the same old stories as his predecessors and feeding them to a new generation. In 2015, three years into his rule, a new history textbook for high school students was still claiming that the "American imperialists" started the Korean War "so that they could annex the entire Korea."[56] "Even today," students were told, "the American imperialists who are occupying the southern Republic [South Korea] are the cause of the Korean people's misfortune and pain." Therefore, it was essential, the text explained, to "guard our beloved general Kim Jong Un with our lives" and work to "fully eradicate the imperialistic American invaders, who are the greatest enemy of our Korean people, and accomplish the historically astounding reunification."[57] The new textbooks accused the "American imperialists and the puppet government [South Korea]" of staging provocative military exercises to stir tensions on the peninsula and set out the need for nuclear weapons and the means to deliver them as incontrovertible fact.[58]

With the United States creating a "war-like atmosphere" on the Korean peninsula and plotting to "invade the North," students are taught that North Korea has been forced to develop its own weapons programs to defend itself. "Our Fatherland secured its dignity through historical events like successfully launching the 'Kwangmyongsong-3' [widely considered to have been a covert long-range ballistic missile test] in December 2012 and successfully conducting the third under-ground nuclear test [in 2013], thereby sternly crushing the American imperialists' nuclear brinkmanship and schemes for invasion," the his-tory textbook explains.[59] Presumably it has since been updated to in-clude the fourth, fifth, and sixth nuclear tests and the launch of two intercontinental ballistic missiles.

This is not the syllabus of a country that is preparing to give up its nuclear weapons anytime soon.

* * *

I heard the same rationale from people up and down the system. To a person, they repeated the official line about why North Korea needed its nuclear weapons, whether they truly believed it or not, insisting that it was an entirely defensive move.

"Our nuclear policy is a result of the US hostile policy against us," Choe Il, North Korea's ambassador to the United Kingdom, told me in 2017. "The US has been threatening us with nuclear power for over sixty years. They have been threatening to launch a nuclear attack and destroy us. We need nuclear power to defend ourselves."

We were talking in the living room of the suburban house that func-tions as North Korea's embassy and official residence in London, which was equipped with a pool table and mahogany leather sofa and arm-chairs and gave off more of a bachelor pad vibe than nuclear-armed rogue state. "The US has been attacking only the weak countries, such as Afghanistan and Libya," Choe said. "If we have nuclear power, the US could not attack us first."

But surely his government's pursuit of nuclear weapons was only impoverishing his people, I pressed him, and making their lives harder by forcing them to live under sanctions. At a time when so many North Koreans were struggling for food, how could they possibly justify the vast expense of the nuclear program, I asked. But Choe stuck fast to the regime's line that without nuclear weapons they would have nothing at all. "We lived under Japanese rule for thirty-six years in the last cen-tury," he said. "The lesson we learned was that having no strength led to us losing our country and becoming a colony. The only way to protect our country is that we strengthen our power enough to suppress any enemy countries. This is the only way to protect our peace and security." He paused for effect. "This is a lesson we feel in our bones."[60]

A junior official in Pyongyang put it to me more succinctly: "We have learned the price of being weak."

Of all the stories the Kim regime told its people, the one about the country's suffering and Kim Il Sung's heroism during the wars of the last century was the most compelling. It was true that the country had endured terrible hardship under colonial rule, that Kim really was a guerrilla fighter, and that the Korean War had been utterly devastating. If you didn't know the truth about who started the Korean War, or how the Second World War ended, the official version of history made sense. Andray Abrahamian, who traveled to North Korea more than thirty times over the course of a decade with the nonprofit organization Choson Exchange, said that people he met did seem to be convinced by the regime's account of the Korean War at least. "The North Korean people genuinely believe it was a defensive war," Abrahamian writes in *Being in North Korea*. "Even for many defectors, most of whom are somewhat cynical about the DPRK, the fact that it wasn't is the hardest thing for them to accept."[61]

"There are no rumors contradicting the official line on the Korean war—nothing to make people think otherwise about this 'truth,'" explained Mina Yoon, who was in her early twenties when she fled North Korea in 2010. "I never heard anything about the Korean War that contradicted what I had learned in school." In fact, when she arrived in South Korea and was told that it was the North that had invaded the South, she thought it was a trick to "brainwash" escapees. "Even if you try to tell the truth about the war to North Korean people, no one would be likely to believe it," Yoon said. "It was unbelievable even for someone like me, who voluntarily left North Korea." As she summed it up, "It looks like Kim Il Sung did a very good job in sealing the truth of the Korean War in complete darkness."[62]

As he neared the end of his first decade in power, Kim Jong Un understood the importance of keeping that truth sealed in darkness and perpetuating his grandfather's myths. That version of the past provided him with a heroic, revolutionary pedigree and an endless fount of enemies to blame for the country's problems. And while the Kim family might have taken the idea to extremes, at its root the message was the same as in Russia and China: that theirs was an extraordinary nation, with a great and glorious history, whose leaders were waging a valiant struggle to defend their interests. In other words, they were the heroes, not the villains of this story.

So as talks with the United States that might have yielded sanctions relief petered out and the prospects of a deal faded in late 2019, Kim returned to this familiar theme. With the television cameras in tow, he mounted a magnificent white stallion and led his generals on horseback to the snow-capped summit of Mount Paektu. They toured the "secret guerrilla camps," huddled around campfires, and galloped through forests of snow-covered pines as he retraced his grandfather's footsteps and claimed to be leading a new heroic struggle against their contemporary enemies.

"Riding a steed across the vast area of Mount Paektu together with the commanding officers who accompanied him," the state news agency said, "he recollected the bloody history of the guerrillas who recorded dignity on the first page of the history of the Korean revolution by shedding their blood in the vast plain of Mount Paektu." Kim called for the whole nation to learn from the guerrillas' example and "instill the indefatigable revolutionary spirit of Mount Paektu" as they confronted "the unprecedented blockade and pressure imposed by the imperialists."[63]

Footage from the expedition was incorporated into a documentary about Kim's "legendary miracle year" that aired daily on North Korean television during the early weeks of 2020. It included a montage of the leader supervising military drills and weapons tests, and a grave warning that the "hostile forces' scheme to isolate and crush us to death is at its height." Viewers were urged to follow his lead and redouble their efforts to thwart those enemies.

The film ended with Kim and his generals galloping into the sunset over soaring, dramatic music and a call to "Advance! Advance! Advance!"[64]

IO

Patriots

The Chinese people will never allow foreign forces to bully, oppress or
enslave us. Whoever nurses delusions of doing that will crack their heads
and spill blood on the Great Wall of steel built from the flesh and blood
of 1.4 billion Chinese people.

—XI JINPING[1]

Beijing, China

Xi Jinping and Vladimir Putin strode out to the Gate of Heavenly
Peace in the center of Beijing. The sky overhead was perfectly blue. The
crowds waved their red flags in perfect unison. This was the entrance to
the Forbidden City when China's last emperors ruled, and it was where
Mao Zedong declared the foundation of the People's Republic in 1949.
But that wasn't why they were here. They had come to commemorate
Victory Day, the anniversary of the end of World War II in China, or
as it was known there, the Chinese People's War of Resistance against
Japanese Aggression and World Anti-Fascist War.

"In that devastating war, the Chinese People's War of Resistance
against Japanese Aggression started first and lasted longest," Xi said
in his speech on September 3, 2015. "The unyielding Chinese people
fought gallantly and finally won total victory over the Japanese milita-
rist aggressors, thus preserving the achievements of China's 5,000-year-
old civilization and defending the cause of peace for mankind."[2] Now,
to celebrate that peace, there would be a massive military parade.

Twelve thousand troops marched into Tiananmen Square in perfect lockstep. When they reached Xi their heads snapped right, a sea

of resolute faces turning to salute their commander in chief. From the crowded press pen, I squinted up at the tiny figures of Xi and Putin on the balcony high above us as the soldiers goose-stepped past below. Most of all, I was struck by the sound, the boots stamping out a relentless drumbeat on the pavement and then the low guttural growl of the tanks. They rumbled past in a cloud of engine smoke and they were so heavy I could feel the ground shaking beneath my feet. Next came a procession of the country's latest, most formidable weaponry. There was the new long-range strategic missile, the Dong Feng (East Wind) 5B, designed to carry a nuclear warhead and capable of reaching targets in Western Europe and the United States, and the Dong Feng-21D anti-ship missile, dubbed the "carrier killer" for its purported ability to sink an aircraft carrier.

Putin shaded his eyes from the sun on the balcony. Xi looked straight ahead. His face was impassive, even slightly bored. Fighter jets roared through the sky above us, followed by a thunderous swarm of attack helicopters that made downtown Beijing look like a scene from *Apocalypse Now*. Clearly this was as much about demonstrating the country's growing strength as it was about remembering the past. But then, both leaders insisted the two were inextricably linked.

Xi Jinping was then midway through his first term as general secretary of the Chinese Communist Party (CCP), while Putin, his increasingly close friend, had been in power for fifteen years. Putin said they had first bonded over family memories of World War II while they shared a late-night shot of vodka and "sliced some sausage" at an Asia-Pacific leaders' summit in 2013, and they evidently also shared an understanding of the conflict's wider resonance.[3] The two leaders deployed their extensive security forces to crush dissent and silence their opponents, but they also both appealed to the history of the war to rally public support.

In Russia, Putin exploited the sacred myth to frame the country's contemporary challenges and cast his enemies as traitors, and in China, too, Xi was intensifying focus on the conflict and turning to the past to serve his contemporary needs. The Victory Day celebrations in 2015 were a case in point. While the extraordinary scale and seamless choreography made this look like a long-held tradition, it was not. In fact, this was the first time the Victory parade had ever been held. Victory Day was one of three new national holidays that had been created the previous year, along with an annual day to commemorate the Nanjing Massacre, which was carried out by Japanese troops during World War II, and Martyrs' Day, which was dedicated to all those who had given their lives to defend the country.[4]

It was not unusual for a country to designate memorial days to honor its fallen, but this was all happening seventy years after the end of the war. It had taken long enough for the Soviet leadership to reinstate Victory Day—almost two decades after Stalin canceled the holiday there—but it took the CCP another half century to come around to the idea.

The new memorial days were just the beginning. Xi called for a renewed effort to study the history of the conflict, although on the party's terms, and while Chinese suffering during the war with Japan had played an important role in the party's post-Tiananmen patriotic education campaign, he now turned up the volume and shifted the emphasis. As well as remembering the country's suffering during the conflict as part of the broader "century of humiliation" China had endured before the party came to power, he said the war should also be remembered as the beginning of the end of that humiliation and the start of the journey to what he called the "China Dream of national rejuvenation."[5]

The victory over Japan was the "first complete victory won by China in its resistance against foreign aggression in modern times," Xi said in his Victory Day speech in 2015. Not only did it "put an end to the national humiliation of China," he explained, but also this "great triumph represented the rebirth of China, opened up bright prospects for the great renewal of the Chinese nation, and set our ancient country on a new journey." What was more, the victory "re-established China as a major country and won the Chinese people the respect of all peace-loving people around the world."

This was an important part of Xi's narrative of the war and another point on which he and Putin agreed: that as the nations that had sacrificed the most to save the world from fascism, the war had earned them the right to respect. They presented themselves as the founders and guardians of the postwar international order, instead of its greatest threat. Putin had illegally annexed Crimea a year earlier and he was fighting a covert war in Ukraine at the time, while Xi was installing surface-to-air missiles and military facilities on artificial islands in the South China Sea. But both leaders claimed they were the ones upholding world peace and it was US hegemony that posed the real danger.

"All countries should jointly uphold the international order and system underpinned by the purposes and principles of the UN Charter [which China was the first to sign]," Xi said. They should "build a new model of international relations based on mutually beneficial cooperation, and advance the noble cause of global peace and development."[6] In his telling, China's growing military strength was simply to defend its interests and ensure the country would never again be pushed around. Even as the tanks and the intercontinental ballistic missiles rolled through Tiananmen Square, the official commentary assured viewers that China's rise would always be peaceful.

"Our generation is lucky to be born at a time when the country will not be bullied by others," remarked one student at Beijing's prestigious Tsinghua University after watching the military parade. "Now we will show the world how strong China is," said an eight-year-old girl.[7]

* * *

When Xi was unveiled as the CCP's new general secretary in November 2012, there were some predictions that he would unleash a series of pragmatic reforms. "Mao's body will be hauled out of Tiananmen Square on his watch," wrote Nicholas Kristof in the *New York Times* in January 2013. "And Liu Xiaobo, the Nobel Peace Prize–winning writer, will be released from prison."[8] Xi's father, Xi Zhongxun, who had served under Mao as one of the first generation of Chinese Communist revolutionaries, had supported economic reforms, Kristof pointed out (he was not alone in his optimism), and Xi's mother had elected to live in the "capitalist enclave" of Shenzhen. His daughter was studying at Harvard in the United States. But as with Kim Jong Un, who took over across the border in North Korea the previous year, those early predictions turned out to be wrong. Instead of loosening his grip, Xi consolidated power and reasserted the party's role in the economy and across all aspects of society. Liu Xiaobo died in detention in 2017, with Mao still firmly ensconced in his mausoleum.

Like Putin and Kim, Xi saw history as a crucial tool for maintaining power. It was the foundation on which the party built its claim to rule and framed its appeals for public support. It was the basis on which they attacked their opponents and the answer to the question as to why China needed the Communist Party at all. As Deng Xiaoping had urged in the aftermath of the Tiananmen crackdown, they needed to continually remind people "what China was like in the old days and what kind of country it was to become" before the rise of the CCP.

Also, like Putin, Xi had seen for himself what happened when a Communist regime lost power. Xi was a mid-ranking party official in the southeastern province of Fujian when he watched the Soviet Union collapse. "All it took was one quiet word from Gorbachev to declare the dissolution of the Soviet Communist Party, and a great party was gone," he later said. He had given considerable thought to how the CCP could avoid the same fate, and it was one of the first issues he raised after becoming general secretary. "Why did the Soviet Union disintegrate? Why did the Soviet Communist Party collapse?" he asked party members in a closed-door speech in December 2012, less than a month after taking office. "An important reason was that their ideals and convictions wavered," he said. "In the end, nobody was a real man, nobody came out to resist."[9]

He repeated that message a few weeks later when he returned to the Soviet collapse during a seminar for senior officials. "The struggle in the ideological sphere was extremely fierce," Xi said of the situation in the Soviet Union at the time. "There was a complete denial of Soviet history, denial of Lenin, denial of Stalin, pursuit of historical nihilism, confusion of thought." With discipline breaking down and the party's history under attack, he said, "the great Soviet Communist Party scattered like birds and beasts. The great Soviet socialist nation fell to pieces."[10]

Xi was determined not to repeat those mistakes. As he saw it, national security was not just a physical or a material concept. They also had to guard against threats in the ideological sphere.[11] And already there were signs of some of the same looming dangers for the CCP as there had been in the Soviet Union. Organizational discipline had collapsed, corruption was spiraling, and ideological control was failing. If they wanted to avoid the same fate they would have to act fast. Public support, Xi warned, was a matter of the party's "survival or extinction."[12] Unlike Gorbachev, he intended to put up a fight.

In the spring of 2013, a secret communique known as Document No. 9 circulated among senior officials. The party faced a "complicated, intense struggle" in the ideological realm, the document warned, setting out a series of "false ideological trends" that must be confronted. These included efforts to promote "Western constitutional democracy," "universal values," "civil society," and "historical nihilism," which meant denying the party's version of history. The goal of this historical nihilism, the document explained, was to undermine the party's legitimacy and challenge its "long-term political dominance." In other words, if the party wanted to hold on to power, it would have to strengthen its grip on the country's history. Officials were urged to wage a "perpetual, complex, and excruciating" struggle, making ideological work a top priority in their daily schedules.[13]

A select group of historians convened for a special conference at the Chinese Academy of Social Sciences (CASS), a government-affiliated research institute, in Beijing the following year and concluded that historical nihilism was one of the main tactics "hostile international forces" were using to try to Westernize and divide China. They called for a more disciplined approach to the study of history that would "safeguard ideological security" and "create a positive image of China."[14]

Just as the party's focus on the country's past "national humiliation" after the Tiananmen crackdown had seen a sudden surge of scholarship on the subject, so too now historical nihilism became a hot topic for research. New papers and initiatives proliferated. *Qiushi* (*Seeking Truth*), the party's ideology journal, devoted a special section on its website to the battle to combat historical nihilism, complete with a banner quote from Xi Jinping: "History is history, truth is truth, and no one can change history or truth."[15]

This wasn't true. The Communist Party had rewritten plenty of the country's history. The extent of the man-made famine under Mao had been erased, as had the scale of the violence during the Cultural Revolution and the Tiananmen massacre. It would be more accurate to say that history and truth were whatever the leadership said they were at that moment, and no one was allowed to challenge that version of events. But the party presented its campaign against historical nihilism as a patriotic mission, and the hunt for historical nihilists was on. It was against this backdrop that a young historian from Beijing attempted to question one of China's most sacred myths from the Second World War.

* * *

Hong Zhenkuai did not look like a radical. When I met him at a busy coffee shop just off Beijing's notoriously congested Third Ring Road, he was wearing smart wire-rimmed glasses and a navy-blue pullover and battling a heavy head cold. He spoke quietly, sometimes barely audible above the coffee grinder and the background music, which seemed to be cycling through the hits of the early 2000s from Dido's *White Flag* to *You're Beautiful* by James Blunt. Hong paused periodically to blow his nose and apologize as he told me the unlikely story of how his research had landed him on the front lines of Xi's battle to control China's past.

Hong had been captivated by the tale of *The Five Heroes of Langya [Wolf's Teeth] Mountain*, which he, and every other Chinese schoolchild over the last five decades, had learned growing up. It was one of the country's best-known war stories and a staple of Communist Party propaganda, recounting how five Chinese soldiers had sacrificed their own lives to save their comrades from the advancing Japanese army during World War II. Statues of the five men stood in pride of place in the country's war museums as monuments to the heroism of Communist troops during the conflict. But like the story of Panfilov's men in Russia, there were reasons to doubt whether it was really true, and Hong had decided to investigate.

According to the official version of the story, it took place in 1941 in the central Chinese province of Hebei, where soldiers from the Communist Party's Eighth Route Army were surrounded and about to be overrun by Japanese forces. Their only hope of breaking out of the encirclement, so the story goes, was to create a diversion and lure the enemy away from the main body of Chinese troops so that they could escape and regroup. The commander selected five men and ordered them to draw the Japanese army up into the mountains and hold out for as long as they could. He gave them each five hand grenades. The men understood what was being asked of them and that there was no hope of surviving the mission, but they were said to have accepted their orders at once and marched off up the mountainside.

The Japanese soldiers took the bait, pursuing the men up the steep slope as the five men ran back and forth to different firing positions to give the impression of a much larger force. When they ran out of bullets and grenades, they threw rocks and heaved enormous boulders down on their attackers. But finally, they found themselves trapped at the edge of a steep cliff with nowhere left to go. They smashed their rifles so that they wouldn't fall into the enemy's hands and gathered together one last time. The most senior officer among them told the men that they had stood the test of battle and proven themselves worthy of becoming members of the Communist Party and that as he was already a member, he would recommend them for admittance. He scrawled a note to that effect and tucked it into his uniform, assuring them that one day the letter would be found, and they would be posthumously admitted to the party. Then they supposedly leaped to their deaths, shouting, "Down with Japanese Imperialism! Long Live the Communist Party of China!"[16]

The story first appeared in a Communist Party newspaper in 1941 after two of the men survived the fall and managed to recount their miraculous tale. It had been reproduced in textbooks, paintings, and films in the years since, and there were claims that at least ninety Japanese soldiers had been killed or wounded in the battle. But the truth may not be so straightforward. Research in Japanese archives by Jiang Keshi, a professor of modern Japanese history at Okayama University, found no evidence of any Japanese losses in the area, although there were indications some fighting did take place.[17] Hong identified further inconsistencies in the account, and after climbing the mountain himself with a local guide, he was satisfied that the incident could not have taken place as it was described. He published his findings in an article in the liberal history journal *Yanhuang Chunqiu* (generally translated as *China Annals* or *China through the Ages*) in the fall of 2013.[18] The publication had managed to coexist with the Communist Party for a quarter of a century, reportedly because of support from senior officials, but with the crackdown on historical nihilism underway, the space for critical examination of Chinese history was shrinking. Soon, both Hong and the journal were under attack.

Two prominent leftist commentators led the assault. In November 2013, retired air force pilot Guo Songmin and economist Mei Xinyu accused Hong and his editor, Huang Zhong, of historical nihilism and denounced them as "sons of bitches" on their social media accounts, which each had more than 250,000 followers.[19] Hong and Huang tried to sue for defamation, but the court ruled in favor of Guo and Mei, finding that the article had attempted to "subvert the heroic image of the 'Five Heroes of Langya [Wolf's Teeth] Mountain'" and "injured the national and historical sentiment of the public."[20] A senior People's Liberation Army (PLA) officer testified during the trial in May 2015 that Hong and Huang had "wantonly demonized [CCP] history, demonized the people's leaders, and smeared revolutionary martyrs and national heroes."[21] As they left the courtroom the two historians were jeered and heckled as "traitors," according to one witness, while Guo and Mei received "resounding applause."[22]

Relatives of two of the five soldiers then sued Hong for libeling the heroes. Here, too, the court ruled against the historian and ordered him to apologize. "The national sentiments, historical memories and the national spirit reflected in the five heroes of Langya Mountain and their story are important sources and components of modern China's socialist core values," ruled the Beijing Xicheng District People's Court. "Thus, it also damages the Chinese nation's spiritual values."[23] As in Russia, it was clear that the official version of history was not up for debate. Presumably to underline that point, Xi Jinping praised "heroic groups such as the Eighth Route Army's 'Five Heroes of Langya Mountain'" on the eve of the 2015 Victory Day celebrations, calling them the "backbone" of our nation. The following day's parade featured a formation in honor of the "Five Heroes."[24]

Hong told me the pressure on historians had been getting steadily worse since Xi took power. "During the Hu Jintao and Wen Jiaobao era [which preceded Xi], *Yanhuang Chunqiu* was allowed to publish articles about history and explore the historical truth," he said. "But not anymore." In 2016, *Yanhuang Chunqiu*'s staff was locked out of its offices and the editorial board was replaced with party loyalists.

"This is shameless," the publication's ninety-three-year-old founder, Du Daozheng, protested. "It's just like the Cultural Revolution."[25] Guo Songmin was invited to write for the revamped publication. Hong Zhenkuai was left unemployed.

"Now I don't have work," Hong said matter-of-factly. "Normal organizations don't dare to have me as an employee." He said he had also been put on a blacklist that meant he couldn't buy train tickets or book flights and his social media accounts were blocked. "Basically, I can't publish anything inside the country. I can only publish on overseas platforms and publications."

While the hardline Mao supporters—sometimes called neo-Maoists—had long tried to police the boundaries of historical inquiry in China and accused scholars they opposed of historical nihilism, Hong said the difference now was that they seemed to have the backing of the senior leadership. "From 2013, the frequency of the term 'historical nihilism' increased significantly," Hong explained, typing it into an academic database on his laptop to demonstrate the sudden proliferation of books and papers on the subject after Xi came to power. "The political situation is going backwards. The ideology is going backwards too," he said. "The far-left ideology is coming back."

But despite the personal consequences he had suffered and his ongoing legal troubles, he said he refused to give up the pursuit of objective historical truth. "I am an intellectual, and from the ancient times, intellectuals have had their own beliefs towards society and this country," he said. "We believe in the freedom of academia, we believe in the independence of human nature, and as a modern intellectual I want to carry on this belief."[26]

Two months after we spoke in February 2018, the Chinese government passed a law making it an offense to "defame, profane or deny the deeds and spirits of heroes and martyrs."[27] Both Hong Zhenkuai and Guo Songmin told me they believed the law was in response to their case.

For his part, Guo insisted he also had no regrets. All history was political, he told me in a Beijing Starbucks early one Sunday morning. In Xi Jinping, he was grateful to have a leader who finally understood the dangers of allowing open discussion of the historical truth. This was where the Soviet Union had gone wrong under Gorbachev, Guo said.

"The Soviet government didn't realize this. They didn't try to stop it, they tolerated it and encouraged it, and that was the reason the USSR collapsed." Xi had made a good start, he thought, but they needed to be on their guard for new attempts at historical nihilism in China. "The risks have been controlled, but the risks have not been eliminated," he warned. In his view, history was much too important to be left to the historians.[28]

* * *

The approach to history in China under Xi was a one-way ratchet. Where in the past scholars had experienced periods of tightening and loosening in terms of the sensitivities of historical research, now there was only tightening. "Since Xi Jinping came to power there has been a very big change," a professor at one of Beijing's top universities told me. He asked me not to identify him because he was worried he would get into trouble. We met at a café away from the campus, but he kept his voice low and glanced nervously around the room as we talked. "Of course, no one will tell you that officially, and it is not written down; no one knows where the line is for certain," he said. "But I know there are some things I cannot say, and if you are an editor, you understand that you will not publish certain articles. This is how things are in China now."[29]

His words reminded me of a famous essay by the China scholar Perry Link, a professor of Chinese language and literature at the University of California–Riverside who coauthored *The Tiananmen Papers*, detailing the Communist Party's crackdown in 1989. Link compared the official approach to censorship to "a giant anaconda coiled in an overhead chandelier." Normally, he wrote, "the great snake doesn't move. It doesn't have to. It feels no need to be clear about its prohibitions. Its constant silent message is 'You yourself decide,' after which, more often than not, everyone in its shadow makes his or her large and small adjustments."[30]

Those calculations had always been a fact of Chinese academic life, the professor explained, but increasingly the great snake was making its presence felt. Multiple cameras had been installed in his classroom and he was nervous that his students might report him to the university administration if he discussed sensitive subjects or contradicted the party's line. That fear was not unfounded. Not long after our conversation, Zhai Juhong, an associate professor at Zhongnan University of Economics and Law in Wuhan, was fired for making "ideologically incorrect" remarks in class after some of her students reported her to administrators, and other academics warned about the increased use of student informers.[31] The party had declared universities a "major battleground" for ideological struggle and banned the use of textbooks promoting "western values."[32] Well-funded research institutes devoted to the study of Xi Jinping Thought were springing up on campuses, meanwhile, as officials called for universities to ensure Xi's teachings reached students and to promote a "patriotic striving spirit" on campus.[33]

"From Deng to Jiang to Hu, the change was gradual," the professor told me, listing the previous three Chinese leaders. "*Yanhuang Chunqiu* was still able to publish articles by scholars with liberal views. But after Xi took office there was a new approach." It was dressed up as patriotism, but really this approach to history was about serving the party's interests. "History is being rewritten to enhance the party's legitimacy," he said. "You see all the how; you know the why." He was an optimist by nature, and he wanted to believe that the situation would eventually improve, but he feared they were heading back to the days of ideological taboos and the "forbidden zones" that had existed under Mao, when it was safer for scholars to "stop thinking and using your head."[34]

I met up with another historian in a busy canteen-style restaurant in Beijing. This time he was perfectly happy for me to use his name because he said the authorities already knew who he was talking to anyway. Zhang Lifan and his wife were already in a booth at the back when I arrived. An immaculately dressed couple in their late sixties, they looked more like a pair of retirees enjoying an early lunch than dodging government surveillance. He wore a light tan sports jacket over a buttoned-up polo shirt, matching tan flat cap laid neatly on the table in front of him. She was an elegant woman with a warm smile and a long, sleeveless cardigan over her sapphire blue sweater. "I'm sorry it's a bit loud in here," Zhang said, "But that means it's safe."

He presented me with his business card, holding it out with both hands in the formal manner. "Zhang Lifan, Historian," it said. "Restore

History, Contribute Common Sense." He said he had arranged to meet an American journalist at a local Starbucks recently, but there were already "people" there waiting for him and it was difficult to talk openly, so it was better to have more background noise. Sure enough, around ten minutes later, a man in a black zip-up windbreaker walked into the restaurant and sat down at a table just across from us. He took out his phone and placed it faceup at the edge of the table. In the entire hour and a half we were there, he didn't order a thing, periodically swigging from a red flask he had brought with him instead. "He's not doing a very good job if he's so obvious," Zhang said and laughed. But then, presumably part of the point was to let him know he was being watched.

"I've been invited for tea for years; it's become part of my life," he said and shrugged, referring to a favored tactic for Chinese security officials, who would invite a person to "drink tea" under the guise of hospitality, but both parties understood the meeting was intended to gather information or deliver warnings. The interest in him had come and gone over the years. "Sometimes they followed me everywhere," he said. "The minute I left an office they would go in and tell the people there not to work with me." The surveillance was particularly intense before the arrest of Bo Xilai, the former party secretary of Chongqing, who was thought to be a leadership contender before his sudden downfall in 2012, he recalled. "But on the day he was arrested, all of a sudden all the cars that had been following me disappeared." When we met in the spring of 2018, the authorities appeared to be interested in him again. The problem, Zhang explained, was that he kept challenging the party's version of history. "Personally, I think that before Xi we were able to comment on the history of the party and the anti-Japanese war [World War II], but it wasn't possible after that."

Challenging the party's account on the war was particularly sensitive, Zhang said, because it undermined the party's appeals to patriotism. "By saying it was the party that led the anti-Japanese war, that binds the party and the country together, making people love the party more," he explained. "It's a basic propaganda tactic. Promoting nationalism and patriotism helps the party. It is all for the purpose of politics." But preventing the objective study of history, he believed, was not a patriotic act at all—just the opposite. "It stops the country learning from history, so that it will repeat the same historical mistakes," he said.

Like Hong Zhenkuai, Zhang was unable to publish his work on domestic Chinese platforms, but he carried on with his research anyway, publishing abroad and speaking out where he could. "An old Chinese saying goes that a person has the strongest will when she or he doesn't have any desire," he told me. "Before, the authorities asked whether I had any desires, anything they could arrange for me. I just happened not to have any. I don't really care about those things. That's why I am able to speak until now."[35] He believed that the objective study of history was important work, and he was determined to keep going. As it said on the business cards: "Restore History, Contribute Common Sense."

* * *

It was easier to go along with the official line.

On July 31, 2015, Xi convened a meeting of the Politburo, the party's senior decision-making body, at the Academy of Military Sciences to review the progress of academic research into the history of the Second World War. He was not satisfied. Given the "great contribution" the Chinese people had made toward the Allied victory and therefore world peace, he told officials, the current scholarship was "still not nearly sufficient" and there must be more "deep systematic research."[36]

For decades, Chinese historians had described the war as an "eight-year War of Resistance" and dated its beginning to the Japanese attack on the outskirts of Beijing in July 1937, which still made the conflict the longest any of the Allied nations had fought. But Japan had invaded the northeastern Chinese region of Manchuria six years earlier, in 1931, and while this had previously been treated primarily as a related but separate regional struggle, Xi now urged historians to approach the conflict as a "fourteen-year War of Resistance," beginning in 1931.[37] There was a historical basis to argue the change, but this was plainly a political decision. Xi also urged scholars to focus on three core aspects of the conflict: its "great significance," its "important place" in the global struggle against fascism, and the "central role" of the Communist Party in the victory.[38] This was the basis on which scholarship on the war should proceed and schools should teach the conflict's history. Anything else, especially accounts that denied the importance of the party's role, would be considered historical nihilism.

In January 2017, the Ministry of Education announced that the conflict would now be known as the "14-year War of Resistance against Japanese Aggression" and all textbooks and teaching materials were to be revised accordingly. They would stress the "instrumental function of the Communist Party" during the war and China's contribution to the worldwide anti-fascist effort, just as Xi had urged.[39] That summer, the People's Education Press, which was controlled by the education ministry, published a new textbook detailing China's modern history from the Opium Wars to the "14-year War of Resistance."[40]

Luo Cunkang, vice curator of the War of Resistance Museum in Beijing, told me that while they had previously divided the conflict into a six-year "regional anti-Japanese war" and then an eight-year "comprehensive anti-Japanese war," it made sense to refer to the entire period as a "14-year war of resistance." The museum had long covered both phases of the conflict, he said, so that they barely had to alter their displays. "Actually, the content of our exhibition hasn't changed much," he said. "It's just that we really emphasize the 14 years as a comprehensive period of time."

The location of the museum told a different story. It was built in 1987 at the site of what was then deemed the start of the war—the Japanese attack on the Marco Polo Bridge on July 7, 1937. Thirty years later, now that the war had almost doubled in length, the site represented the midway point. But Luo was breezy and upbeat about the change, insisting that it was just a matter of emphasis. "Right now we accommodate more than a thousand visitors every day, mainly primary and secondary school students," he said. "When we explain our exhibits to them, we always stress that the history of China's anti-Japanese war was fourteen years. In our publications, and materials, and promotions materials, we really highlight that as well."

Xi Jinping had visited the museum in July 2014 with the entire Politburo Standing Committee—the party's seven-man top leadership group—and that visit was now an exhibit itself, complete with large color photographs and quotes from Xi. "China's government is paying more and more attention to history education," Luo told me approvingly. "The status of our museum is getting higher and higher. I feel that the role of our museum as an educator is more valuable." With the savvy of the veteran bureaucrat that he was, Luo peppered his answers with the latest slogans from Xi. "I encourage myself as well as my colleagues every day to work harder on passing on this anti-Japanese war spirit to achieve the great rejuvenation of China, and realize the China Dream," Luo said. "Therefore, I think my work is not just about the past; it is also about today."[41] That last part at least was accurate.

As I left the museum, a large group of high school students was lining up outside, notebooks in hand, to begin their tour. A red banner above the entrance exhorted them to "Use Xi Jinping Thought" as their guiding principle.

In schools themselves, the country's teachers had long had to navigate limits on the materials they could draw from for lessons. In any case, they were preparing their students for a nationwide—and notoriously tough—college-entrance exam known as the Gaokao, which rewarded memorizing the required facts rather than exploring a diverse range of views. But whereas before 2012 different provinces could choose from a small number of permitted texts, under Xi, the curriculum was increasingly standardized. From 2017 all high schools were required to use the same textbooks for History, Chinese Language, and Moral Education, and by 2019, the history textbooks had reduced discussion of the Cultural Revolution to a single page (as opposed to four pages in an earlier edition), while the section on China's territorial claims, such as in the South China Sea, Taiwan, and Hong Kong, had expanded.[42] In July 2020, the Ministry of Education instructed teachers to add the country's handling of the Covid-19 pandemic to their lesson plans as an example of the advantages of the Chinese system, which would encourage "patriotism, love for the party, and love for socialism."[43]

Patriotic education was not just for schoolchildren. As with the post-Tiananmen campaign in the 1990s, Xi called for the whole country to undergo a "spiritual red baptism" and learn from "the hardships suffered by the revolutionary generation."[44] Over the next four years, between 2016 and 2020, the government spent $370 million developing "red" tourism sites across the country, which included Red Army bases, the locations of famous battles, and the sites of important party meetings.[45] The state news agency Xinhua claimed more than 1.4 billion people had visited red tourism sites in 2019—up from 140 million in 2004—which meant that either the entire population was now flocking to these sites or there were some serious repeat visitors, and perhaps a little exaggeration.[46]

One of the most popular destinations was Jinggangshan, a mountain range in southeastern China where the Red Army, which would later become known as the People's Liberation Army (PLA), was founded. Visitors could rent uniforms and walk along the narrow trails the soldiers used. "Many tourists like me love to wear the Red Army uniforms, which reflects our memories of those historical times," said Li Ping, a tourist who had traveled more than a thousand miles from Beijing to visit. "In my opinion, the uniform is the most fashionable clothes here in Jinggangshan."[47] Party members could renew their vow to "sacrifice everything for the party" at the Monument to the Revolutionary Martyrs on the mountaintop, or line up to see the chair Xi Jinping sat in during his visit, an exhibit that would not have been out of place in North Korea.

"It feels deeply emotional to be here," kindergarten principal Gao Hongli told reporters from Bloomberg News. She was visiting with a delegation of a hundred fellow preschool principals, all wearing Red Army uniforms. "We're going to take the red spirit we've learned here back to each of our kindergartens," she said.[48]

Visiting these sites also made good business sense. It was a way to demonstrate respect for the party and its version of history, and before long some of the country's wealthiest individuals were making their own pilgrimages. In the summer of 2018, Pony Ma (also known as Ma Huateng), the founder of internet giant Tencent and China's second-richest person at the time, visited the party's wartime headquarters in Yan'an. He was dressed in a Red Army uniform, complete with a red star on his cap, and accompanied by other leading tech executives including Liu Qiangdong, the chief executive of JD.com, one of the country's most popular internet shopping sites.[49] The following year, the founders and chief executive officers of forty-five leading tech start-ups were pictured taking part in a study tour of revolutionary sites in Fujian province to "imbue themselves in the red revolutionary spirit."[50] Where Facebook founder Mark Zuckerberg reportedly ended team meetings with the mantra "company over country," this was the opposite of the sentiment Xi sought to promote. If you wanted your business to prosper in China, it was wise to acknowledge that the interests of the party and the country came first.[51]

Previous patriotic education initiatives had been compared to a radio program that young people could turn down or tune out if they weren't interested, but the intensity and the range of programming under Xi was harder to ignore. "Patriotic education has penetrated to unthinkable depths within popular culture over the past eight years [since 2012]," wrote Zheng Wang, a professor of diplomacy and international relations at Seton Hall University and the author of *Never Forget National Humiliation: Historical Memory in Chinese Politics and Foreign Relations*. Chinese television had long been dominated by films and dramas about the war with Japan—in 2013 one scholar estimated that war-themed content made up around 70 percent of programming—and there was no sign of that production slowing down.[52] "These programs are available anytime and everywhere," said Wang. "They are a part of Chinese daily life that can never be switched off."[53]

The party called for more "patriotic plots" in movies too, urging producers and directors to study Xi Jinping Thought and maintain a "clear ideological bottom line."[54] Chinese studios had been making what were known as "main melody films"—in tune with the party's ideological goals—since the days of Mao. But as Xi reasserted the party's leading role across all aspects of society, the film industry was brought under the direct supervision of the Central Propaganda Department in 2018. Hollywood studios had long churned out unabashedly jingoistic fare that showed American heroes saving the day, but there was no central authority approving the scripts to ensure the country's leadership came out of it looking good. The size of the Chinese cinema market and strict caps on the number of foreign films admitted each year also created a strong commercial incentive for even the most powerful Hollywood studios to avoid upsetting the Chinese government. Presumably this helped explain why the animated children's movie *Abominable* featured a map showing the "nine-dash line" China uses to mark its territorial claims in the South China Sea, the Taiwan and Japan flags disappeared from Tom Cruise's jacket in the *Top Gun* sequel, and the Hong Kong–based characters in *Transformers: Age of Extinction* were shown appealing to the "central government" for help.[55]

"It is now commonly accepted that there will be no Chinese villains in any Hollywood film in the years to come since China's box office is too important," a report from the free speech advocacy organization PEN concluded in 2020. "The Chinese government is essentially offered a co-producer's chair of their own, to not only advance a specific political agenda through film but to shape the film's narrative to better mirror CCP propaganda."[56]

World War II was a popular subject for Chinese film and TV studios, as it was in Hollywood and Europe, and it was not just government censors that policed dramatizations of the conflict's history. With just days to go before its premiere at the Shanghai International Film Festival in 2019, the $80 million war epic *The Eight Hundred* was abruptly withdrawn due to "technical difficulties."[57] The China Red Culture Association, which was largely made up of retired cadres and scholars and linked to a government-affiliated think tank, complained that the film focused too heavily on the role of Kuomintang (KMT) troops—the Communist Party's domestic rivals—and portrayed them too heroically. They were particularly offended by a scene that showed the soldiers defending the KMT flag under heavy fire, reminiscent of the famous image of the US Marines raising the American flag during the Battle of Iwo Jima.

The Eight Hundred was set during the Battle of Shanghai, where KMT forces fought in 1937, and the KMT's contribution to the broader conflict had been acknowledged since the mid-1980s. But showing that reality on the big screen, in such an epic production, was going too far, decided the Red Culture Association. In fact, it was dangerous. Guo Songmin, who had led the attacks on Hong Zhenkuai over his article about the heroes of Langya Mountain, argued that the film would "hurt the Chinese people, especially the soldiers who gave their lives to build the new China." "It is a reversal of history, and misleads the audience," the group's leader Wang Benzhou complained. "If left unchecked, it will certainly deprive the entire Communist Party of its historical basis."[58]

The Eight Hundred reappeared the following year with the flag at a safe distance, its distinctive white sun symbol edited out, and the civilian population playing a more prominent role in the conflict, ferrying crucial supplies to the soldiers and keeping their spirits up. This was more in keeping with the official narrative that the war was fought by the Chinese people in general, rather than the Nationalist troops in particular, and did not contradict the idea that the Communist Party was providing the overall leadership even if there was no way to crowbar them into the Battle of Shanghai.

As in Russia, the government was not imposing this top-down narrative on a wholly unwilling public so much as enforcing the boundaries of historical debate and mobilizing one part of society against another. The neo-Maoists, for instance, felt they finally had a government that was taking the protection of history seriously, and the enthusiasm of the veterans and their families taking part in commemoration ceremonies to mark the wartime anniversaries was not manufactured.

Zhao Yan, the granddaughter of the late KMT general Peng Shiliang, was among them. Her family had been designated as counterrevolutionaries under Mao and persecuted during the Cultural Revolution. But Peng's name was cleared and he was finally recognized as a martyr in 1985 when the story of the war was revised under Deng. Now, under Xi, he was celebrated.

She pulled out a red cardboard box from a large pile of papers and souvenirs in her tiny magazine store and opened it up. Inside was the commemorative medal her grandfather had been posthumously awarded, brightly polished gold against the red velvet lining. She beamed proudly as she showed it off, holding it up in the light so that I could take a picture. But that wasn't all. Zhao pulled out a series of photos of the family visiting a new memorial in Hunan province in 2015 that commemorated Peng as one of those who had died fighting there. She pointed to herself and her husband standing solemnly on either side of the statue. Another photo showed her mother, Peng's daughter, wiping tears from her eyes. She said local government officials had attended the ceremony and put them all up in a five-star hotel. For a family that had once had to hide its past and pretend that Peng didn't exist, it was hard to believe it was real.

"I felt proud and relieved," Zhao told me. "It was comforting. My grandfather was no longer a counterrevolutionary; he was a revolutionary martyr." Now, she liked to boast that her grandfather was a famous war hero. She had taped his portrait to the wall, and when customers asked who he was, and even when they didn't, she told them his name and that he had died "for the country and the people." She had watched Xi presiding over the Victory Parade in September 2015 on television and she thoroughly approved of what she saw. "Xi Jinping acknowledges the past," she said happily. "He is seeking truth from facts." Objectively speaking, Xi was acknowledging a highly selective version of the past, based on the party's rendering of the facts. But it was the version of history Zhao wanted to hear, and she repeated the phrase, eyes gleaming, "Xi Jinping is seeking truth from facts."[59]

* * *

Every morning on my way to work in Beijing I passed a huge billboard at the base of a skyscraper reminding passersby that the Communist Party was the mainstay of the Chinese People's War of Resistance against Japanese Aggression. It had gone up as part of the Victory Day celebrations in 2015, but then it just stayed there, quietly enforcing the party's version of history among the high-end shopping malls and luxury apartment blocks of the central business district. It was probably not deliberate, but the juxtaposition fitted the official line: that the party's leadership back then was essential, as it was now as the foundation of China's economic rise. The wartime past was prologue to a glorious future, just as long as the party was in charge.

Like Putin and Kim, Xi drew selectively from history to make that case, and the war with Japan formed an important part of that narrative. According to Xi's rendering, the conflict was the turning point in China's long history of humiliation. It was the first time the country had fought back successfully against foreign aggression and achieved its "first complete victory" in the long "century of humiliation." The Communist Party was not in power at the time, but it was portrayed as the crucial factor in that victory—leading the struggle, devising the critical tactics, and uniting the Chinese people in their fight. Keeping up that story meant keeping a tight hold on the past and ensuring there were no serious challenges to the official myth. But as in North Korea, the war with Japan was not the only conflict contemporary rulers called upon. As the circumstances required, successive Chinese leaders also invoked the history of the Korean War.

Known as the "War to Resist US Aggression and Aid Korea" in China, there was considerably more ambiguity over how the war started in Beijing than there was in Pyongyang. But both countries presented the conflict as evidence of American "imperialism" and both insisted it had ended in a humiliating defeat for the United States. In China, the conflict's profile had risen and fallen over the years with the party's priorities and the state of Sino-US relations. Mao Zedong had downplayed the twentieth anniversary of the start of the war in 1970, for example, ahead of talks with the Nixon administration, while Jiang Zemin had ramped up commemorations for the fiftieth anniversary in 2000 after the US bombing of the Chinese embassy in Belgrade in 1999.[60]

But as tensions flared and the trade war between China and the United States intensified in 2019, the Korean War once again returned to prominence in Beijing. As talks broke down in May 2019 and Donald Trump threatened to impose sweeping tariffs on Chinese goods and ban Huawei from US networks, China's state broadcaster CCTV broke into its scheduled programming and began screening black-and-white Korean War movies. "We are using movies to echo the current era," a spokesperson for the channel explained.[61]

In 2020, as Sino-US relations deteriorated further and analysts in both countries began to warn of a new Cold War, Xi summoned the memory of the Korean War—or his version of the history of that war—to deliver a stark warning to Washington.

"Seventy years ago, imperialist invaders brought the flames of war burning to the doorway of the new China," Xi said in a speech to mark the seventieth anniversary of China's entry into the conflict. "After arduous battles, Chinese and [North] Korean troops, armed to their teeth, defeated their opponents, shattering the myth of the invincibility of the US military." China did not go looking for trouble, he warned, but nor was it afraid to stand up for itself and "use the language that invaders understand—to fight war with war."[62]

The lesson Xi sought to draw from both the Korean War and World War II was that as long as the Communist Party was in power, China would face down its foreign adversaries now as it had done then. China would never be pushed around or humiliated again. He made that point explicitly in a speech to celebrate the hundredth anniversary of the Communist Party's founding in July 2021.

"China's success hinges on the Party," Xi told the vast crowd in Tiananmen Square. "Without the Communist Party of China, there would be no new China and no national rejuvenation." It was the "foundation and lifeblood" of the country, he said, "and the crux upon which the interests and wellbeing of all Chinese people depend." With the party in charge, Xi declared, "we will never allow any foreign force to bully, oppress, or subjugate us." The crowd roared its approval. "Whoever nurses delusions of doing that will crack their heads and spill blood on the Great Wall of steel built from the flesh and blood of 1.4 billion Chinese people."[63]

During the celebrations that night, thousands of tiny drones lit up the sky over Shanghai, spelling out: "There would be no new China without the Communist Party."[64]

The message was that the party and the country's fate were one and the same. If you were a patriot—someone who wanted what was best for China—then you would support the party's continuing rule. If you opposed the party, you were opposing the country's development and security too. You were either with the party or you were against China. It was up to you.

* * *

Early one morning in March 2018, I took the high-speed train from Beijing to Bengbu in eastern China. It was a journey of more than five hundred miles, but it took just under four hours, weaving our way out through the gray concrete sprawl of the capital in the early dawn and then hurtling across the open countryside. Bengbu was named after the pearls that used to be found in its river, but these days its fortunes were tied to its rail links to Beijing and Shanghai, which developers promised would bring "new glory" to the area.[65] Dense clusters of high-rise apartment blocks were sprouting up all over the city and the suburbs thrummed with the sound of construction. A large billboard by the side of the eight-lane highway proclaimed: "Bengbu: A Nice City Building Chinese Dream."

I was heading for Bengbu High School No. 2 to sit in on a history class and speak to some of the students there about what they were learning about China's experiences during World War II. I would like to say I had carefully selected the school after extensive research, but in truth it was the only one that hadn't immediately said no to the idea of a foreign journalist visiting. I could read what was written in the textbooks, but I wanted to understand how the teachers approached the material and what impression it made on students, and the head of the school's history department thought this was a fine idea. It was one of their most important subjects and she was proud of the lessons they taught.

The students filed into the classroom clutching their folders to their chests and keeping their eyes on the ground. They radiated the universal awkwardness of teenagers anywhere who wanted to avoid having to make small talk with the unknown guest at all costs. Huang Yufeng, the department head, on the other hand, came barreling into the room like a tornado. "Welcome! Welcome!" she cried. "You must try some Chinese tea!" Huang was a blur of activity in a hot pink trench coat and matching lipstick, simultaneously summoning up a huge vat of hot water and corralling us all to pose for a group photo. History was her lifelong passion, she said, and she was delighted to see the country's leadership taking the subject so seriously since Xi had come to power. There was no more important subject for young people to learn. "I always tell my students that learning history is learning patriotism," Huang said. "History is basically patriotic education—teaching students to love their country and their history."[66]

The class teacher Zhu Baolin was a mild-mannered man in his early thirties. His dark hair was cropped short and he wore glasses and a black sweatshirt emblazoned with a large picture of the moon. Once the formalities were out of the way, Zhu fired up his computer and launched into a lesson about the horrors of the war with Japan. He showed the class a slide with a screenshot of ninety-two-year-old veteran Liu Aimin, taken from a CCTV documentary, and recounted the story of how he had survived by hiding under the bodies of his comrades and pretending to be dead. Liu was one of only thirteen men from his unit to survive the war, he said. Zhu later told me he deliberately selected images of real people and real stories to capture the students' attention and bring the subject to life.

Another slide showed a series of human heads hanging from a wooden post and a number of dead bodies on the ground. It was surprisingly graphic. There was a slide about the "comfort stations" where Chinese women were held captive and raped by Japanese soldiers. The students silently scribbled their notes. "We want to let the students know what damage the war caused to ordinary citizens," Zhu said. "That civilians suffered the most." He ended his lesson with an image of Xi Jinping and a quote from one of his speeches: "War is like a mirror, which makes people cherish peace."

Afterward, I asked some of the students what they had thought of the lesson and what came to mind when they thought about the war.

"Dead bodies," said sixteen-year-old Yao Mingming. "The Japanese invasion and the Japanese soldiers were so cruel. It hurt my feelings to see my ancestors lying on the ground." She had short dark hair and round glasses and said she liked to watch *Game of Thrones* in her spare time. She told me she thought it was their duty as Chinese citizens to learn about their history. "Our motherland is full of scars," she said. "When we see the downfall we suffered and the achievements we made, it makes us want to unite and devote ourselves to studying or working and make this society better."

"China actually had many invasions," Zhang Qianhui, who was seventeen, added matter-of-factly. "And all because of China's weakness. China was not strong enough." She recited a line from a poem she had memorized: "Every inch of the land is covered by blood."

This past weakness was a key theme in their comments and in line with one of the party's main talking points—that the country had suffered so terribly because it was weak before the Communist Party came to power. It was certainly possible that the students were answering to please their teachers, who were still in the room and nodding along as they spoke. But their responses sounded thoughtful and heartfelt, and whether or not they truly believed what they were saying, these were the answers they would have to reproduce if they wanted to do well in their final exams.

"With our great economy right now it's very hard for us to imagine what kind of hardship the country went through," said sixteen-year-old

Yang Yuzhe, who spoke softly and wore a pale pink coat. "We can only try to experience this by historical evidence, historical facts, and historical statements. Only by doing so are we able to understand what kind of struggle they went through in the past so that we could have a decent life." She told me she had cried when she first took part in a ceremony at elementary school to mark the anniversary of the Japanese attack on September 18, 1931 (unofficially known as National Humiliation Day and now designated as the start of the war). "We rang the school bell to remind us how we suffered during this time, to bring us back to this day. I remember I was crying because I thought that China was always a very strong country, but I didn't know the recent history so I was very sad and upset. From then on, I knew that China must be strong again."

They had all had to go through two weeks of military training with a local People's Liberation Army unit the previous summer, but they said the soldiers were nice and they had enjoyed learning the revolutionary songs. "Studying history helps me identify myself as a Chinese citizen and take pride in being Chinese," Zhang said. "I'm proud of China's old past glory and I'm proud of China's ability to go through the darkness and recover from it." Her passion was writing and poetry, but she said she also understood the need to build up the country's military strength. "Because China was weak it went through a hundred years of humiliation and hardship. I guess that is why it is necessary to be strong—it is the only way to protect itself from being invaded again."

It was dark by the time we had finished talking and the students were late for their next class. As I walked back across the school grounds, the lights were still on in many of the classrooms, the students inside still hunched over their books. In one class they were watching *Amazing China*, a propaganda film about the country's great progress under Xi, from reducing poverty to advances in space, science, and military technology. The moon gleamed brightly overhead as the narrator's voice boomed out across the campus, reeling off one amazing achievement after another.

Conclusion

Power

What makes a nation is the past, what justifies one nation against others is the past.

—ERIC HOBSBAWN[1]

Volgograd, Russia

On a bitterly cold, dark morning in December 2020, Denis Chistyakov went to check his grandfather Vasily's mail. There was one letter that looked important—and urgent. Inside was a summons from the Investigative Committee, Russia's equivalent of the Federal Bureau of Investigation (FBI). They were calling his grandfather in for questioning as a witness to suspected genocide by German forces during the Battle of Stalingrad.

It made no sense, Chistyakov complained, to drag his ninety-four-year-old grandfather out in the depths of winter at the height of the coronavirus pandemic to ask him about something that had happened almost eighty years ago. He would have been fifteen or sixteen years old in 1942, fighting as a young volunteer in the Red Army—what could he possibly remember that would help the investigation, he demanded. The officer he spoke to said he understood why he was upset, and he was not the first to react that way, but they were summoning witnesses from across the country and his grandfather was on the list.[2]

The Kremlin had designated 2020 the Year of Memory and Glory in honor of the seventy-fifth anniversary of victory in the Great Patriotic

War. But it was also the year of a crucial vote on changing the constitution that would allow Vladimir Putin to stay in power until 2036.
The result was never in doubt, but Putin wanted a high turnout and an
emphatic victory to give the impression of resounding public support,
and the memory of the war was an important part of his appeal to
voters. The clause on term limits was wrapped in with popular initiatives enshrining the "historical truth" of the conflict and the sanctity
of the country's war heroes, as well as banning same-sex marriage, and
Putin delivered his final speech before the vote from a new war memorial. Standing beneath the twenty-five-meter-tall bronze statue of a
Soviet soldier, he praised the "Great Victory" and railed against those
he said were trying to erase their glorious history.[3] His pitch was less
about the bright future he would deliver and more about how he would
defend their sacred past.

The Victory Day parade had been postponed from its usual date in
May because of the pandemic, but it took place on the eve of the vote in
June instead, even though Russian hospitals were still overwhelmed by
patients with Covid-19. The Immortal Regiment moved online, where
participants could upload photos of their relatives to a virtual procession instead of marching through the streets, and the authorities did
their best to summon up as much patriotic sentiment as was possible in
the circumstances. For months beforehand, the names of every Soviet
soldier killed in the war scrolled down the side of the screen on state
television. The war was there when you woke up in the morning and it
was there when you went to bed at night.

Putin was pictured touring a new cathedral dedicated to the Russian
armed forces in Patriot Park, a military theme park on the outskirts of
Moscow. The vast temple was colored khaki-green on the outside and
featured an elaborate stained-glass ceiling with images of Soviet war
medals and the orange-and-black ribbon of St. George. The entrance
steps were made from melted-down German tanks and guns. Visitors
were told they were striking a symbolic blow to the enemy with every
step.[4] The president looked around the site with his defense minister,
Sergei Shoigu, and Patriarch Kirill, the head of the Russian Orthodox
Church, who offered thanks for Putin's leadership and a prayer for him
to continue his "demanding service to our nation."[5] He had once described him as a "miracle of God."[6] Flanked by the patriarch in his

long black robes and the glittering golden domes of the new cathedral, Putin's message to viewers was clear: God and history were on his side.

But there was a harder edge to the commemoration these days. The surging pride that had accompanied the 2014 annexation of Crimea had long since faded. The Kremlin's control over information was being eroded by a younger generation that was turning to social media and encrypted messaging channels for their news instead of state television. Polls showed the vast majority of Russians still agreed that the victory in the Great Patriotic War was the most important event in their history, but Putin's own approval ratings were slipping as real incomes fell and the economy stalled. The public healthcare system had been struggling long before the coronavirus pandemic and there were rumors of another attempt to raise the pension age. But the more uncertain the future looked, and in the absence of any other ideas, Putin kept pulling the same old lever again and again, railing against foreign enemies for the country's problems and doubling down on the memory of the war and the great battle he claimed to be fighting to protect it.

The Russian president wrote, or at least put his name to, a sprawling nine-thousand-word essay in the American *National Interest* magazine in June 2020 on the "real lessons" of World War II, marshalling selective facts to suit his case and declaring that the Soviet Union had won an "epic, crushing victory over Nazism and saved the entire world."[7] Patriotism, he declared that summer, was Russia's national idea. "There can be nothing else here."[8] As he presented it, true patriots supported his leadership. Everyone else was a traitor or a "fifth columnist" who was trying to keep Russia down and undermine the memory of their glorious victory.

The changes to the constitution were approved by more than three-quarters of voters, according to the official results on July 1, although there was no independent scrutiny of the ballot and the amendments were enacted before the first vote was even cast. The following day, Putin convened his top officials for a meeting of the Victory Committee—responsible for coordinating commemoration of World War II—and instructed them to begin investigating Nazi war crimes, including genocide against Soviet citizens during the conflict. They should "constantly work on this," he told the group, which included the long-time head of the Investigative Committee Aleksandr Bastrykin and explained the summons veterans started receiving that winter.[9] Within months, the first verdicts were in. To the surprise of no one, a court in the northwestern region of Novgorod ruled that German soldiers were indeed guilty of genocide against Soviet civilians.[10]

Commemorating the war and policing the Kremlin's version of history was now a top political priority and government agencies rushed to outdo each other in responding to Putin's call. The Investigative Committee set up a new department to investigate the falsification of history and attempts to rehabilitate Nazism.[11] Parliament amended the education law to require schools to foster a "sense of patriotism" in their students and "respect for the memory of the defenders of the Fatherland."[12] One lawmaker proposed making it illegal to compare Soviet and Nazi actions during the war, which Putin commended, and a draft bill soon materialized.[13] Russia's foreign ministry reimagined the Soviet invasion of Poland in September 1939 as a "liberation campaign," claiming that the population had "greeted the Soviet soldiers with jubilation."[14]

The state also made clear that it alone would be the keeper of the country's memory. After years of harassment and intimidation, Memorial, the organization that was founded in 1987 to document Soviet-era atrocities, whose members once held up quotes from Gorbachev to defend themselves, was liquidated by Russia's Supreme Court along with its affiliated human rights center. During the hearing, state prosecutor Alexei Zhafyarov accused the organization of violating the terms of its designation as a "foreign agent" and undermining the memory of the Soviet victory in World War II by focusing on the crimes of the past. "Why do we, the offspring of victors, have to repent and be embarrassed, instead of being proud of our glorious past?" he demanded.[15] Only an organization that was in the pay of foreign governments would dedicate such close attention to the negative aspects of Soviet history, he argued.

On the first day of the new school year in September 2020, Putin delivered the first lesson, and of course it was about the war and how their enemies were attempting to rewrite its history. The Kremlin photographs of the event showed Putin sitting behind an enormous desk in front of a large Russian flag, solemnly addressing a large video screen. "Collaborationists" were trying to tarnish the memory of the victory, he warned the children, just like the traitors who had collaborated with the enemy during the war. "Those who agree with the rewriters of history can easily be called the collaborationists of today," he told them.[16] The children stared back in silence from their classrooms in boxes on the screen, sitting up straight with the posture of students who had clearly been told to be on their best behavior.

As Putin was lecturing the schoolchildren, Russia's leading opposition figure, Aleksei Navalny, was in a medically induced coma in Germany, where he had been evacuated for treatment after narrowly surviving an assassination attempt with a Soviet-era nerve agent. When he returned to Russia, he was arrested and sent to prison for violating the terms of his probation, then dragged into court again to face a new charge of slandering ninety-four-year-old Ignat Artemenko, a veteran of the Great Patriotic War, which became a criminal offense in both Russia and China.[17] It was not enough that Navalny had been poisoned and jailed. As Putin's popularity declined, he was no longer prepared to tolerate even the slightest trace of dissent and his rival had to be smeared as a man who insulted elderly war heroes. When Artemenko fell ill during the trial and an ambulance had to be called, the prosecutor asked for the record to show "that it was Aleksei Anatolyevich Navalny who brought him to this state."[18]

From his prison cell, Navalny reported that he was forced to watch Russian state television for more than eight hours a day. "We watch films about the Great Patriotic War, or how one day, forty years ago, our athletes defeated the Americans or Canadians," Navalny told the *New York Times*. "You have to sit in a chair and watch TV." If someone falls asleep, the guards shout, "Don't sleep, watch!" He said the experience had given him his clearest insight yet into Putin's strategy to hold on to power. "The present and the future are being substituted with the past—the truly heroic past, or embellished past, or completely fictional past," he wrote. "All sorts of past must constantly be in the spotlight to displace thoughts about the future and questions about the present."[19]

* * *

This was the same logic the Kim regime had been operating under in North Korea for decades. Successive leaders invoked the memory of the wartime past and claimed to be defending the country's security. The worse the situation was in the present, the more they turned to history and conjured foreign enemies to blame. Kim Jong Un had sealed North Korea's borders at the start of the coronavirus pandemic, and by the summer of 2021, there were reports of serious food shortages and price spikes. There were fears that the country was on the brink of another famine like the catastrophe of the 1990s. But Kim demanded his citizens focus their attention on what he said was the threat of imminent attack.

"Hostile forces," by which he meant the United States and South Korea, were strengthening their capabilities and preparing to launch a "preemptive attack," he warned in July 2021. He urged "all the military and political cadres to put the greatest efforts into bolstering up the combat efficiency of their units."[20] The transition from Trump to Biden in the White House made no difference, he told senior officials at a party congress. The United States will always be "our biggest enemy," he said. "No matter who is in power in the U.S., the true nature of the U.S. and its fundamental policies towards North Korea never change."[21]

The official portraits of Kim that year showed him in military uniform for the first time, with gold stars on his epaulettes and a black rifle resting casually on his desk.[22] The image was of a resolute wartime president, like his grandfather, with the rifle suggesting the enemy was near at hand and he might return to the fight at any moment. Just like his father and his grandfather before him, Kim claimed to be waging a great battle against their imperialist enemies—fighting at all times and on all fronts to protect his people, improve their lives, and develop the economy—all the while pumping money into the nuclear and missile programs he insisted they needed to keep them safe.

Five hundred miles to the west in Beijing, Xi Jinping was intensifying his own focus on China's history. In February 2021, he launched a mass line campaign, which he was said to have personally planned, calling for all Chinese Communist Party members to study their history and oppose historical nihilism. "Know history and love the party, know history and love the country," he declared.[23] But it was not just party officials who were expected to learn and abide by that version of history. Across the country, people were told to be on guard for attempts to stoke historical nihilism. China's internet regulator set up a special hotline for citizens to report instances of historical nihilism they saw online and claimed to have deleted more than two million posts containing "harmful" discussions of history by May 2021.[24] They published a list of topics it was now forbidden to mention, including whether the Five Heroes of Langya Mountain really leapt to their deaths and the extent of the Communist forces' fighting during the war.[25] The first prison sentences were handed down to those convicted of slandering Chinese war heroes.

Like Putin and Kim, Xi used the past to frame the country's contemporary challenges and demonstrate the necessity of his leadership, claiming to be delivering victory after victory and leading the struggle against their enemies, just as his predecessors had done during previous conflicts. Xi urged Chinese citizens to carry forward the "great spirit of resisting aggression" from World War II with the party now, as then, "fighting as the central pillar."[26] And there were important lessons to be learned from the Korean War too. *The Battle at Lake Changjin*, a new government-backed movie about the conflict that was said to be the most expensive film ever made in China, smashed box office records in 2021 with its rendering of how Chinese troops had stood up to US bullying and aggression, just as Xi claimed to be doing now.[27] "The victory in the War to Resist U.S. Aggression and Aid Korea was a victory of justice, a victory of peace, and a victory of the people," Xi said,[28] although in fact the conflict ended in a truce.

Xi himself was depicted in official media outlets as the commander in chief of a great "people's war" against extreme poverty and the coronavirus pandemic, channeling the memory of the Second World War.[29] Despite the obfuscation and censorship that characterized the early weeks of the outbreak, Xi was lauded for his visionary leadership and declared the handling of the crisis a "victory for China." The education ministry ordered schools to add the pandemic response to the curriculum as a "vivid lesson" in the superiority of China's political system.[30] A new official history released in the spring of 2021, meanwhile, reduced discussion of the Great Leap Forward, and the terrible famine that followed, as well as the Cultural Revolution still further, and devoted more than a quarter of its pages to the accomplishments of Xi's rule. That fall, the Chinese Communist Party adopted a resolution codifying the party's version of history and the "Major Achievements and Historical Experience of the Party over the Past Century." The text summed up the primary lesson, echoing Xi's earlier speech: "the leadership of the Party is the foundation and lifeblood of the Party and the Country, and the pillar upon which the interests and wellbeing of all Chinese people depend."[31] In other words, China's future prosperity and security depended on the CCP's continued rule. An editorial in the *People's Daily* praised the resolution as an "action guide" that would enable the country to "take history as a mirror and learn from it . . . and realize the great rejuvenation of the Chinese nation."[32] But it was a mirror that showed only what the Communist Party wanted to see.

* * *

All nations tell themselves stories about the past and draw selectively from their history, but in Russia, China, and North Korea, these narratives are becoming increasingly entrenched. And these leaders are not going anywhere anytime soon. Putin and Xi have removed the legal barriers that would have forced them to step down when their current terms end, and regardless of whether they retain their formal titles they will wield power in Russia and China for the rest of their lives. Kim is still a young man, thought to be in his late thirties, and if he lives as long as his grandfather he could rule North Korea for another half century.

Experience has taught these men the power of appealing to history and, therefore, the importance of keeping it under tight control. The greater the challenges they perceive in the present and the less assured the future, the more they will turn to their version of the past—rallying support behind these sacred myths, vowing to reclaim lost greatness and avenge past weakness, and denouncing anyone who opposes them as traitors.

Those who come after them will have little incentive to abandon these tactics and perhaps even more need to exploit these historical wounds.

This matters because we all have to live with the world they have conjured. While these historical narratives are distorted, selective, and, in North Korea's case, partly made up, the weapons programs and the grievances they have nurtured in response are real. These past wars are the lens through which future rivalries and territorial disputes will be framed, as domestic audiences are told that they must stand firm in the face of foreign bullying and aggression, build up their military strength, and never concede an inch. As the Chinese Community Party enshrined in its 2021 history resolution: "Constant concessions will only invite more bullying and humiliation."[33]

This warped version of history is the backdrop against which future wars will be fought. As I write this in January 2022, Russian forces are massed on the border of Ukraine, where they have already annexed Crimea and started a war, but Putin claims it is Moscow that is the victim of a great historical betrayal and the defender of innocent lives. North Korea has resumed missile testing, including what it claims are hypersonic missiles, as Kim Jong Un insists that developing the country's nuclear and missile arsenals is the only way to defend itself and deter an attack on its territory. China has stepped up military drills near Taiwan and sent hundreds of military aircraft into its air defense identification zone (ADIZ), as well as building vast military facilities to enforce its claims in the South China Sea, where it dismisses international criticism of its actions as Western attempts to interfere in China's internal affairs and "terminate China's development."[34] Beijing is likely to respond in future disputes as it has in this case, longtime China observer Orville Schell has written: "aggrieved, hostile, and determined."[35]

Aggrieved hostility is the safer political bet for all three leaders. Having fetishized strength and unyielding resolve, compromise can be a risky endeavor. In her study of nationalist protest movements, Cornell University political scientist Jessica Chen Weiss notes that the last two regimes to rule China—the Kuomintang (KMT) government and the Qing dynasty—"fell to popular movements that accused the government of failing to defend the nation from foreign predations."[36] It is far better to be seen as a tough-talking strongman and resolute defender of the state.

This behavior is not unique to autocrats. It is not unusual for democratic leaders to appeal to a glorious, uncomplicated version of the past and gloss over the dark and shameful episodes of the country's history. Nostalgia is a powerful drug. It is intoxicating to believe you belong to a great nation, born of magnificent heroes, and that your country is a force for good in the world. But the danger is when this becomes the only permitted version of history and those who try to challenge it are labeled traitors and historical nihilists, because we should be clear about whose interests this serves.

"History as pom-pom waving," as the historian Simon Schama has called it, creates the veneer of patriotism instead of actually working to tackle the country's problems and reckon with the complex legacies of the past.[37] This approach to history protects those in power and the status quo. As George Orwell once wrote, and as Putin, Xi, and Kim understand all too well: "Who controls the past controls the future."

NOTES

Epigraph
1. George Orwell, *Nineteen Eighty-Four* (New York: New American Library, 1983), 204.

Introduction
1. Mao Zedong, "对'中央音乐学院的意见'的批示" ["Comments on 'Opinions of the Central Conservatory of Music'"], Marxists Internet Archive, September 27, 1964, https://www.marxists.org/chinese/maozedong/1968/5-117.htm.
2. "Выступление на военно-морском параде," President of Russia website, May 9, 2014, http://kremlin.ru/events/president/transcripts/20992. The UN General Assembly adopted a resolution in March 2014 calling the referendum invalid and the United States and most European countries said it was a violation of international law. See "General Assembly Adopts Resolution Calling upon States Not to Recognize Changes in Status of Crimea Region," United Nations, March 27, 2014, https://www.un.org/press/en/2014/ga11493.doc.htm; Ben Hoyle and David Taylor, "Bring on the Sanctions, Says Sneering Kremlin," *The Times*, March 18, 2014, https://www.thetimes.co.uk/article/bring-on-the-sanctions-says-sneering-kremlin-ttovcmpnv8m; Roland Oliphant, "Crimeans Vote Peacefully in Referendum, but Have Little Choice," *The Telegraph*, March 16, 2014, https://www.telegraph.co.uk/news/worldnews/europe/ukraine/10701676/Crimeans-vote-peacefully-in-referendum-but-have-little-choice.html.
3. "Address by President of the Russian Federation," President of Russia website, March 18, 2014, http://en.kremlin.ru/events/president/news/20603.

"The West" can be a problematic and contested term, and in any case, as Michael McFaul points out, the group of states invoked by the term is not a monolithic or even unified actor. I use it to convey the views advanced by Putin and other officials that they face opposition from Western actors, chief among them the United States; see Michael McFaul, "Putin, Putinism, and the Domestic Determinants of Russian Foreign Policy," *International Security* 45, no. 2 (2020): 95–139, https://doi.org/10.1162/isec_a_00390.

4. Before the annexation of Crimea, Putin's approval rating had dropped to 61 percent, which, while still high by most international standards, was low by his own; see "Indicators: Putin's Approval Rating," Levada Center, https://www.levada.ru/en/ratings/. It's worth noting the complexities of conducting polls in an authoritarian system such as Russia; see, for instance, Kirill Rogov and Maxim Ananyev, "Public Opinion and Russian Politics," in *The New Autocracy: Information, Politics, and Policy in Putin's Russia*, ed. Daniel Treisman (Washington, DC: Brookings Institution Press, 2018), 191–216; Timothy Frye, Scott Gehlbach, Kyle L. Marquardt, and Ora John Reuter, "Is Putin's Popularity Real?," *Post-Soviet Affairs* 33, no. 1 (2017):1–15, doi:10.1080/1060586X.2016.1144334.

5. "Gorbachev: Crimean Referendum 'Happy Event,'" Associated Press, March 18, 2014, https://apnews.com/article/offd5fd755994a9680d82a2bb12788d8.

6. Shaun Walker, *The Long Hangover: Putin's New Russia and the Ghosts of the Past* (New York: Oxford University Press, 2018), 182.

7. Sergey Radchenko, "Vladimir Putin Wants to Rewrite the History of World War II," *Foreign Policy*, January 21, 2020, https://foreignpolicy.com/2020/01/21/vladimir-putin-wants-to-rewrite-the-history-of-world-war-ii/; "Встреча с ветеранами Великой Отечественной войны и представителями патриотических объединений," President of Russia website, January 18, 2020, http://kremlin.ru/events/president/news/62609.

8. Steven Lee Myers, "Shutting Down Historical Debate, China Makes It a Crime to Mock Heroes," *New York Times*, November 2, 2021, https://www.nytimes.com/2021/11/02/world/asia/china-slander-law.html.

9. Timothy Frye notes that personal popularity deters challenges from the elite and discourages ordinary citizens from mobilizing against an autocratic ruler; thus, maintaining popular support is important for regime stability. See Timothy Frye, *Weak Strongman: The Limits of Power in Putin's Russia* (Princeton, NJ: Princeton University Press, 2021), 51–52. Similarly, Timur Kuran explains that when public opinion turns demonstrably against a regime, the outcome can be mass protests and even revolution, so even the most autocratic regimes have an incentive to maintain at least the appearance of public support. See Timur Kuran, *Private Truths, Public Lies: The Social Consequences of Preference Falsification* (Cambridge, MA: Harvard University Press, 1997), 89–90.

10. Michael Crowley, "Trump Calls for 'Patriotic Education' to Defend American History from the Left," *New York Times*, September 17, 2020, https://www.nytimes.com/2020/09/17/us/politics/trump-patriotic-education.html; "Trump's 1776 Commission Critiques Liberalism in Report Derided by Historians," *New York Times*, January 18, 2021, https://www.nytimes.com/2021/01/18/us/politics/trump-1776-commission-report.html; "Executive Order on Advancing Racial Equity and Support for Underserved Communities through the Federal Government," White House website, January 20, 2021, https://www.whitehouse.gov/briefing-room/presidential-actions/2021/01/20/executive-order-advancing-racial-equity-and-support-for-underserved-communities-through-the-federal-government/.

11. Peter Hobson, "How Russian Authorities Hijacked a WWII Remembrance Movement," *Moscow Times*, May 6, 2016, https://www.themoscowtimes.com/2016/05/06/how-russian-authorities-hijacked-a-wwii-remembrance-movement-a52776.

Chapter 1

1. Václav Havel, *The Power of the Powerless* (London: Vintage Classics, 2018), 21. In this and other chapters on North Korea, other than where subjects have already been identified on camera, I have not included names, dates, or other identifying details in the text.

2. United Nations, "DPR Korea Needs and Priorities 2020," UN Resident Coordinator for DPR Korea, April 22, 2020, https://reliefweb.int/sites/reliefweb.int/files/resources/2020_DPRK_Needs_and-Priorities_Plan.pdf.

3. Bradley K. Martin, *Under the Loving Care of the Fatherly Leader: North Korea and the Kim Dynasty* (New York: Thomas Dunne Books, 2004), 30.

4. Bradley K. Martin, *Under the Loving Care of the Fatherly Leader: North Korea and the Kim Dynasty* (New York: Thomas Dunne Books, 2004), 15.

5. Kim Il Sung, *With the Century*, vol. 1 (Pyongyang: Foreign Languages Publishing House, 1992), 62. Kim returned to Korea for two years' schooling from 1923 to 1925, but otherwise he lived in northeast China and the Soviet Union until his return to Korea in September 1945.

6. Sydney A. Seiler, *Kim Il-sŏng 1941–1948, The Creation of a Legend, the Building of a Regime* (Lanham, MD: University Press of America, 1994), 23.

7. Kim Il Sung, *With the Century*, vol. 3 (Pyongyang: Foreign Languages Publishing House, 1993), 62.

8. Hwang Jang-yop, "The Problems of Human Rights in North Korea (I)," Network for North Korean Democracy and Human Rights (Seoul: NKnet, 2000), available at http://www2.law.columbia.edu/course_00S_L9436_001/North%20Korea%20materials/hwang%20jang1.html; Bradley K. Martin, *Under the Loving Care of the Fatherly Leader: North Korea and the Kim Dynasty* (New York: Thomas Dunne Books, 2004), 12.

9. Kim Il Sung, *With the Century*, vol. 1 (Pyongyang: Foreign Languages Publishing House, 1992), preface.

10. Party History Research Institute, *History of Revolutionary Activities of the Great Leader Comrade Kim Il Sung* (Pyongyang: Foreign Languages Publishing House, 1983), 175.

11. Party History Research Institute, *History of Revolutionary Activities of the Great Leader Comrade Kim Il Sung* (Pyongyang: Foreign Languages Publishing House, 1983), 176.

12. Party History Research Institute, *History of Revolutionary Activities of the Great Leader Comrade Kim Il Sung* (Pyongyang: Foreign Languages Publishing House, 1983), 177.

13. Andrei Lankov, *From Stalin to Kim Il Sung: The Formation of North Korea 1945–1960* (New Brunswick, NJ: Rutgers University Press, 2002), 6.

14. Suh Dae-Sook, *Kim Il Sung: The North Korean Leader* (New York: Columbia University Press, 1988), 52–53.

15. Andrei Lankov, *From Stalin to Kim Il Sung: The Formation of North Korea 1945–1960* (New Brunswick, NJ: Rutgers University Press, 2002), 54.

16. "Soviet Report on Communists in Korea, 1945," Wilson Center History and Public Policy Program Digital Archive, AGShVS RF. F. 172. OP 614631. D. 23 pp. 21–26. Translated by Gary Goldberg. http://digitalarchive.wilsoncenter.org/document/114890.

17. Sydney A. Seiler, *Kim Il-sŏng 1941–1948: The Creation of a Legend, the Building of a Regime* (Lanham, MD: University Press of America, 1994), 97–99.

18. Sergei N. Goncharov, John W. Lewis, and Xue Litai, *Uncertain Partners: Stalin, Mao, and the Korean War* (Stanford, CA: Stanford University Press, 1993), 327.

19. Sydney A. Seiler, *Kim Il-sŏng 1941–1948: The Creation of a Legend, the Building of a Regime* (Lanham, MD: University Press of America, 1994), 99.

20. Kim Ch'an-jong, *"BBalch'isan manga, kim il-song kwa 88 tongnip yodan" [Funeral March of the Partisans, Kim Il-song and the 88th Independent Brigade], Sindonga*, July 1992, 380–381, in Sydney A. Seiler, *Kim Il-sŏng 1941–1948: The Creation of a Legend, the Building of a Regime* (Lanham, MD: University Press of America, 1994), 46.

21. Sydney A. Seiler, *Kim Il-sŏng 1941–1948: The Creation of a Legend, the Building of a Regime* (Lanham, MD: University Press of America, 1994), 46.

22. Sydney A. Seiler, *Kim Il-sŏng 1941–1948: The Creation of a Legend, the Building of a Regime* (Lanham, MD: University Press of America, 1994), 117. Seiler notes that there is still some confusion as to the rank of uniform Kim wore, and indeed whether he was wearing the Soviet uniform at all.

23. Sydney A. Seiler, *Kim Il-sŏng 1941–1948: The Creation of a Legend, the Building of a Regime* (Lanham, MD: University Press of America, 1994), 117–118. This is an alternative transliteration of Kim Il Sung.

24. Bradley K. Martin, *Under the Loving Care of the Fatherly Leader: North Korea and the Kim Dynasty* (New York: Thomas Dunne Books, 2004), 52; Sydney A. Seiler, *Kim Il-sŏng 1941–1948, The Creation of a Legend, the Building of a Regime* (Lanham, MD: University Press America, 1994), 52; Sheila Miyoshi Jager, *Brothers at War: The Unending Conflict in Korea* (New York and London: Norton, 2013), 24.

25. B. R. Myers, *North Korea's Juche Myth* (Busan: Sthele Press, 2015), 208; see also the cover of Lim Un, *The Founding of a Dynasty: An Authentic Biography of Kim Il-sŏng* (Tokyo: Jiyu-sha, 1982). I am grateful to B. R. Myers for drawing my attention to this image and his correspondence on the subject.

26. Bradley K. Martin, *Under the Loving Care of the Fatherly Leader: North Korea and the Kim Dynasty* (New York: Thomas Dunne Books, 2004), 52; see also Sheila Miyoshi Jagger's account of the event in *Brothers at War: The Unending Conflict in Korea* (New York: Norton, 2013), 24–25.

27. Sydney A. Seiler, *Kim Il-sŏng 1941–1948, The Creation of a Legend, the Building of a Regime* (Lanham, MD: University Press America, 1994), 56.

28. O. Yong-jin, *An Eyewitness Report* (Pusan: Kungmin Sasang Chidowan, 1952), 141–143, in Robert A. Scalapino and Chong-sik Lee, *Communism in Korea, Part I: The Movement* (Los Angeles: University of California Press, 1972), 324–325; see also Sheila Miyoshi Jager, *Brothers at War: The Unending Conflict in Korea* (New York and London: Norton, 2013), 25.

29. Bradley K. Martin, *Under the Loving Care of the Fatherly Leader: North Korea and the Kim Dynasty* (New York: Thomas Dunne Books, 2004), 733n24.

30. Bradley K. Martin, *Under the Loving Care of the Fatherly Leader: North Korea and the Kim Dynasty* (New York: Thomas Dunne Books, 2004), 55; Sheila Miyoshi Jager, *Brothers at War: The Unending Conflict in Korea* (New York and London: Norton, 2013), 40–41.

31. Adrian Buzo notes the appeal of Kim's "outward conformity" and absence of an independent power base for the Soviets, who saw him as a "known quality." Adrian Buzo, *Politics and Leadership in North Korea: The Guerilla Dynasty* (London: Routledge, 2018), 13.

32. "Soviet Report on Communists in Korea, 1945," 1945, History and Public Policy Program Digital Archive, AGShVS RF. F. 172. OP 614631. D. 23 pp. 21–26. Translated by Gary Goldberg. http://digitalarchive. wilsoncenter.org/document/114890.

33. Sergei N. Goncharov, John W. Lewis, and Xue Litai, *Uncertain Partners: Stalin, Mao, and the Korean War* (Stanford, CA: Stanford University Press, 1993), 327.

34. Suh Dae-Sook, *Kim Il Sung: The North Korean Leader*
     (New York: Columbia University Press, 1988), 63–65.
35. Suh Dae-Sook, *Kim Il Sung: The North Korean Leader*
     (New York: Columbia University Press, 1988), 72.
36. Anna Louise Strong, *In North Korea: First Eyewitness Report*
     (New York: Soviet Russia Today, 1949), 22–23.

Chapter 2

1. *Krasnaya Zvezda* [Red Star], May 9, 1945, in Nina Tumarkin, "The
    Great Patriotic War as Myth and Memory," *European Review* 11, no. 4
    (2003): 595–611 (*Red Star* was the official Soviet military newspaper).
    A section of this chapter and chapter 10 is adapted with permission from
    an article in the *Asan Forum*: Katie Stallard-Blanchette, "Who Controls
    the Past Controls the Future: The Political Use of WWII History in Russia
    and China," *Asan Forum* (September–October 2019), September 9, 2019,
    http://www.theasanforum.org/who-controls-the-past-controls-the-future-
    the-political-use-of-wwii-history-in-russia-china/.
2. Hans van de Ven, *China at War: Triumph and Tragedy in the Emergence of
    the New China* (Cambridge, MA: Harvard University Press, 2018), 208.
3. Rupert Wingfield-Hayes, "Witnessing Japan's Surrender in China," BBC
    News, September 2, 2015, https://www.bbc.com/news/magazine-34126445.
4. Chi Pang-yuan, *Juliuhe (The Great Flowing River)* (Taipei: Yuanjian
    Tianxia, 2014), 218–219, in Hans van de Ven, *China at War: Triumph and
    Tragedy in the Emergence of the New China* (Cambridge, MA: Harvard
    University Press, 2018), 215.
5. "W.J. Sebald's Memo Summarizing Radio Intelligence Following Japan's
    Surrender," Department of Defense, August 15, 1945, *U.S. Declassified
    Documents Online*, Gale Document Number: GALE|CK2349067533,
    http://tinyurl.gale.com/tinyurl/BjqYn4.
6. Agnes Norman, "Immediate Needs," *China Newsweek*, December 20,
    1945, in "Chinese National Relief and Rehabilitation Administration and
    the United Nations," UK National Archives, WO 208/484, in Hans van
    de Ven, *China at War: Triumph and Tragedy in the Emergence of the New
    China* (Cambridge, MA: Harvard University Press, 2018), 223; "Railway
    Lines Had Been Torn Up Ruth E. Pardee, "First Aid for China," *Pacific
    Affairs* 19, no. 1 (1946): 75–89, https://doi.org/10.2307/2752222.
7. US president Franklin D. Roosevelt lobbied for China's inclusion (then the
    Republic of China) and British prime minister Winston Churchill pressed
    for France to be included as a bulwark against possible German or Soviet
    ambitions in Europe, resulting in the five permanent members of the
    UNSC we know today.
8. Sergey Radchenko, "China Lost World War II," *Foreign Policy*, September
    3, 2015, https://foreignpolicy.com/2015/09/03/china-lost-world-war-2-china-
    world-war-ii-victory-parade/.

9. Hans van de Ven, *China at War: Triumph and Tragedy in the Emergence of the New China* (Cambridge, MA: Harvard University Press, 2018), 203–204.

10. Daqing Yang, "China: Meanings and Contradictions of Victory," in *Memory, Identity, and Commemorations of World War II: Anniversary Politics in Asia Pacific*, ed. Daqing Yang and Mike Mochizuki (Lanham, MD: Lexington Books, 2018), 6

11. Rana Mitter, *Forgotten Ally: China's World War II 1937–1945* (New York: Mariner Books, Houghton Mifflin Harcourt Publishing, 2014), 10–11.

12. Rana Mitter, *Forgotten Ally: China's World War II 1937–1945* (New York: Mariner Books, Houghton Mifflin Harcourt Publishing, 2014), 373–374.

13. Arthur Waldron, "China's New Remembering of World War II: The Case of Zhang Zizhong," *Modern Asian Studies* 30, no. 4, Special Issue: War in Modern China (October 1996): 945–978. Waldron notes that only one of the ten carvings on the Monument of the People's Heroes in Tiananmen Square, built in 1958, portrays a "scene from the guerrilla war against the Japanese (1937–1945)," focusing on the CCP resistance, and ignoring the larger battles fought by the KMT. A museum and memorial hall dedicated to the conflict was erected on the outskirts of Beijing in 1987.

14. Interview in Shanghai, March 2017.

15. Alexander Werth, *Russia at War: 1941–1945* (New York: E. P. Dutton & Co., 1964), 969.

16. George F. Kennan, *Memoirs: 1925–1950* (Boston: Little, Brown and Company, 1967), 240–241.

17. Robert Service, *Stalin: A Biography* (Cambridge, MA: Belknap Press of Harvard University Press, 2005), 480–481. The parade took place on June 24, 1945.

18. Georgii Konstantinovich Zhukov, *The Memoirs of Marshal Zhukov* (New York: Delacorte Press, 1971), 653–654.

19. *Pravda*, June 25, 1945, in Nina Tumarkin, *The Living and the Dead: The Rise and Fall of the Cult of World War II in Russia* (New York: Basic Books, 1994), 93.

20. Michael Ellman and S. Maksudov, "Soviet Deaths in the Great Patriotic War: A Note." *Europe-Asia Studies* 46, no. 4 (1994): 671–680, http://www.jstor.org/stable/152934.

21. Robert Service, *Stalin: A Biography* (Cambridge, MA: Belknap Press of Harvard University Press, 2005), 485.

22. Harrison E. Salisbury, "Zhukov: Rising Star in the Kremlin," *New York Times Magazine*, May 8, 1955, in Aleksandr Fursenko and Timothy Naftali, *Khrushchev's Cold War: The Inside Story of an American Adversary* (New York: W. W. Norton & Company, 2007), 28.

23. Khleviuk, *Politburo TsK VKP (b) i Soviet Ministrov SSSR 1945–1953*, 204–206, Reshetnikov, Vasily, "Drama marshala Novikova," *Krasnaia zvezda*, June 5, 1993, in Vladislav M. Zubok, *A Failed Empire: The Soviet Union in the Cold War from Stalin to Gorbachev* (Chapel Hill: University of North Carolina Press, 2007), 53–54.

24. Vladislav M. Zubok, *A Failed Empire: The Soviet Union in the Cold War from Stalin to Gorbachev* (Chapel Hill: University of North Carolina Press, 2007), 54–55, 59.

25. *Pravda*, May 9, 1946, in Matthew P. Gallagher, *The Soviet History of World War II: Myths, Memories, and Realities* (New York: Frederick A. Praeger, 1963), 40–41.

26. "Speech Delivered by Stalin at a Meeting of Voters of the Stalin Electoral District, Moscow, February 9, 1946," History and Public Policy Program Digital Archive, Gospolitizdat, Moscow, 1946, from the Pamphlet collection, J. Stalin, *Speeches Delivered at Meetings of Voters of the Stalin Electoral District, Moscow* (Moscow: Foreign Language Publishing House, 1950), http://digitalarchive.wilsoncenter.org/document/116179.

27. Robert Service, *Stalin: A Biography* (Cambridge, MA: Belknap Press of Harvard University Press, 2005), 528.

28. Kees Boterbloem, *Life and Times of Andrei Zhdanov, 1896–1948* (Montreal: McGill-Queen's University Press, 2004), 112–119, in Vladislav M. Zubok, *A Failed Empire: The Soviet Union in the Cold War from Stalin to Gorbachev* (Chapel Hill: University of North Carolina Press, 2007), 53.

29. Nina Tumarkin, *The Living and the Dead: The Rise and Fall of the Cult of World War II in Russia* (New York: Basic Books, 1994), 104.

30. Mark Edele, "Soviet Veterans as an Entitlement Group, 1945–1955," *Slavic Review* 65, no. 1 (2006): 111–137. Edele notes that the full text of this decision was never published; instead, short notices appeared in *Pravda*, December 24, 1947, and *Vedomosti Verkhovnogo Soveta SSSR*, no. 45, on December 26, 1947.

31. Matthew P. Gallagher, *The Soviet History of World War II: Myths, Memories, and Realities* (New York: Frederick A. Praeger, 1963), 17.

32. Richard Taylor, *Film Propaganda: Soviet Russia and Nazi Germany*, 2nd ed. rev. (London: I. B. Tauris, 1998), 100, in Denise J. Youngblood, *Russian War Films: On the Cinema Front, 1914–2005* (Lawrence: University Press of Kansas, 2007), 100–101.

33. A. M. Vasilevsky, *Delo vsei Zhizni* (Moscow: Gospolotitizdat, 1973), 3, in Lazar Lazarev, "Russian Literature on the War and Historical Truth," in *World War 2 and the Soviet People: Selected Papers from the Fourth World Congress for Soviet and East European Studies, Harrogate, 1990*, ed. John Garrard and Carol Garrard (New York: St. Martin's Press, 1993), 31.

34. Lazar Lazarev, "Russian Literature on the War and Historical Truth," in *World War 2 and the Soviet People: Selected Papers from the Fourth World*

Congress for Soviet and East European Studies, Harrogate, 1990, ed. John Garrard and Carol Garrard (New York: St. Martin's Press, 1993), 31.

35. Petro Vershyhora, "o 'byvalykh liudiakh' i ikh kritikakh," *Zvezda*, no. 6 (1948): 106, in Amir Weiner, "The Making of a Dominant Myth: The Second World War and the Construction of Political Identities within the Soviet Polity," *Russian Review* 55, no. 4 (1996): 638–660, doi:10.2307/ 131868.

36. Lazar Lazarev, "Russian Literature on the War and Historical Truth," in *World War 2 and the Soviet People: Selected Papers from the Fourth World Congress for Soviet and East European Studies, Harrogate, 1990*, ed. John Garrard and Carol Garrard (New York: St. Martin's Press, 1993), 31; see also Nina Tumarkin, *The Living and the Dead: The Rise and Fall of the Cult of World War II in Russia* (New York: Basic Books, 1994), 104.

37. Izabella Tabarovsky, "Russia's Lost War," *Wilson Quarterly*, Fall 2020, https://www.wilsonquarterly.com/quarterly/the-ends-of-history/russias-lost-war/; see also Nina Tumarkin, *The Living and the Dead: The Rise and Fall of the Cult of World War II in Russia* (New York: Basic Books, 1994), 98.

38. Svetlana Alexievich, *The Unwomanly Face of War: An Oral History of Women in World War II*, trans. Richard Pevear and Larissa Volokhonsky (New York: Random House, 2017), xlii, also quoted in part in Izabella Tabarovsky, "Russia's Lost War," *Wilson Quarterly*, Fall 2020, https:// www.wilsonquarterly.com/quarterly/the-ends-of-history/russias-lost-war/.

39. Matthew P. Gallagher, *The Soviet History of World War II: Myths, Memories, and Realities* (New York: Frederick A. Praeger, 1963), 45; "Analysis of Soviet Foreign Propaganda Broadcasts," U.S. Central Intelligence Agency, July 23, 1946, *U.S. Declassified Documents Online*, http://tinyurl.gale.com/tinyurl/BjqdqX, Gale Document Number: GALE|CK2349533951.

40. Sergei N. Goncharov, John W. Lewis, and Litai Xue, *Uncertain Partners: Stalin, Mao and the Korean War* (Stanford, CA: Stanford University Press, 1993), 144; Kathryn Weathersby, "Soviet Aims in Korea and the Origins of the Korean War, 1945–1950: New Evidence from Russian Archives," Cold War International History Project Working Paper No. 8, Woodrow Wilson International Center for Scholars (Washington, DC: November 1993).

Chapter 3

1. As quoted in Wang Jisi, "China's Search for a Grand Strategy," *Foreign Affairs*, March/April 2011, https://www.foreignaffairs.com/articles/china/ 2011-02-20/chinas-search-grand-strategy.

2. Kim Il Sung, "Every Effort for Victory in the War: Radio Address to the Entire Korean People, June 26, 1950," in *Kim Il Sung: Selected Works*, vol.

1, ed. The Party History Institute of the C. C. of the Workers Party of Korea (Pyongyang: Foreign Languages Publishing House, 1976), 287–291.

3. The Korean peninsula had been divided into northern and southern sectors by the United States and USSR at the end of World War II, but the plan to reunite the peninsula was abandoned and separate states were established in 1948, formally known as the Democratic People's Republic of Korea (DPRK) and the Republic of Korea (ROK).

4. "North Korea Celebrates Liberation Day," Moscow, Soviet Far East Service, via Komsomolsk, August 23, 1947, *Foreign Broadcast Information Service (FBIS) Daily Reports,* Daily Report, Foreign Radio Broadcasts (BIS-FRB-47-132), August 29, 1947.

5. Sergei N. Goncharov, John W. Lewis, and Xue Litai, *Uncertain Partners: Stalin, Mao and the Korean War* (Stanford, CA: Stanford University Press, 1993), 145–146; detail on not informing Mao of the final timing is from Samuel F. Wells Jr., *Fearing the Worst: How Korea Transformed the Cold War* (New York: Columbia University Press, 2020), 116. Mao had his own agenda at the time as he sought Stalin's support for an offensive to wrest back control of Taiwan from the KMT and both Kim and Mao sought to beat each other to the off; see Sergei N. Goncharov, John W. Lewis, and Xue Litai, *Uncertain Partners: Stalin, Mao and the Korean War* (Stanford, CA: Stanford University Press, 1993), 148–149; Shen Zhihua and Li Danhui, *After Leaning to One Side: China and Its Allies in the Cold War* (Washington, DC: Woodrow Wilson Center Press and Stanford University Press, 2011), 31–33.

6. Sergei N. Goncharov, John W. Lewis, and Xue Litai, *Uncertain Partners: Stalin, Mao and the Korean War* (Stanford, CA: Stanford University Press, 1993), 150.

7. "The Political Situation in Korea during the Period of Military Operations," August 11, 1950, History and Public Policy Program Digital Archive, AVP RF f. 0102. op. 6, p. 21, d. 47, pp. 29–40. Translated for NKIDP by Gary Goldberg. https://digitalarchive.wilsoncenter.org/document/114916 (report sources quote to *Minju Joseon,* July 7, 1950).

8. "The Ambassador in Korea (Muccio) to the Secretary of State," June 26, 1950, in *Foreign Relations of the United States, 1950, Korea,* vol. 7, ed. John P. Glennon and S. Everett Gleason (Washington, DC: Government Printing Office, 1976), Document 94, https://history.state.gov/historicaldocuments/frus1950v07/d94.

9. "Mao Telegram Confirming the Scheduled Entry of the Volunteers," October 18, 1950, in Sergei N. Goncharov, John W. Lewis, and Xue Litai, *Uncertain Partners: Stalin, Mao and the Korean War* (Stanford, CA: Stanford University Press, 1993), 198.

10. While South Korea's president Moon Jae-in pushed for an end of war declaration in 2021, no agreement had been reached by the time of this writing in January 2022. For a detailed account of the history of the

conflict and its consequences see Bruce Cumings, *The Korean War: A History* (New York: Modern Library, 2011); Sheila Miyoshi Jager, *Brothers at War: The Unending Conflict in Korea* (New York and London: Norton, 2013); Samuel F. Wells Jr., *Fearing the Worst: How Korea Transformed the Cold War* (New York: Columbia University Press, 2020).

11. "Outstanding Leadership and Brilliant Victory (Excerpts)," *Korea Pictorial* (Pyongyang: Korea Pictorial, 1993), Woodrow Wilson International Center for Scholars, History and Public Policy Program Digital Archive, http://digitalarchive.wilsoncenter.org/document/155225.

12. The Research Institute of History, Academy of Sciences of the Democratic People's Republic of Korea, *History of the Just Fatherland Liberation War of the Korean People* (Pyongyang: Foreign Languages Publishing House, 1961), 303–304.

13. The Research Institute of History, Academy of Sciences of the Democratic People's Republic of Korea, *History of the Just Fatherland Liberation War of the Korean People* (Pyongyang: Foreign Languages Publishing House, 1961), 304.

14. "Outstanding Leadership and Brilliant Victory (Excerpts)," *Korea Pictorial* (Pyongyang: Korea Pictorial, 1993), Woodrow Wilson International Center for Scholars, History and Public Policy Program Digital Archive, http://digitalarchive.wilsoncenter.org/document/155225.

15. "Outstanding Leadership and Brilliant Victory (Excerpts)," *Korea Pictorial* (Pyongyang: Korea Pictorial, 1993), Woodrow Wilson International Center for Scholars, History and Public Policy Program Digital Archive, http://digitalarchive.wilsoncenter.org/document/155225.

16. Bruce Cumings, *The Korean War: A History* (New York: Modern Library, 2011), 159.

17. "Dean Rusk Interviewed by Thomas J. Schoenbaum and Thomas W. Ganschow circa 1985," Dean Rusk Oral History Collection, Richard B. Russell Library for Political Research and Studies, http://russelllibrarydocs.libs.uga.edu/Rusk_OH_KK.pdf.

18. Eric Pace, "George Barrett of the Times, Cited for War Coverage, Dies," *New York Times*, November 22, 1984, https://www.nytimes.com/1984/11/22/obituaries/george-barrett-of-the-times-cited-for-war-coverage-dies.html; see also US National Archives, 995.000 file, box 6175, George Barrett dispatch of February 8, 1951, in Bruce Cumings, "Nuclear Threats against North Korea: Consequences of the 'Forgotten' War," *Asia-Pacific Journal* 3, no. 1 (January 13, 2005), https://apjjf.org/-Bruce-Cumings/2055/article.html.

19. "Report from the Embassy of the Polish Republic in Korea for the Period of July through August 1951," September 1, 1951, History and Public Policy Program Digital Archive, Polish Foreign Ministry Archive. Obtained by Jakub Poprocki and translated by Maya Latynski. http://digitalarchive.wilsoncenter.org/document/114933.

20. This is not to say there were no atrocities against civilians by US forces. Troops from the US Seventh Cavalry Regiment massacred civilians at the village of No Gun Ri in July 1950 in an incident that was uncovered by the Associated Press, leading to a Pentagon investigation and subsequent expression of regret from President Bill Clinton. See Charles J. Hanley, Sang-Hun Choe, and Martha Mendoza, *The Bridge at No Gun Ri: A Hidden Nightmare from the Korean War* (New York: Holt, 2001).

21. The Research Institute of History, Academy of Sciences of the Democratic People's Republic of Korea, *History of the Just Fatherland Liberation War of the Korean People* (Pyongyang: Foreign Languages Publishing House, 1961), 127.

22. Adam Cathcart, "Notes on the Sinchon Massacre," May 16, 2015, https://adamcathcart.com/2015/05/16/notes-on-the-sinchon-massacre/; Patrick Tapy, "The Sincheon Massacre: Historical Fact and Historical Revision," *Sino-NK*, September 17, 2013, https://sinonk.com/2013/09/17/the-sincheon-massacre-historical-fact-and-historical-revision/.

23. The Research Institute of History, Academy of Sciences of the Democratic People's Republic of Korea, *History of the Just Fatherland Liberation War of the Korean People* (Pyongyang: Foreign Languages Publishing House, 1961), 127–128.

24. O. Hye-gyong (오혜경), *Choeak e ch'an mije-ui Choseon ch'imnyaksa* (죄악에 찬 미제의 조선 침략사) (Pyongyang: Publisher of Science Encyclopedia [Gwahak baekgwa sajun choolpansa], 2010), 157.

25. O. Hye-gyong (오혜경), *Choeak e ch'an mije-ui Choseon ch'imnyaksa* (죄악에 찬 미제의 조선 침략사) (Pyongyang: Publisher of Science Encyclopedia [Gwahak baekgwa sajun choolpansa], 2010), 147–148.

26. The Research Institute of History, Academy of Sciences of the Democratic People's Republic of Korea, *History of the Just Fatherland Liberation War of the Korean People* (Pyongyang: Foreign Languages Publishing House, 1961), 2.

27. "Kim Jong Un Visits Sinchon Museum," KCNA, November 25, 2014, http://www.kcna.co.jp/item/2014/201411/news25/20141125-01ee.html; "Kim Visits Sinchon Museum, Calls for Stronger Ideological Education," *Daily NK*, July 24, 2015, http://www.dailynk.com/english/read.php?catId=nk01700&num=13361.

28. Interview in Sejong, South Korea, April 2018.

29. Interview in Washington, DC, October 2019.

30. Later formulations tended to skip over the details of how the fighting started and refer instead to the "outbreak" of the war. See, for example, "Resist U.S. Aggression and Aid Korea," PRC Ministry of Foreign Affairs website, https://www.fmprc.gov.cn/mfa_eng/ziliao_665539/3602_665543/3604_665547/t18022.shtml.

31. A. Doak Barnett, *Communist China: The Early Years 1949–55* (New York: Frederick A. Praeger, 1964), 9–10.

32. "Zhonggong Shanghai shi Penglai quwei xuanchuanbu guanyu yiban sixiang qingkuang ji shishi xuanjiao gongzuo baogao" [Report written by the propaganda division of the Penglai district committee in Shanghai concerning the general thought situation as well as propaganda working on current issues], November 13, 1950, in No. A22-2-20-25, SMA, in Masuda Hajimu, "The Korean War through the Prism of Chinese Society: Public Reactions and the Shaping of 'Reality' in the Communist State, October–December 1950," *Journal of Cold War Studies* 14, no. 3 (2012): 3–38.

33. "Shenyang, Lvda zuijin qunzhong sixiang dongtai ji dite huodong zhuangkuang," [Recent thought trends among people in Shenyang and Lvda etc. and the situation of enemy agent activities], *Neibu cankao*, November 30, 1950, in Masuda Hajimu, "The Korean War through the Prism of Chinese Society: Public Reactions and the Shaping of 'Reality' in the Communist State, October–December 1950," *Journal of Cold War Studies* 14, no. 3 (2012): 3–38.

34. "Shenyang, Lvda zuijin qunzhong sixiang huodong ji dite huodong zhuangkuang," *Neibu cankao*, November 30, 1950, in CSC, CUHK, in Masuda Hajimu, "The Korean War through the Prism of Chinese Society: Public Reactions and the Shaping of 'Reality' in the Communist State, October—December 1950," *Journal of Cold War Studies* 14, no. 3 (2012): 3–38.

35. Liu Shaoqi, *Jian guo yi lai Liu Shaoqi wengao* [Collected works of Liu Shaoqi after the establishment of the country] (Beijing: Zhongyang wenxian chubanshe, 2005), 593; "Report on the Situation Regarding Young Students, Workers, and Military Staff in Schools," memorandum from the Beijing Municipal Committee to the Central Committee, December 19, 1950, in "Beijing yu Kan-Mei yuan-Chao," *Lengzhan guojishi yanjiu* 2 (Spring/Summer 2005): 404–405; H. Y. Hsu, "Notes by H. Y. Hsu," January 4, 1951, in "Extension of the Power of Ruling Chinese Communists over the Political, Social and Economic Life of the Whole of China," FO371/92193, TNAUK, in Masuda Hajimu, "The Korean War through the Prism of Chinese Society: Public Reactions and the Shaping of 'Reality' in the Communist State, October–December 1950," *Journal of Cold War Studies* 14, no. 3 (2012): 3–38.

36. "Student Life in China Today," December 15, 1950, in Masuda Hajimu, "The Korean War through the Prism of Chinese Society: Public Reactions and the Shaping of 'Reality' in the Communist State, October–December 1950," *Journal of Cold War Studies* 14, no. 3 (2012): 3–38.

37. Interview in Washington, DC, May 2019, conducted with Felix Boecking.

38. Andrew T. Roy, *Never a Dull Moment: A Memoir of Family and China* (Nanjing, China: Nanjing University Press, 2017), 239–250.

39. Milton Leitenberg, "China's False Allegations of the Use of Biological Weapons by the United States during the Korean War," Cold War

International History Project Working Paper No. 78, March 2016, https://
www.wilsoncenter.org/publication/chinas-false-allegations-the-use-
biological-weapons-the-united-states-during-the-korean.

Chapter 4

1. This inscription is the last line of a poem by Leningrad siege survivor Olga
    Berggolts, which was incorporated into the memorial to the victims of the
    siege and the war dead on the Leningrad Front, and is inscribed on many
    Soviet war memorials.
2. *Pravda*, January 11, 1955, in Nina Tumarkin, *Lenin Lives: The Lenin Cult
    in Soviet Russia* (Cambridge, MA: Harvard University Press, 1997), 257.
    For details of Khrushchev's efforts to resurrect the cult of Lenin see Nina
    Tumarkin, *Lenin Lives: The Lenin Cult in Soviet Russia* (Cambridge,
    MA: Harvard University Press, 1997), 252–269.
3. TsDNIVO (Center for the Documentation of History of Volgograd
    oblast'), 71/37/32/93, in Polly Jones, *Myth, Memory, Trauma: Rethinking the
    Stalinist Past in the Soviet Union, 1953–70* (New Haven, CT: Yale University
    Press, 2013), 115.
4. XXII S"ezd Kommunisticheskoi Partii Sovetskogo Soiuza.
    Stenograficheskii otchet, vol. 3 (Moscow, 1962), 121, in Nina Tumarkin,
    Lenin Lives: The Lenin Cult in Soviet Russia (Cambridge, MA: Harvard
    University Press, 1997), 259. Details of the revived Lenin cult in this
    paragraph are from Nina Tumarkin, *Lenin Lives: The Lenin Cult in Soviet
    Russia* (Cambridge, MA: Harvard University Press, 1997), 257–259.
5. Polly Jones, *Myth, Memory, Trauma: Rethinking the Stalinist Past in the
    Soviet Union, 1953–70* (New Haven, CT: Yale University Press, 2013), 1;
    Aleksandr Fursenko and Timothy Naftali, *Khrushchev's Cold War: The
    Inside Story of an American Adversary* (New York: Norton, 2007), 410.
6. William Taubman, *Khrushchev: The Man and His Era*
    (New York: Norton), 305.
7. William Taubman, *Khrushchev: The Man and His Era* (New York: Norton),
    591–593. Khrushchev also deployed Soviet troops to crush the Hungarian
    Revolution in 1956, indicating the limits of his tolerance for dissent; see
    William Taubman, *Khrushchev: The Man and His Era* (New York: Norton),
    298–299.
8. According to Vladislav Zubok, 2,700 US citizens visited the Soviet Union
    and more than 700,000 Soviet citizens traveled abroad in 1957 alone;
    Vladislav M. Zubok, *Failed Empire: The Soviet Union in the Cold War
    from Stalin to Gorbachev* (Chapel Hill: University of North Carolina Press,
    2007), 172.
9. Vladislav M. Zubok, *Failed Empire: The Soviet Union in the Cold War
    from Stalin to Gorbachev* (Chapel Hill: University of North Carolina Press,
    2007), 172, 175.

10. Vladislav M. Zubok, *Failed Empire: The Soviet Union in the Cold War from Stalin to Gorbachev* (Chapel Hill: University of North Carolina Press, 2007), 174.

11. Joseph Brodsky, "Spoils of War," *On Grief and Reason: Essays* (New York: Farrar, Straus, Giroux, 1995), 3–21, in Vladislav M. Zubok, *Failed Empire: The Soviet Union in the Cold War from Stalin to Gorbachev* (Chapel Hill: University of North Carolina Press, 173.

12. Vasily Aksenov, *In Search of Melancholy Baby* (New York: Random House, 1987), in Vladislav M. Zubok, *Failed Empire: The Soviet Union in the Cold War from Stalin to Gorbachev* (Chapel Hill: University of North Carolina Press, 2007), 173.

13. "Vladimir Putin's World War II Reading List," HistoryNet, February 2011, https://www.historynet.com/vladimir-putins-world-war-ii-reading-list.htm.

14. Ustinov's and Grigorenko's comments, respectively. "Meeting of Politburo of CPSU, July 12, 1984," *CWIHP Bulletin*, no. 4 (Fall 1994): 81; and Petr Grigorenko, *V podpolie mozhno vstretit tolko kris* (Moscow: Zvenia, 1997), 312–315, both in Vladislav M. Zubok, *Failed Empire: The Soviet Union in the Cold War from Stalin to Gorbachev* (Chapel Hill: University of North Carolina Press, 2007), 170.

15. William Taubman, *Khrushchev: The Man and His Era* (New York: Norton), 16. For a detailed study of elite power struggles and political manouevring by Khrushchev see Joseph Torigian, *Prestige, Manipulation, and Coercion: Elite Power Struggles in the Soviet Union and China after Stalin and Mao* (New Haven, CT: Yale University Press, 2022).

16. Nina Tumarkin, *The Living and the Dead: The Rise and Fall of the Cult of World War II in Russia* (New York: Basic Books, 1994), 128.

17. Interview by telephone, July 2021.

18. "Zasedaniia Prezidiuma TsK KPSS ot 1 aprelia 1965, 'O prazdnovanii 20-letiia pobedy sovetskogo naroda v Velikoi Otechestvennoi Voine Sovetskogo Soiuza za 1941-1945gg.' Protokol No. 197" (1965), RGANI, 3/16/659, sheet 129, in Jeremy Hicks, *The Victory Banner over the Reichstag: Film, Document, and Ritual in Russia's Contested Memory of World War II* (Pittsburgh, PA: University of Pittsburgh Press, 2020), 125.

19. "Teksty televizionnykh peredach za aprel'-iiun'1965g.," GARF, 6903/26/575, sheet 146, in Jeremy Hicks, *The Victory Banner over the Reichstag: Film, Document, and Ritual in Russia's Contested Memory of World War II* (Pittsburgh, PA: University of Pittsburgh Press, 2020), 126.

20. "Zasedaniia Prezidiuma KPSS ot 15 aprelia 1965g. XXII sozvyz. Protokol No. 199" (1965), RGANI, 3/18/337, sheet 8, in Jeremy Hicks, *The Victory Banner over the Reichstag: Film, Document, and Ritual in Russia's Contested Memory of World War II* (Pittsburgh, PA: University of Pittsburgh Press, 2020), 125.

21. Jeremy Hicks, *The Victory Banner over the Reichstag: Film, Document, and Ritual in Russia's Contested Memory of World War II* (Pittsburgh, PA: University of Pittsburgh Press, 2020), 125–126.

22. "Obzory pisem telezitelei za fevral' 1965 g.," GARF, 6903/10/65, sheet 6, Vladimir Stepaniuk, Korrespondent GRI TsT (DIP 1-go kanala) s 1961–2004, "Vekhi istorii glavnoi redaktsii informatsii TsT," in Jeremy Hicks, *The Victory Banner over the Reichstag: Film, Document, and Ritual in Russia's Contested Memory of World War II* (Pittsburgh, PA: University of Pittsburgh Press, 2020), 128.

23. Interview by video call, July 2021.

24. Jeremy Hicks, *The Victory Banner over the Reichstag: Film, Document, and Ritual in Russia's Contested Memory of World War II* (Pittsburgh, PA: University of Pittsburgh Press, 2020), 124. "This was more than a state-sponsored cult," concludes Mark Edele in his study of the Soviet veterans' movement; rather, it was "a living religion, deeply rooted in a population still trying to make sense of the unintelligible horror of this war." Mark Edele, *Soviet Veterans of the Second World War: A Popular Movement in an Authoritarian Society, 1941–1991* (Oxford: Oxford University Press, 2008), 9.

25. Eric Homberger, "The Story of the Cenotaph," *The Times Literary Supplement* 896 (November 1976): 1427, in George L. Mosse, *Fallen Soldiers: Reshaping the Memory of the World Wars* (New York: Oxford University Press, 1990), 95.

26. George L. Mosse, *Fallen Soldiers: Reshaping the Memory of the World Wars* (New York: Oxford University Press, 1990), 94–95. This is not to suggest such memorials are wholly or in some cases at all motivated by cynicism, but rather that those in power both recognized the genuine desire to commemorate the fallen and ascribe meaning to their loss and the political resonance such conflicts command, particularly with the advent of modern mass wars fought by citizens armies and the increasing impact on civilians.

27. Scott Palmer, "How Memory Was Made: The Construction of the Memorial to the Heroes of the Battle of Stalingrad," *Russian Review* 68, no. 3 (July 2009): 373–407, https://www.jstor.org/stable/20621047.

28. Nina Tumarkin, *The Living and the Dead: The Rise and Fall of the Cult of World War II in Russia* (New York: Basic Books, 1994), 32.

29. Nina Tumarkin, *The Living and the Dead: The Rise and Fall of the Cult of World War II in Russia* (New York: Basic Books, 1994), 133–134.

30. Polly Jones, *Myth, Memory, Trauma: Rethinking the Stalinist Past in the Soviet Union, 1953–70* (New Haven, CT: Yale University Press, 2013), 232.

31. RGANI, 5/58/29/38-40, in Polly Jones, *Myth, Memory, Trauma: Rethinking the Stalinist Past in the Soviet Union, 1953–70* (New Haven, CT: Yale University Press, 2013), 234.

32. Polly Jones, *Myth, Memory, Trauma: Rethinking the Stalinist Past in the Soviet Union, 1953–70* (New Haven, CT: Yale University Press, 2013), 235. Other writers suffered more serious fates during this period, such as Andrei Sinyavsky and Yuli Daniel, who were convicted of anti-Soviet agitation after publishing satirical works under pseudonyms abroad and sentenced to serve seven and five years, respectively, in labor camps in February 1966 in the first public show trial since the Stalin era.

33. RGALI, 2464/3/166, 167, in Polly Jones, *Myth, Memory, Trauma: Rethinking the Stalinist Past in the Soviet Union, 1953–70* (New Haven, CT: Yale University Press, 2013), 224–225.

34. Matthew Luxmoore, "Russian Minister Says Authenticity of War Legend beyond Dispute, 'Amoral' to Dig Further," Radio Free Europe/Radio Liberty, December 3, 2018, https://www.rferl.org/a/russian-minister-says-authenticity-of-war-legend-beyond-dispute-amoral-to-dig-further-/29635477.html.

35. Nina Tumarkin, *The Living and the Dead: The Rise and Fall of the Cult of World War II in Russia* (New York: Basic Books, 1994), 139.

36. Lazar Lazarev, "Russian Literature on the War and Historical Truth," in *World War 2 and the Soviet People: Selected Papers from the Fourth World Congress for Soviet and East European Studies, Harrogate, 1990*, ed. John Garrard and Carol Garrard (New York: St. Martin's Press, 1993), 34–35; see also Nina Tumarkin, *The Living and the Dead: The Rise and Fall of the Cult of World War II in Russia* (New York: Basic Books, 1994), 134.

37. Lazar Lazarev, "Russian Literature on the War and Historical Truth," in *World War 2 and the Soviet People: Selected Papers from the Fourth World Congress for Soviet and East European Studies, Harrogate, 1990*, ed. John Garrard and Carol Garrard (New York: St Martin's Press, 1993), 35.

38. Nora Levin, *The Jews in the Soviet Union since 1917: The Paradox of Survival*, vol. 1 (New York: New York University Press, 1988), 424–425, in Amir Weiner, *Making Sense of War: The Second World War and the Fate of the Bolshevik Revolution* (Princeton, NJ: Princeton University Press, 2002), 208.

39. Polly Jones, *Myth, Memory, Trauma: Rethinking the Stalinist Past in the Soviet Union, 1953–70* (New Haven, CT: Yale University Press, 2013), 250.

40. Answers to the Italian Journalist Oriana Fallaci, *People's Daily*, August 21 and 23, 1980, http://en.people.cn/dengxp/vol2/text/b1470.html.

41. Wasyl Shimoniak, *Communist Education: Its History, Philosophy and Politics* (Chicago: Rand McNally, 1970), 165, in David M. Gist, "The Militarization of Soviet Youth," *Naval War College Review* 30, no. 1 (1977): 115–133.

42. Anna Sanina, *Patriotic Education in Contemporary Russia: Sociological Studies in the Making of the Post-Soviet Citizen* (Stuttgart: ibidem-Verlag, 2017), 70.

43. O. A. Sarkisian, "The History Teacher and the School Komsomol Organization," *Soviet Education*, August 1973, 106; Leon Gouré, *The Military Indoctrination of Soviet Youth* (New York: National Strategy Information Center, 1973), 31, 50, in David M. Gist, "The Militarization of Soviet Youth," *Naval War College Review* 30, no. 1 (1977): 115–133.

44. Details in this paragraph are from David M. Gist, "The Militarization of Soviet Youth," *Naval War College Review* 30, no. 1 (1977): 115–133; Leon Gouré, *The Military Indoctrination of Soviet Youth* (New York: National Strategy Information Center, 1973), 43–45.

45. Daniel Kalder, "Dictator-Lit: Comrade Brezhnev Goes to War," *The Guardian*, October 9, 2009, https://www.theguardian.com/books/booksblog/2009/oct/09/dictator-lit-leonid-brezhnev-malaya-zemlya.

46. Sergei Medvedev, *The Return of the Russian Leviathan*, trans. Stephen Dalziel (Medford, MA: Polity Press, 2020), 201.

47. Vladimir Putin, *First Person: An Astonishingly Frank Self-Portrait by Russia's President*, with Nataliya Gevorkyan, Natalya Timakova, and Andrei Kolesnikov, trans. Catherine A. Fitzpatrick (New York: PublicAffairs, 2000), 42.

Chapter 5

1. CCCPC (Central Committee of the Communist Party of China), "Aiguo zhuyi jiaoyu shishi gangyao" [Outline on the implementation of patriotic education], *Renmin Ribao* [People's Daily], September 6, 1994, in Zheng Wang, *Never Forget National Humiliation: Historical Memory in Chinese Politics and Foreign Relations* (New York: Columbia University Press, 2014), 103.

2. Louisa Lim, *The People's Republic of Amnesia: Tiananmen Revisited* (New York: Oxford University Press, 2014), 110.

3. Details in this paragraph from Ezra F. Vogel, *Deng Xiaoping and the Transformation of China* (Cambridge, MA: Harvard University Press, 2011), 625–627. While the protests are generally remembered as a student democracy movement, the protesters included workers as well as students and their complaints included corruption, economic inequality, access to employment opportunities, and choice over work assignments, as well as complaints over foreign trade deals; see, for instance, Geremie Barmé, "Mirrors of History: On a Sino-Japanese Moment and Some Antecedents," *Asia-Pacific Journal: Japan Focus* 3, no. 5 (May 19, 2005), https://apjjf.org/-Geremie-Barme/1713/article.html.

4. Ezra F. Vogel, *Deng Xiaoping and the Transformation of China* (Cambridge, MA: Harvard University Press, 2011), 629.

5. Timothy Brook, *Quelling the People: The Military Suppression of the Beijing Democracy Movement* (Stanford, CA: Stanford University Press, 1998), 135.

6. Louisa Lim, *The People's Republic of Amnesia: Tiananmen Revisited* (New York: Oxford University Press, 2014), 18.

7. Timothy Brook, *Quelling the People: The Military Suppression of the Beijing Democracy Movement* (Stanford, CA: Stanford University Press, 1998), 146.

8. Ezra F. Vogel, *Deng Xiaoping and the Transformation of China* (Cambridge, MA: Harvard University Press, 2011), 630–631; Timothy Brook, *Quelling the People: The Military Suppression of the Beijing Democracy Movement* (Stanford, CA: Stanford University Press, 1998), 168–169.

9. Details of Wang Nan's death are from Louisa Lim, *The People's Republic of Amnesia: Tiananmen Revisited* (New York: Oxford University Press, 2014), 111–113; Zhang Xianling, "Weile Jilu Lishi de Zhenshi" [In Order to Record the Historical Truth], May 26, 2004, http://64memo.com/b5/16310.htm.

10. Deng Xiaoping, "Address to Officers at the Rank of General and Above in Command of the Troops Enforcing Martial Law in Beijing, June 9, 1989," in *Selected Works of Deng Xiaoping*, vol. 3 (Beijing: Foreign Language Press, 1994), https://dengxiaopingworks.wordpress.com/2013/03/18/address-to-officers-at-the-rank-of-general-and-above-in-command-of-the-troops-enforcing-martial-law-in-beijing/.

11. Louisa Lim, *The People's Republic of Amnesia: Tiananmen Revisited* (New York: Oxford University Press, 2014), 25.

12. James Lilley with Jeffrey Lilley, *China Hands: Nine Decades of Adventure, Espionage, and Diplomacy in Asia* (New York: PublicAffairs, 2004), 309, in Ezra F. Vogel, *Deng Xiaoping and the Transformation of China* (Cambridge, MA: Harvard University Press, 2011), 617.

13. Fox Butterfield, "TV Weekend; China's Leader Calls Massacre 'Nothing,'" *New York Times*, May 18, 1990, https://www.nytimes.com/1990/05/18/arts/tv-weekend-china-s-leader-calls-massacre-nothing.html, in Louisa Lim, *The People's Republic of Amnesia: Tiananmen Revisited* (New York: Oxford University Press, 2014), 25.

14. Ezra F. Vogel, *Deng Xiaoping and the Transformation of China* (Cambridge, MA: Harvard University Press, 2011), 640. Anne-Marie Brady writes that the lesson the party learned from both the Cultural Revolution and the events of 1989 was that "force is only a limited and short-term means of social control in a modern society; the most sustainable means of social control is persuasion." Anne-Marie Brady, *Marketing Dictatorship: Propaganda and Thought Work in Contemporary China* (Lanham, MD: Rowman and Littlefield, 2008), 191.

15. Deng Xiaoping, "Address to Officers at the Rank of General and Above in Command of the Troops Enforcing Martial Law in Beijing, June 9, 1989," in *Selected Works of Deng Xiaoping*, vol. 3 (Beijing: Foreign Language Press, 1994), https://dengxiaopingworks.wordpress.com/2013/03/18/address-to-officers-at-the-rank-of-general-and-above-in-command-of-the-troops-enforcing-martial-law-in-beijing/.

16. "Resolution on Certain Questions in the History of Our Party since the Founding of the People's Republic of China," June 27, 1981, History

and Public Policy Program Digital Archive, translation from the *Beijing Review* 24, no. 27 (July 6, 1981): 10–39, http://digitalarchive.wilsoncenter. org/document/121344.

17. Tania Branigan, "China's Great Famine: The True Story," *The Guardian*, January 1, 2013, https://www.theguardian.com/world/2013/jan/01/ china-great-famine-book-tombstone. Other examples include the anti-Rightist movement of 1957, the Cultural Revolution from 1966 to 1976, the Democracy Wall movement of 1979, and the student-led protests of 1986, 1987, and 1989; see Louisa Lim, *The People's Republic of Amnesia: Tiananmen Revisited* (New York: Oxford University Press, 2014), 5.

18. In response to the question "What Ideals Do You Think University Students Should Establish?" in 1986, 38.1 percent of students chose "Communism," 16.4 percent "Socialism," and 28.1 percent "Only patriotism, social ideals are not necessary," and there were no responses or the option was not provided for "Rely on one's own skills to survive." In 1988, 6.1 percent responded "Communism," 5 percent "Socialism," 40.1 percent "Only patriotism, social ideals are not necessary," and 29.2 percent "Rely on one's own skills to survive." Details of survey size and methodology were not provided. Lü Jia, "Zhengzhi shehuihua guochengzhong de wuqu" [Mistakes in the process of political socialization], *Qingnian Yanjiu*, no. 1 (January 1992): 32–37, in Stanley Rosen, "The Effect of Post-4 June Re-Education Campaigns on Chinese Students," *China Quarterly*, no. 134 (1993): 310–334, www.jstor.org/stable/ 654304.

19. *People's Daily*, February 17, 1986, in Jie Chen, "The Impact of Reform on the Party and Ideology in China," *Journal of Contemporary China*, no. 9 (Summer 1995): 22–34, https://doi.org/10.1080/10670569508724221.

20. Suisheng Zhao, *A Nation-State by Construction: Dynamics of Modern Chinese Nationalism* (Stanford, CA: Stanford University Press, 2004), 211.

21. *Guangming Ribao*, March 19, 1981, in Jie Chen, "The Impact of Reform on the Party and Ideology in China," *Journal of Contemporary China*, no. 9 (Summer 1995): 22–34, https://doi.org/10.1080/10670569508724221.

22. Xing Fensi, *Gongren Ribao*, September 20, 1979, in Charles Burton, *Political and Social Change in China since 1978* (New York: Greenwood Publishing, 1990), 5; see also Jie Chen, "The Impact of Reform on the Party and Ideology in China," *Journal of Contemporary China*, no. 9 (Summer 1995): 22–34, https://doi.org/10.1080/10670569508724221.

23. Deng Xiaoping, "We Are Confident That We Can Handle China's Affairs Well," *People's Daily*, September 16, 1989, http://en.people.cn/dengxp/vol3/ text/d1040.html.

24. Li Guoda, ed., *Qiye xuanchuan sixiang gongzuo shiyong duben* [Practical Handbook of Enterprise Propaganda and Thought Work] (Beijing: Yejin gongye chubanshe, 1996), 292, in Anne-Marie Brady,

Marketing Dictatorship: Propaganda and Thought Work in Contemporary China (Lanham, MD: Rowman & Littlefield, 2008), 44.

25. "Jiang Zemin zongshuji zhixin Li Tieying He Dongchang qiangdiao jinxing zhongguo jinxiangdaishi he guoqing jiaoyu" [General Secretary Jiang Zemin's letter to Li Tieying and He Dongchang stressed to conduct education on Chinese modern and contemporary history], *Renmin Ribao*, June 1, 1991, in Zheng Wang, *Never Forget National Humiliation: Historical Memory in Chinese Politics and Foreign Relations* (New York: Columbia University Press, 2014), 98; see also Alison A. Kaufman, "The 'Century of Humiliation' and China's National Narratives," US-China Economic and Security Review Commission testimony, March 10, 2011, https://www.uscc.gov/sites/default/files/3.10.11Kaufman.pdf; Peter Hays Gries, *China's New Nationalism: Pride, Politics, and Diplomacy* (Berkeley: University of California Press, 2005), 43–53.

26. Zheng Wang, *Never Forget National Humiliation: Historical Memory in Chinese Politics and Foreign Relations* (New York: Columbia University Press, 2014), 102–103.

27. Orville Schell and John Delury, *Wealth and Power: China's Long March to the Twenty-First Century* (New York: Random House, 2014), 7; see also Rush Doshi, "The Chinese Communist Party Has Always Been Nationalish," July 1, 2021, https://foreignpolicy.com/2021/07/01/chinese-communist-party-nationalist-centennial/, https://foreignpolicy.com/2021/07/01/chinese-communist-party-nationalist-centennial/; Adam Tooze, "Why There Is No Solution to Our Age of Crisis without China," *New Statesman*, July 21, 2021, https://www.newstatesman.com/politics/2021/07/why-there-no-solution-our-age-crisis-without-china.

28. Mao Zedong, *Selected Works of Mao Zedong*, vol. 5 (Beijing: Foreign Languages Press, 1977), 17.

29. Zheng Wang, "Not Rising, but Rejuvenating: The Chinese Dream," *The Diplomat*, February 5, 2013, https://thediplomat.com/2013/02/chinese-dream-draft/; William A. Callahan, "National Insecurities: Humiliation, Salvation, and Chinese Nationalism," *Alternatives: Global, Local, Political* 29, no. 2, (2004): 199–218.

30. Wang Yugao, *Shilue Gaoben* [Shilue Manuscripts], Archives of President Chiang Kai-shek, Academia Historica, Hsintien, Taiwan, May 9, 1928, Grace Huang, "Chiang Kai-shek's Politics of Shame and Humiliation, 1928–34," Paper presented at the Institut Barcelona D'Estudis Internacional (IBEI), Barcelona, Spain, June 11, 2009, in Zheng Wang, *Never Forget National Humiliation: Historical Memory in Chinese Politics and Foreign Relations* (New York: Columbia University Press, 2014), 80–81.

31. William A. Callahan, "History Identity and Security: Producing and Consuming Nationalism in China," *Critical Asian Studies* 38, no. 2 (2006): 179–208.

32. "Guochi Ri Yi" [Things one should do on National Humiliation Day], *Shenbao*, May 9, 1922, in William A. Callahan, "History Identity and Security: Producing and Consuming Nationalism in China," *Critical Asian Studies* 38, no. 2 (2006): 179–208. Callahan notes that the idea of a National Humiliation Day was not unique to China, with similar practices having been adopted in the past in South Korea, India, the United Kingdom, and the United States.

33. William A. Callahan, "History Identity and Security: Producing and Consuming Nationalism in China," *Critical Asian Studies* 38, no. 2 (2006): 179–208; see also Louisa Lim, *The People's Republic of Amnesia: Tiananmen Revisited* (New York: Oxford University Press, 2014), 138.

34. CCCPC (Central Committee of the Communist Party of China), "Aiguo zhuyi jiaoyu shishi gangyao" [Outline on the implementation of patriotic education], *Renmin Ribao* [People's Daily], September 6, 1994, in Zheng Wang, *Never Forget National Humiliation: Historical Memory in Chinese Politics and Foreign Relations* (New York: Columbia University Press, 2014), 115.

35. Jiang Zemin, "Speech at the 6th Plenary Session of the 14th CCP National Congress," *Renmin Ribao*, October 10, 1996, in Zheng Wang, *Never Forget National Humiliation: Historical Memory in Chinese Politics and Foreign Relations* (New York: Columbia University Press, 2014), 124.

36. National Education Council, "Zhongxiaoxue jiaqiang jindai xiandaishi he guoqing jiaoyu de zongti gangyao" [General outline on strengthening education on Chinese modern and contemporary history and national conditions] (Beijing: Government Printing Office, 1991), in Zheng Wang, *Never Forget National Humiliation: Historical Memory in Chinese Politics and Foreign Relations* (New York: Columbia University Press, 2014), 99. Patriotic education in general had been carried out in Chinese schools since the early years of the People's Republic of China, however, and as recently as 1983–1984 the Propaganda Department had called for patriotic education to be strengthened; see Elizabeth J. Perry, "Cultural Governance in Contemporary China: 'Re-Orienting' Party Propaganda," Harvard-Yenching Institute Working Paper Series, 2013.

37. Wu Zijiao, "Zeyang jinxing guochi jiaoyu?" [How can we conduct national humiliation education?], *Anhui jiaoyu* 6 (June 1990): 22–23, in William A. Callahan, *China: The Pessoptimist Nation* (New York: Oxford University Press, 2010), 36.

38. Details in this paragraph are from Suisheng Zhao, *A Nation-State by Construction: Dynamics of Modern Chinese Nationalism* (Stanford, CA: Stanford University Press, 2004), 218–222.

39. "Beijing Students Watch Patriotic Films," Xinhua, May 16, 1994, in Suisheng Zhao, *A Nation-State by Construction: Dynamics of Modern Chinese Nationalism* (Stanford, CA: Stanford University Press, 2004), 218.

40. Anne-Marie Brady, *Marketing Dictatorship: Propaganda and Thought Work in Contemporary China* (Lanham, MD: Rowman and Littlefield, 2008), 76.

41. Suisheng Zhao, *A Nation-State by Construction: Dynamics of Modern Chinese Nationalism* (Stanford, CA: Stanford University Press, 2004), 240.

42. CCCPC (Central Committee of the Communist Party of China), "Aiguo zhuyi jiaoyu shishi gangyao" [Outline on the implementation of patriotic education], *Renmin Ribao* [People's Daily], September 6, 1994, in Zheng Wang, *Never Forget National Humiliation: Historical Memory in Chinese Politics and Foreign Relations* (New York: Columbia University Press, 2014), 115.

43. Steven Mufson, "China's New Nationalism," *Washington Post National Weekly Ed.*, April 1–7, 1996, in Suisheng Zhao, *A Nation-State by Construction: Dynamics of Modern Chinese Nationalism* (Stanford, CA: Stanford University Press, 2004), 214.

44. Sarah Lubman, "Students at Beijing University Trying to 'De-programme' Freshmen Exposed to Year of Indoctrination," *Chronicle of Higher Education*, October 17, 1990, A46–A47, in Stanley Rosen, "The Effect of Post-4 June Re-Education Campaigns on Chinese Students," *China Quarterly*, no. 134 (1993): 310–334, www.jstor.org/stable/654304.

45. Stanley Rosen, "The Effect of Post-4 June Re-Education Campaigns on Chinese Students," *China Quarterly*, no. 134 (1993): 310–334, www.jstor.org/stable/654304.

46. Stanley Rosen, "The Effect of Post-4 June Re-Education Campaigns on Chinese Students," *China Quarterly*, no. 134 (1993): 310–334, www.jstor.org/stable/654304.

47. Stanley Rosen, "The Effect of Post-4 June Re-Education Campaigns on Chinese Students," *China Quarterly*, no. 134 (1993): 310–334,www.jstor.org/stable/654304.

48. "Throughout the Mao years," writes Rana Mitter, ". . . memory of the immensely destructive war against Japan was reduced to official commemorations or stylized presentations as part of performances honoring the Communist Victory. The Chinese Communist Party (CCP) did not need to draw much on the legacy of the war years, since it had a founding myth and ideology of its own: the Chinese Communist revolution." Rana Mitter, *China's Good War: How World War II Is Shaping a New Nationalism* (Cambridge, MA: Harvard University Press, 2020), 251; see also Yinan He, "Remembering and Forgetting the War: Elite Mythmaking, Mass Reaction, and Sino-Japanese Relations, 1950–2006," *History and Memory* 19, no. 2 (2007): 43–74, https://doi.org/10.2979/his.2007.19.2.43.

49. Rana Mitter, *China's Good War: How World War II Is Shaping a New Nationalism* (Cambridge, MA: Harvard University Press, 2020), 251–252.

50. As Howard French notes in *Everything under the Heavens*, the profile of the war was not a constant and the scale of commemorations varied over the years according to broader domestic and geopolitical concerns. In 2008, for instance, French writes, "the country's leaders discreetly let the Marco Polo anniversary [then considered the start of the war] pass without commemoration in order to facilitate negotiations with Japan over the joint development of undersea gas fields in the East China Sea. . . . [W]henever it seemed expedient, China's past leaders had also been willing to acknowledge Japanese efforts over the years to acknowledge and make amends for their country's past aggression and atrocities." Howard W. French, *Everything under the Heavens: How the Past Helps Shape China's Push for Global Power* (London: Scribe, 2017), 20.

51. Interview by video call, July 2020.

52. Rana Mitter, *China's Good War: How World War II Is Shaping a New Nationalism* (Cambridge, MA: Harvard University Press, 2020), 70–71.

53. "Weida de quanmin kangzhan" [The great all-nation war of resistance], Xinhua, and "Zhongguo kangri zhanzheng shi quanminzu de fan qinlue zhangzheng" [China's War of Resisting Japan is a war against aggression by the entire nation], *Renmin Ribao*, August 23, 1985, in Daqing Yang, "China: Meanings and Contradictions of Victory," in *Memory, Identity, and Commemorations of World War II: Anniversary Politics in Asia Pacific*, ed. Daqing Yang and Mike Mochizuki (Lanham, MD: Lexington Books, 2018), 4. Arthur Waldron also dates the start of China's "new remembering" to 1985. Arthur Waldron, "China's New Remembering of World War II: The Case of Zhang Zizhong," *Modern Asian Studies* 30, no. 4, Special Issue: War in Modern China (October 1996): 945–978.

54. James C. Hsiung and Steven I. Levine, eds., *China's Bitter Victory: The War with Japan 1937–1945* (Armonk, NY: M. E. Sharpe, 1992), xii note 1, in Arthur Waldron, "China's New Remembering of World War II: The Case of Zhang Zizhong," *Modern Asian Studies* 30, no. 4, Special Issue: War in Modern China (October 1996): 945–978.

55. Rana Mitter, "Behind the Scenes at the Museum: Nationalism, History and Memory in the Beijing War of Resistance Museum, 1987–1997," *China Quarterly* 161 (2000): 279–293, doi:10.1017/S0305741000004033.

56. Iris Chang, *The Rape of Nanking: The Forgotten Holocaust of World War II* (New York: Basic Books, 1998), 199; William A. Callahan, *China: The Pessoptimist Nation* (New York: Oxford University Press, 2010), 164. NB: These new museums were not wholly top-down efforts—private museums also opened up; see Rana Mitter, *China's Good War: How World War II Is Shaping a New Nationalism* (Cambridge, MA: Harvard University Press, 2020), 140–141.

57. Rana Mitter, "Behind the Scenes at the Museum: Nationalism, History and Memory in the Beijing War of Resistance Museum, 1987–1997," *China Quarterly* 161 (2000): 279–293, doi:10.1017/S0305741000004033.

58. Parks M. Coble, "China's 'New Remembering' of the Anti-Japanese War of Resistance, 1934–1945," *China Quarterly*, no. 190 (2007): 394–410.

59. Arthur Waldron, "China's New Remembering of World War II: The Case of Zhang Zizhong," *Modern Asian Studies* 30, no. 4, Special Issue: War in Modern China (October 1996): 945–978.

60. Interview in Shanghai, March 2018.

Chapter 6

1. Seventy-four percent of respondents agreed with this statement. Nikolai Popov, *The Russian People Speak: Democracy at the Crossroads* (Syracuse, NY: Syracuse University Press, 1995), 57, in Thomas Sherlock, *Historical Narratives in the Soviet Union and Post-Soviet Russia: Destroying the Settled Past, Creating an Uncertain Future* (New York: Palgrave Macmillan, 2007), 113.

2. Alexander Kabakov, "Unizhenie" [Humiliation], *Moskovskie novosti*, March 12, 1989, 5, in Arkady Ostrovsky, *The Invention of Russia: The Journey from Gorbachev's Freedom to Putin's War* (London: Atlantic Books, 2015), 83.

3. David Remnick, *Lenin's Tomb: The Last Days of the Soviet Empire* (New York: Vintage Books/Random House, 1994), 202–203.

4. *Komsomolskaya Pravda*, April 19, 1990, in David Remnick, *Lenin's Tomb: The Last Days of the Soviet Empire* (New York: Vintage Books/Random House, 1994), 202.

5. Thomas Sherlock, *Historical Narratives in the Soviet Union and Post-Soviet Russia: Destroying the Settled Past, Creating an Uncertain Future* (New York: Palgrave Macmillan, 2007), 111–112.

6. Anatoly Chernyaev, *My Six Years with Gorbachev*, trans. and ed. Robert D. English and Elizabeth Tucker (University Park: Pennsylvania State University Press, 2000), 241; see also Conor O'Clery, *Moscow, December 25 1991: The Last Day of the Soviet Union* (London: Transworld Ireland, 2011), 165.

7. Mikhail Gorbachev, *Memoirs* (New York: Doubleday, 1995), 631.

8. David Remnick, *Lenin's Tomb: The Last Days of the Soviet Empire* (New York: Vintage Books/Random House, 1994), 461.

9. David Remnick, *Lenin's Tomb: The Last Days of the Soviet Empire* (New York: Vintage Books/Random House, 1994), 481. Detail on Yeltsin's bulletproof vest is from Boris Yeltsin, *The Struggle for Russia*, trans. Catherine A. Fitzpatrick (New York: Random House, 1994), 61.

10. David Remnick, *Lenin's Tomb: The Last Days of the Soviet Empire* (New York: Vintage Books/Random House, 1994), 467.

11. Mikhail Gorbachev, *Memoirs* (New York: Doubleday, 1995), 633–639.

12. David Remnick, *Lenin's Tomb: The Last Days of the Soviet Empire* (New York: Vintage Books/Random House, 1994), 495.

13. David Remnick, *Lenin's Tomb: The Last Days of the Soviet Empire* (New York: Vintage Books/Random House, 1994), 502.

14. David Remnick, *Lenin's Tomb: The Last Days of the Soviet Empire* (New York: Vintage Books/Random House, 1994), 46; see also Vera Tolz, "'*Glasnost*' and the Rewriting of Soviet History," Radio Liberty Research, May 18, 1987 (RL189/87); Geremie Barmé, "History for the Masses," in *Using the Past to Serve the Present: Historiography and Politics in Contemporary China*, ed. Jonathan Unger (New York: M. E. Sharpe, 1993), 284.

15. Arkady Ostrovsky, *The Invention of Russia: The Journey from Gorbachev's Freedom to Putin's War* (London: Atlantic Books, 2015), 74.

16. David Remnick, *Lenin's Tomb: The Last Days of the Soviet Empire* (New York: Vintage Books/Random House, 1994), 106.

17. Izabella Tabarovsky, "History Must Be Measured in Human Beings," Wilson Center, December 6, 2018, https://www.wilsoncenter.org/blog-post/history-must-be-measured-human-beings.

18. Yegor Ligachev, *Inside Gorbachev's Kremlin: The Memoirs of Yegor Ligachev* (New York: Pantheon Books, 1993), 285–287.

19. David Remnick, *Lenin's Tomb: The Last Days of the Soviet Empire* (New York: Vintage Books/Random House, 1994), 327.

20. Nina Tumarkin, *The Living and the Dead: The Rise and Fall of the Cult of World War II in Russia* (New York: Basic Books, 1994), 197; see also Michael Ellman and S. Maksudov, "Soviet Deaths in the Great Patriotic War: A Note," *Europe-Asia Studies* 46, no. 4 (1994): 671–680, http://www.jstor.org/stable/152934; Esther B. Fein, "Soviets Confirm Nazi Pacts Dividing Europe," *New York Times*, August 19, 1989, https://www.nytimes.com/1989/08/19/world/soviets-confirm-nazi-pacts-dividing-europe.html.

21. Nina Tumarkin, *The Living and the Dead: The Rise and Fall of the Cult of World War II in Russia* (New York: Basic Books, 1994), 197.

22. The first quote and background details in this paragraph are from a telephone interview in July 2021; all other quotes are from Nina Tumarkin, *The Living and the Dead: The Rise and Fall of the Cult of World War II in Russia* (New York: Basic Books, 1994), 190–193.

23. Nina Tumarkin, *The Living and the Dead: The Rise and Fall of the Cult of World War II in Russia* (New York: Basic Books, 1994), 200.

24. Vladimir Putin, *First Person: An Astonishingly Frank Self-Portrait by Russia's President*, with Nataliya Gevorkyan, Natalya Timakova, and Andrei Kolesnikov, trans. Catherine A. Fitzpatrick (New York: PublicAffairs, 2000), 18. Although Putin is listed as the author and the book is billed as an autobiography, it is actually a series of interviews with Putin and his close friends and family that was intended to introduce him to the Russian public and burnish his image ahead of his first presidential election, so the details and the picture it presents should be seen in that context.

25. Vladimir Putin, *First Person: An Astonishingly Frank Self-Portrait by Russia's President*, with Nataliya Gevorkyan, Natalya Timakova, and Andrei Kolesnikov, trans. Catherine A. Fitzpatrick (New York: PublicAffairs, 2000), 42.

26. Vladimir Putin, *First Person: An Astonishingly Frank Self-Portrait by Russia's President*, with Nataliya Gevorkyan, Natalya Timakova, and Andrei Kolesnikov, trans. Catherine A. Fitzpatrick (New York: PublicAffairs, 2000), 41.

27. Details of Putin's posting in Dresden are from Vladimir Putin, *First Person: An Astonishingly Frank Self-Portrait by Russia's President*, with Nataliya Gevorkyan, Natalya Timakova, and Andrei Kolesnikov, trans. Catherine A. Fitzpatrick (New York: PublicAffairs, 2000), 70–75; Masha Gessen, *The Man without a Face: The Unlikely Rise of Vladimir Putin* (New York: Riverhead Books, 2012), 63–65; Chris Bowlby, "Vladimir Putin's Formative German Years," BBC News, March 27, 2015, https://www.bbc.com/news/magazine-32066222.

28. Chris Bowlby, "Vladimir Putin's Formative German Years," BBC News, March 27, 2015, https://www.bbc.com/news/magazine-32066222.

29. It's worth noting this is Putin's account of the incident and there is no independent verification that this exchange took place as he describes it, or indeed at all, but it at least conveys the key lesson he says he learned from his posting. Vladimir Putin, *First Person: An Astonishingly Frank Self-Portrait by Russia's President*, with Nataliya Gevorkyan, Natalya Timakova, and Andrei Kolesnikov, trans. Catherine A. Fitzpatrick (New York: PublicAffairs, 2000), 79.

30. Vladimir Putin, *First Person: An Astonishingly Frank Self-Portrait by Russia's President*, with Nataliya Gevorkyan, Natalya Timakova, and Andrei Kolesnikov, trans. Catherine A. Fitzpatrick (New York: PublicAffairs, 2000), 79.

31. Boris Yeltsin, *Midnight Diaries*, trans. Catherine A. Fitzpatrick (New York: PublicAffairs, 2000), 6. Putin's recollection of the conversation contains many of the same details but does not mention Yeltsin's comment about the "era of Putin." Vladimir Putin, *First Person: An Astonishingly Frank Self-Portrait by Russia's President*, with Nataliya Gevorkyan, Natalya Timakova, and Andrei Kolesnikov, trans. Catherine A. Fitzpatrick (New York: PublicAffairs, 2000), 204–205.

32. Daniel Treisman, "Presidential Popularity in a Hybrid Regime: Russia under Yeltsin and Putin," *American Journal of Political Science* 55, no. 3 (2011): 590–609, http://www.jstor.org/stable/23024939.

33. Peter Baker and Susan Glasser, *Kremlin Rising: Vladimir Putin's Russia and the End of Revolution* (New York: Scribner, 2005), 60.

34. Mikhail Novikov, "Ne dai zasokhnut' Rodine svoeii!," *Kommersant Daily*, August 8, 1997, 1, in Arkady Ostrovsky, *The Invention of Russia: The*

Journey from Gorbachev's Freedom to Putin's War (London: Atlantic Books, 2015), 234.

35. Michael R. Gordon, "Post-Communist Russia Plumbs Its Soul, in Vain, for New Vision," *New York Times*, March 31, 1998, https://www.nytimes. com/1998/03/31/world/post-communist-russia-plumbs-its-soul-in-vain-for-new-vision.html.

36. Vladimir Putin, "Russia on the Turn of the New Millennium," December 30, 1999, available in Russian on the *Nezavisimaia Gazeta* website: https:// www.ng.ru/politics/1999-12-30/4_millenium.html, and in English translation via the University of Oregon: https://pages.uoregon.edu/ kimball/Putin.htm; see also Fiona Hill and Clifford G. Gaddy, *Mr. Putin: Operative in the Kremlin* (Washington, DC: Brookings Institution Press, 2015), 39–40.

37. Vladimir Putin, *First Person: An Astonishingly Frank Self-Portrait by Russia's President*, with Nataliya Gevorkyan, Natalya Timakova, and Andrei Kolesnikov, trans. Catherine A. Fitzpatrick (New York: PublicAffairs, 2000), 205.

38. Vladimir Putin, *First Person: An Astonishingly Frank Self-Portrait by Russia's President*, with Nataliya Gevorkyan, Natalya Timakova, and Andrei Kolesnikov, trans. Catherine A. Fitzpatrick (New York: PublicAffairs, 2000), 205.

39. Arkady Ostrovsky, *The Invention of Russia: The Journey from Gorbachev's Freedom to Putin's War* (London: Atlantic Books, 2015), 284.

40. Arkady Ostrovsky, *The Invention of Russia: The Journey from Gorbachev's Freedom to Putin's War* (London: Atlantic Books, 2015), 285.

41. Opinion poll by VTsIOM, January 21–24, 2000, http://www. temadnya.ru/spravka/29dec2000/96.html, in Arkady Ostrovsky, *The Invention of Russia: The Journey from Gorbachev's Freedom to Putin's War* (London: Atlantic Books, 2015), 285.

42. Jill Dougherty, "How the Media Became One of Putin's Most Powerful Weapons," *The Atlantic*, April 21, 2015, https://www.theatlantic.com/ international/archive/2015/04/how-the-media-became-putins-most-powerful-weapon/391062/; Arkady Ostrovsky, *The Invention of Russia: The Journey from Gorbachev's Freedom to Putin's War* (London: Atlantic Books, 2015), 292–294.

43. "Acting President Vladimir Putin Arrived in Grozny," President of Russia website, March 20, 2000, http://en.kremlin.ru/events/president/news/ 38841; Natalia Gevorkyan and Andrei Kolesnikov, "Zheleznyi Putin," *Kommersant*, March 10, 2000, https://www.kommersant.ru/doc/142144, in Elizabeth A. Wood, "Performing Memory: Vladimir Putin and the Celebration of WWII in Russia," *Soviet and Post-Soviet Review* 38 (2011), 172–200.

44. Catherine Belton, *Putin's People: How the KGB Took Back Russia and Then Took on the West* (New York: Farrar, Straus and Giroux, 2020), 202.

45.   Peter Baker and Susan Glasser, *Kremlin Rising: Vladimir Putin's Russia and the End of Revolution* (New York: Scribner, 2005), 38.

46.   Peter Baker and Susan Glasser, *Kremlin Rising: Vladimir Putin's Russia and the End of Revolution* (New York: Scribner, 2005), 40.

47.   "Statement on the Bills on State Symbols Introduced at the State Duma," President of Russia website, December 4, 2000, http://en.kremlin.ru/events/president/transcripts/21137.

48.   "Speech at a Gala Reception Dedicated to the 55th Anniversary of Victory in the Great Patriotic War," President of Russia website, May 9, 2000, http://en.kremlin.ru/events/president/transcripts/21423. Putin became acting president when Boris Yeltsin resigned on December 31, 1999. He won the presidential election that followed on March 26, 2000, and was sworn in as president on May 7, 2000.

49.   Elizabeth A. Wood, "Performing Memory: Vladimir Putin and the Celebration of WWII in Russia," *Soviet and Post-Soviet Review* 38 (2011), 172–200.

50.   "Владимир Путин подписал указ о создании Российского организационного комитета 'Победа'" [Vladimir Putin signed decree on the creation of the Russian organising committee "Victory"], press release, President of Russia website, August 7, 2000, http://kremlin.ru/events/president/news/38875.

51.   Government spending on patriotic education programs rose from 178 million rubles (approx. $2.7 million) in 2001–2005 to 497 million rubles (approx. $7.4 million) in 2006–2010. Nataliya Danilova, *The Politics of War Commemoration in the UK and Russia* (New York: Palgrave Macmillan, 2015), 176. Youth clubs: Judyth L. Twigg, "What Has Happened to Russian Society?," in *Russia after the Fall*, ed. Andrew C. Kuchins (Washington, DC: Carnegie Endowment for International Peace, 2002), 96; Cheng Chen, *The Return of Ideology: The Search for Regime Identities in Postcommunist Russia and China* (Ann Arbor: University of Michigan Press, 2016), 82; "Владимир Путин подписал указ о создании Российского организационного комитета 'Победа'" [Vladimir Putin signed decree on the creation of the Russian organising committee "Victory"], press release, President of Russia website, August 7, 2000, http://kremlin.ru/events/president/news/38875, in "Patriotic Mobilisation in Russia," International Crisis Group, July 4, 2018, https://www.crisisgroup.org/europe-central-asia/caucasus/russianorth-caucasus/251-patriotic-mobilisation-russia.

52.   Cheng Chen, *The Return of Ideology: The Search for Regime Identities in Postcommunist Russia and China* (Ann Arbor: University of Michigan Press, 2016), 71.

53.   "Opening Remarks at Meeting with the Government Cabinet," President of Russia website, May 5, 2008, http://en.kremlin.ru/events/president/transcripts/24938.

Chapter 7

1. Isa Blagden, *The Crown of a Life*, vol. 3 (London: Hurst and Blackett, 1869), 155. A variation of this quote has been attributed to Lenin, Goebbels, and others.

2. In-hua Kim, "Ask a North Korean: Were North Koreans Genuinely Grieving When Kim Il Sung Died?," NK News, January 30, 2020, https://www.nknews.org/2020/01/ask-a-north-korean-were-north-koreans-genuinely-grieving-when-kim-il-sung-died/. In-hua Kim is a pseudonym.

3. "Kim Il Sung, N. Korea's Longtime Leader, Dies: Asia: Death of Communist Dictator at 82 Comes Weeks before North-South Meeting. Experts Expect Instability," *Los Angeles Times*, July 9, 1994, https://www.latimes.com/archives/la-xpm-1994-07-09-mn-13445-story.html. Footage of the announcement and public reaction can be found at https://www.youtube.com/watch?v=GDq2YIsfIiE, https://www.nbcnews.com/video/from-the-archives-kim-il-sung-dies-43496003916, https://www.youtube.com/watch?v=cZ_pyTr-K88.

4. In-hua Kim, "Ask a North Korea: Were North Koreans Genuinely Grieving When Kim Il Sung Died?," NK News, January 30, 2020, https://www.nknews.org/2020/01/ask-a-north-korean-were-north-koreans-genuinely-grieving-when-kim-il-sung-died/.

5. Barbara Demick, *Nothing to Envy: Ordinary Lives in North Korea* (New York: Spiegel & Grau, 2015), 99–101.

6. Interview by telephone, June 2020.

7. David E. Sanger, "Kim Il Sung Dead at Age 82; Led North Korea 5 Decades; Was Near Talks with South," *New York Times*, July 9, 1994, https://www.nytimes.com/1994/07/09/world/kim-il-sung-dead-at-age-82-led-north-korea-5-decades-was-near-talks-with-south.html; "DPRK: Slow-Motion Succession; the Secretary's Morning Intelligence Summary," US Department of State Bureau of Intelligence and Research (INR), August 25, 1994, The National Security Archive, Washington, DC, Document 12, https://www.documentcloud.org/documents/5750509-National-Security-Archive-Doc-12-DPRK-Slow.

8. Sam Jameson, "S. Korea Places Troops on Alert," *Los Angeles Times*, July 10, 1994, https://www.latimes.com/archives/la-xpm-1994-07-10-mn-14107-story.html (or a relative, as was more likely in the North Korean case).

9. Stephan Haggard and Marcus Noland, *Famine in North Kores: Markets, Aid and Reform* (New York: Columbia University Press, 2007), 58; Kongdan Oh and Ralph C. Hassig, *North Korea through the Looking Glass* (Washington, DC: Brookings Institution Press, 2000), 52, in Sandra Fahy, *Marching through Suffering: Loss and Survival in North Korea* (New York: Columbia University Press, 2015), 187.

10. Fyodor Tertitsky dates the first version of Kim's biography to the 1949 edition of the Korean Central Yearbook, *Chosŏn chungang nyŏn'gam 1949* [Korean Central Yearbook 1949] (Pyongyang: Chosŏn chungang

t'ongsinsa, 1949). Tertitsky writes that one of the Soviet officers who helped oversee the biography thought the exaggeration was so egregious that he resigned his post; see Fyodor Tertitskiy, "A Blatant Lie: The North Korean Myth of Kim Il-sung Liberating the Country from Japan," *Korea Observer* 49, no. 2 (2018), https://doi.org/10.29152/KOIKS.2018.49.2.219.

11.   *Kim Il-sŏng changgun-ŭi ryakchŏn* [A Short Biography of Commander Kim Il-sung] (Pyongyang: Chosŏn Rodongdang Chungang Wiwŏnhoe Sŏnjŏn Sŏndongbu, 1952), 32, in Fyodor Tertitskiy, "A Blatant Lie: The North Korean Myth of Kim Il-sung Liberating the Country from Japan," *Korea Observer* 49, no. 2 (2018), https://doi.org/10.29152/KOIKS.2018.49.2.219.

12.   "Information on the Situation in the DPRK," April 1955, History and Public Policy Program Digital Archive, RGANI, Fond 5, Opis 28, Delo 314, listi 34–59. Obtained for NKIDP by James Person and translated for NKIDP by Gary Goldberg. https://digitalarchive.wilsoncenter.org/document/114590. ()

13.   "Record of the Third Congress of the Korean Workers' Party by L.I. Brezhnev," April 30, 1956, History and Public Policy Program Digital Archive, GARF, Fond 5446, Opis 98, Delo 721, Listy 221–228. Translated by Gary Goldberg. https://digitalarchive.wilsoncenter.org/document/120183.

14.   "Letter from Ri Sang-jo to the Central Committee of the Korean Workers Party," October 5, 1956, History and Public Policy Program Digital Archive, RGANI, Fond 5, Opis 28, Delo 410, Listy 233–295. Obtained by Nobuo Shimotomai and translated by Gary Goldberg. https://digitalarchive.wilsoncenter.org/document/114152.

15.   Andrei Lankov, *Crisis in North Korea: The Failure of De-Stalinization, 1956* (Honolulu: University of Hawaii Press, 2005), 205.

16.   Andrei Lankov, *North of the DMZ: Essays on Daily Life in North Korea* (Jefferson, NC: McFarland & Company, 2007), 40.

17.   Hwang Jang-yop, "The Problems of Human Rights in North Korea," original article posted by Network for North Korean Democracy and Human Rights, available at http://www2.law.columbia.edu/course_00S_L9436_001/North%20Korea%20materials/hwang%20jang1.html.

18.   "Comment on the Internal Korean Workers Party Brochure, 'The Revolutionary Traditions of Our Party Established during the Period of the Armed Anti-Japanese Struggle,'" May 16, 1963, History and Public Policy Program Digital Archive, SAPMO-BA, Berlin, DY 30, IV A 2/20/250. Translated for NKIDP by Bernd Schaefer. https://digitalarchive.wilsoncenter.org/document/110116.

19.   "Comment on the Internal Korean Workers Party Brochure, 'The Revolutionary Traditions of Our Party Established during the Period of the Armed Anti-Japanese Struggle,'" May 16, 1963, History and Public Policy Program Digital Archive, SAPMO-BA, Berlin, DY 30, IV A 2/

20/250. Translated for NKIDP by Bernd Schaefer. https://digitalarchive. wilsoncenter.org/document/110116. Scholars such as B. R. Myers have argued that *Juche* should be seen more as a catchy slogan than a coherent ideology and caution against overstating its importance; see B. R. Myers, *North Korea's Juche Myth* (Busan: Sthele Press, 2015).

20. Fyodor Tertitskiy, "A Blatant Lie: The North Korean Myth of Kim Il-sung Liberating the Country from Japan," *Korea Observer* 49, no. 2 (2018), https://doi.org/10.29152/KOIKS.2018.49.2.219.

21. Fyodor Tertitskiy, "A Blatant Lie: The North Korean Myth of Kim Il-sung Liberating the Country from Japan," *Korea Observer* 49, no. 2 (2018), https://doi.org/10.29152/KOIKS.2018.49.2.219.

22. *Kim Il-sŏng tongji ryakchŏn* [A concise biography of the respected comrade Kim Il-sung] (Pyongyang: Chosŏn Rodongdang Ch'ulp'ansa, 1972) in Fyodor Tertitskiy, "A Blatant Lie: The North Korean Myth of Kim Il-sung Liberating the Country from Japan," *Korea Observer* 49, no. 2 (2018), https://doi.org/10.29152/KOIKS.2018.49.2.219; Baik Bong, *Kim Il Sung: Biography [I]* (Beirut, Lebanon: Dar Al-Talia, 1973), 532–533.

23. "GDR Ambassador Pyongyang to Ministry for Foreign Affairs, Berlin," November 12, 1974, History and Public Policy Program Digital Archive, Political Archive of the Foreign Office, Ministry of Foreign Affairs (PA AA, MfAA), C 6862. Obtained and translated for NKIDP by Bernd Schaefer. https://digitalarchive.wilsoncenter.org/document/113928.

24. DPRK Academy of Social Sciences, *Dictionary of Political Terminologies* (Pyongyang: Academy of Social Science, 1970), 414, in Kim Ilpyong and Lee Dong-bok, "After Kim: Who and What in North Korea," *World Affairs* 142, no. 4 (1980): 246–267, http://www.jstor.org/stable/20671834; see also Adrian Buzo, *Politics and Leadership in North Korea: The Guerilla Dynasty* (New York: Routledge, 2018), 75.

25. "GDR Ambassador Pyongyang to Ministry for Foreign Affairs, Berlin," April 14, 1975, History and Public Policy Program Digital Archive, Political Archive of the Foreign Office, Ministry of Foreign Affairs (PA AA, MfAA), C 6862. Obtained and translated for NKIDP by Bernd Schaefer. https://digitalarchive.wilsoncenter.org/document/113929.

26. Andrei Lankov, *From Stalin to Kim Il Sung: The Formation of North Korea 1945–1960* (New Brunswick, NJ: Rutgers University Press, 2002), 74; Adrian Buzo, *Politics and Leadership in North Korea: The Guerilla Dynasty* (New York: Routledge, 2018), 75.

27. Kim Jong Il, *On the Art of the Cinema* (Honolulu, HI: University Press of the Pacific, 2001, reprint of 1989 ed.), 4–5.

28. Kim Jong Il, *On the Art of the Cinema* (Honolulu, HI: University Press of the Pacific, 2001, reprint of 1989 ed.), 79, 90–91.

29. Paul Fischer, *A Kim Jong-Il Production: The Extraordinary True Story of a Kidnapped Filmmaker, His Star Actress, and a Young Dictator's Rise to Power* (New York: Flatiron Books, 2015), 237.

30. "A Visit to the DPRK: A Report from the Delegation of the American-Korean Friendship and Information Center to the Democratic People's Republic of Korea," 1972, History and Public Policy Program Digital Archive, *Korea Focus* 1, no. 2 (Spring 1972): 23–29. Obtained by Brandon Gauthier. https://digitalarchive.wilsoncenter.org/document/121132.

31. Andrei Lankov, *From Stalin to Kim Il Sung: The Formation of North Korea 1945–1960* (New Brunswick, NJ: Rutgers University Press, 2002), 70.

32. Lee Sang-min, "The Personality Cult in the North Korean Political Process (II)," *Vantage Point*, September 1989, 1–2, in Bradley K. Martin, *Under the Loving Care of the Fatherly Leader: North Korea and the Kim Dynasty* (New York: Thomas Dunne Books, 2004).

33. "Untitled Report from Stanisław Jewdoszuk, Polish Diplomat in Pyongyang," July 29, 1982, History and Public Policy Program Digital Archive, AMSZ, Department II, 43/86, w. 2. Obtained by Marek Hańderek and translated by Jerzy Giebułtowski. https://digitalarchive.wilsoncenter.org/document/208557.

34. "Telegram from the Hungarian Embassy in Pyongyang, 'KWP's Congress,'" November, 1980, History and Public Policy Program Digital Archive, MNL OL XIV-J-1-j Korea 25-001140/1980. Obtained by North Korean Materials Archive, IFES, Kyungnam University, and translated by Imre Májer. https://digitalarchive.wilsoncenter.org/document/123766.

35. Paul Fischer, *A Kim Jong-Il Production: The Extraordinary True Story of a Kidnapped Filmmaker, His Star Actress, and a Young Dictator's Rise to Power* (New York: Flatiron Books, 2015), 95.

36. *Kim Jong-il: Biography*, vol. 1 (Pyongyang: Foreign Languages Publishing House, 2005), 4, in Christopher Richardson, "Hagiography of the Kims and the Childhood of Saints: Kim Jong-il," Sino NK, August 12, 2014, https://sinonk.com/2014/08/12/hagiography-of-the-kims-and-the-childhood-of-saints-kim-jong-il/.

37. Hwang Jang-yop, "The Problems of Human Rights in North Korea," original article posted by Network for North Korean Democracy and Human Rights, available at http://www2.law.columbia.edu/course_00S_L9436_001/North%20Korea%20materials/hwang%20jang1.html.

38. Kim Il Sung, *With the Century: 8* (Pyongyang: Foreign Languages Publishing House, 1998), 250.

39. Andrei Lankov, *North of the DMZ: Essays on Daily Life in North Korea* (Jefferson, NC: McFarland & Company, 2007), 40.

40. *Kim Jong-il: Biography*, vol. 1 (Pyongyang: Foreign Languages Publishing House, 2005), 26–27, in Christopher Richardson, "Hagiography of the Kims and the Childhood of Saints: Kim Jong-il," Sino NK, August 12, 2014, https://sinonk.com/2014/08/12/hagiography-of-the-kims-and-the-childhood-of-saints-kim-jong-il/.

41. Hazel Smith, "Intelligence Failure and Famine in North Korea," *Asia-Pacific Journal* 2, no. 5 (May 1, 2004), https://apjjf.org/-Hazel-Smith/1634/article.html.

42. Sandra Fahy, *Marching through Suffering: Loss and Survival in North Korea* (New York: Columbia University Press, 2015), 11.

43. In email correspondence, September 2021.

44. Marcus Noland, Sherman Robinson, and Tao Wang, "Famine in North Korea: Causes and Cures," *Economic Development and Cultural Change* 49, no. 4 (July 2991): 741–767, in Sandra Fahy, *Marching through Suffering: Loss and Survival in North Korea* (New York: Columbia University Press, 2015), 190.

45. Sandra Fahy, *Marching through Suffering: Loss and Survival in North Korea* (New York: Columbia University Press, 2015), 40.

46. Sandra Fahy, *Marching through Suffering: Loss and Survival in North Korea* (New York: Columbia University Press, 2015), 120.

47. Details and quotes in this paragraph are from Patrick McEachern, *Inside the Red Box: North Korea's Post-Totalitarian Politics* (New York: Columbia University Press, 2010), 72–73.

48. *Questions and Answers on the Songun Idea* (Pyongyang: Foreign Languages Publishing House, 2012), 42–43.

49. Adrian Buzo, *Politics and Leadership in North Korea: The Guerilla Dynasty* (New York: Routledge, 2018), 162. Sandra Fahy notes that even with this priority, the military still suffered from its own shortages of food and basic supplies. "The military was part of the fabric of the rest of society," she told me via email. "Like the rest, they were stunted in growth, malnourished, and starving."

Chapter 8

1. "Заседание Совета по культуре и искусству" [Meeting of the Council for Culture and Art], President of Russia website, October 27, 2020, http://kremlin.ru/events/president/news/64288.

2. "Ukraine Crisis: Putin Signs Russia-Crimea Treaty," BBC News, March 18, 2014, https://www.bbc.com/news/world-europe-26630062; William Hague, "Russia Faces Global Isolation—Again," *The Telegraph*, March 22, 2014, https://www.telegraph.co.uk/news/worldnews/europe/russia/10716194/Russia-faces-global-isolation-again.html.

3. In fact, surveys carried out in March 2014 before the conflict in eastern Ukraine began showed a majority of citizens in the Donetsk and Luhansk regions preferred to stay part of Ukraine, with 85 percent of respondents opposed to Russian military intervention. See Harley Balzer, "The Ukraine Invasion and Public Opinion," *Georgetown Journal of International Affairs* 16, no. 1 (2015): 79–93, http://www.jstor.org/stable/43773670.

4. Interviews in Donetsk, January 2015.

5. There were elements of truth in some of these claims—far-right groups did take part in the 2014 Maidan protests in Kyiv, although they were in the minority; the ultra-nationalist "Azov battalion" was fighting with the Ukrainian national guard; the former leader of a radical nationalist

party was appointed to the National Security and Defense Council; and the new parliament made an attempt to overturn a law protecting the status of the Russian language, although the interim president vetoed the move and it was swiftly abandoned—but the idea that a fascist junta had seized control or that neo-Nazis were roaming the streets was a Kremlin fiction. See Serhiy Kudelia, "Domestic Sources of the Donbas Insurgency," PonarsEurasia—Policy Memo No. 351, September 2014, http://www.ponarseurasia.org/memo/domestic-sources-donbas-insurgency; Elise Giuliano, "The Origins of Separatism: Popular Grievances in Donetsk and Luhansk," PonarsEurasia—Policy Memo No. 396, October 2015, http://www.ponarseurasia.org/memo/origins-separatism-popular-grievances-donetsk-and-luhansk.

6. "V Konstantinovke separatist 'ozhivili' tank-pamyatnik," Segodnia.ua, June 5, 2014, https://www.segodnya.ua/regions/donetsk/v-konstantinovke-separatisty-ozhivili-tank-pamyatnik-526553.html, in Julie Fedor, Markku Kangaspuro, Jussi Lassila, and Taitiana Zhurzhenko, eds., *War and Memory in Russia, Ukraine and Belarus* (London: Palgrave Macmillan, 2017), 2.

7. The Tulip Revolution in Kyrgyzstan in 2005 also added to these fears. Former US ambassador to Russia Michael McFaul argues that the US-led invasion of Iraq in 2003 marked the beginning of the rift in Russia's relationship with the United States, with the color revolutions in Ukraine and Georgia subsequently marking a "significant turning point in Putin's thinking about the United States, as the Russian leader blamed the Bush administration for fostering regime change in both countries." See Michael McFaul, "Putin, Putinism, and the Domestic Determinants of Russian Foreign Policy," *International Security* 45, no. 2 (2020): 95–139. https://doi.org/10.1162/isec_a_00390.

8. Mikhail Boycko, "Opasna li 'oranzhevaia chuma,'" *Nezavisimaia Gazeta*, December 13, 2012, http://www.ng.ru/columnist/2012-02-13/100_chuma.html, in Matthew Luxmoore, "'Orange Plague': World War II and the Symbolic Politics of Pro-State Mobilization in Putin's Russia," *Nationalities Papers* 47, no. 5 (2019): 822–839, doi:10.1017/nps.2018.48.

9. "На Воробьевых горах проходит альтернативный митинг не согласных с итогами выборов," Rosbalt.ru, December 24, 2011, https://www.rosbalt.ru/moscow/2011/12/24/928119.html.

10. "Митинг на Воробьёвых горах 24 декабря 2011 года," YouTube, December 29, 2011, https://www.youtube.com/watch?v=eZykHP5_onA, in Matthew Luxmoore, "'Orange Plague': World War II and the Symbolic Politics of Pro-State Mobilization in Putin's Russia," *Nationalities Papers* 47, no. 5 (2019): 822–839, doi:10.1017/nps.2018.48.

11. "Ruling Party MP Stomps on Russian Opposition's Symbol," RT, October 26, 2012, https://www.rt.com/russia/white-ribbon-opposition-sidyakin-290/.

12. "Umremte zhe pod Moskvoi," Lenta.ru, February 23, 2012, https:// lenta.ru/articles/2012/02/23/zaputina/; "Miting v podderzhku Putina v Luzhnikakh. Reportazh," Pravda, February 23, 2012, https://www. youtube.com/watch?v= MXxDdOZM4Fg, in Matthew Luxmoore, "'Orange Plague': World War II and the Symbolic Politics of Pro-State Mobilization in Putin's Russia," *Nationalities Papers* 47, no. 5 (2019): 822– 839, doi:10.1017/nps.2018.48.

13. "Проезд кортежа Путина—7 мая 2012 года [28 дней спустя]," YouTube/CrzTsr, May 12, 2012, https://www.youtube.com/watch?v=BHl-zSkQYSw. In 2018, they abandoned the televised motorcade altogether and filmed Putin walking through the gilded halls of the Kremlin to his inauguration instead; see "Vladimir Putin's Long, Long, Long Walk to His Inauguration (2018)," YouTube/ABC News (Australia), May 8, 2018, https://www.youtube.com/watch?v=b07KldU9kAo.

14. Andrew Higgins and Peter Baker, "Russia Claims U.S. Is Meddling over Ukraine," *New York Times*, February 6, 2014, https://www.nytimes.com/ 2014/02/07/world/europe/ukraine.html.

15. Matthew Luxmoore, "'Orange Plague': World War II and the Symbolic Politics of Pro-State Mobilization in Putin's Russia," *Nationalities Papers* 47, no. 5 (2019): 822–839, doi:10.1017/nps.2018.48.

16. Il'ia Azar, "Rasserzhennye Patrioty," Meduza, February 21, 2015, https:// meduza.io/feature/2015/02/21/rasserzhennye-patrioty, in Matthew Luxmoore, "'Orange Plague': World War II and the Symbolic Politics of Pro-State Mobilization in Putin's Russia," *Nationalities Papers* 47, no. 5 (2019): 822–839, doi:10.1017/nps.2018.48.

17. The connection between Western liberalism and fascism might not be obvious, but they had been lumped together by pro-Kremlin groups since the early 2000s as forces that were supposedly working together to destroy Russia and its traditional values. "Fascist organizations in Russia . . . serve as allies to Russia's liberals," claimed the *Nashi* (Ours) youth movement created by Kremlin strategist Vladislav Surkov in 2005 after the first Ukrainian and Georgian color revolutions. "Only by spreading our ideational influence over the young generation can we counter the youth's involvement in extremist organizations of a fascist and liberal bent." "Manifest molodezhnogo dvizheniia Nashi," April 18, 2005, https://web. archive.org/web/20050417235355/http://www.nashi.su/pravda/83974709, in Matthew Luxmoore, "'Orange Plague': World War II and the Symbolic Politics of Pro-State Mobilization in Putin's Russia," *Nationalities Papers* 47, no. 5 (2019): 822–839, doi:10.1017/nps.2018.48.

18. Efrem Lukatsky, "Russia Evokes Nazi Horrors to Bash Ukraine," Associated Press, April 30, 2014, https://apnews.com/article/37686ff581ee4 e0390609f5a57133309; see also Shaun Walker, *The Long Hangover: Putin's New Russia and the Ghosts of the Past* (New York: Oxford University Press, 2018), 225–226.

19. "Vladimir Putin Answered Journalists' Questions on the Situation in Ukraine," President of Russia website, March 4, 2014, http://en.kremlin.ru/events/president/news/20366.

20. "Vladimir Putin Answered Journalists' Questions on the Situation in Ukraine," President of Russia website, March 4, 2014, http://en.kremlin.ru/events/president/news/20366; United Nations Security Council 7125th meeting (S/PV.7125), UN Digital Library, March 3, 2014, https://undocs.org/pdf?symbol=en/S/PV.7125.

21. "State-run News Station Accused of Making Up Child Crucifixion," *Moscow Times*, July 14, 2014, https://www.themoscowtimes.com/2014/07/14/state-run-news-station-accused-of-making-up-child-crucifixion-a37289. The false claims about the supposed attack were made in the summer of 2014, after the annexation of Crimea, as part of the coverage of the broader conflict in eastern Ukraine.

22. Polling by the independent Levada Center in March 2014 found 90 percent of respondents said television was their main source of national and international news, although this figure was down to 73 percent in August 2018 as online sources and social media platforms became increasingly popular; see "Channels of Information," Levada Center, October 12, 2018, https://www.levada.ru/en/2018/10/12/channels-of-information/; Joshua Yaffa, *Between Two Fires: Truth, Ambition, and Compromise in Putin's Russia* (New York: Tim Duggan Books, 2020), 63–64.

23. Timothy Frye, *Weak Strongman: The Limits of Power in Putin's Power* (Princeton, NJ: Princeton University Press, 2021), 147. Frye cites a Levada Center poll conducted in May 2014, for example, which found that only 31 percent of respondents said they either fully supported or "more or less" supported sending Russian troops to Ukraine, and that figure was down to 20 percent by August 2015.

24. Shaun Walker, "Vladimir Putin: Gay People at Winter Olympics Must 'Leave Children Alone,'" *The Guardian*, January 17, 2014, https://www.theguardian.com/world/2014/jan/17/vladimir-putin-gay-winter-olympics-children.

25. "Address by President of the Russian Federation," President of Russia website, March 18, 2014, http://en.kremlin.ru/events/president/news/20603.

26. "Putin's Approval Rating," Levada Center, https://www.levada.ru/en/ratings/.

27. Samuel A. Greene and Graeme B. Robertson, *Putin v. the People: The Perilous Politics of a Divided Russia* (New Haven, CT: Yale University Press, 2019), 106–107.

28. Samuel A. Greene and Graeme B. Robertson, *Putin v. the People: The Perilous Politics of a Divided Russia* (New Haven, CT: Yale University Press, 2019), 9, in Timothy Frye, *Weak Strongman: The Limits of Power*

in Putin's Power (Princeton, NJ: Princeton University Press, 2021), 59–60. Frye notes that during the post-Crimea surge, survey respondents reported more positive views of Russia's economic future and believed that corruption was declining, even though there was no objective evidence to support these views, writing that the annexation of Crimea "made Russians feel better about their lives on many levels, even those unconnected to the event."

29. Samuel A. Greene and Graeme B. Robertson, *Putin v. the People: The Perilous Politics of a Divided Russia* (New Haven, CT: Yale University Press, 2019), 89.

30. "Парад Победы на Красной площади," President of Russia website, May 9, 2014, http://kremlin.ru/events/president/transcripts/20989.

31. Alexei Miller, "Russia and Europe in Memory Wars," Norwegian Institute of International Affairs, 2020, NUPI Working Paper 887, https://www.nupi.no/nupi_eng/content/download/21330/943540/version/10/file/NUPI_Working_Paper_887_Miller.pdf.

32. "Law to Counter Attempts to Infringe on Historical Memory in Relation to Events of World War II," President of Russia website, May 5, 2014, http://en.kremlin.ru/events/president/news/20912.

33. Alexei Anishchuk, "Russia's Putin Outlaws Denial of Nazi Crimes," Reuters, May 5, 2014, https://www.reuters.com/article/us-russia-putin-nazi-law/russias-putin-outlaws-denial-of-nazi-crimes-idUSBREA440IV20140505.

34. "The Case of Vladimir Luzgin," Columbia University Global Freedom of Expression database, https://globalfreedomofexpression.columbia.edu/cases/case-vladimir-luzgin/.

35. Mark Edele, "Fighting Russia's History Wars: Vladimir Putin and the Codification of World War II," *History and Memory* 29, no. 2 (2017): 90–124, doi:10.2979/histmemo.29.2.05.

36. Mark Edele, "Fighting Russia's History Wars: Vladimir Putin and the Codification of World War II," *History and Memory* 29, no. 2 (2017): 90–124, doi:10.2979/histmemo.29.2.05.

37. Ivan Kurilla, "The Implications of Russia's Law against the 'Rehabilitation of Nazism,'" PONARS Eurasia Policy Memo No. 331, August 2014, https://www.ponarseurasia.org/wp-content/uploads/attachments/Pepm331_Kurilla_August2014_0.pdf.

38. Mark Edele, "Fighting Russia's History Wars: Vladimir Putin and the Codification of World War II," *History and Memory* 29, no. 2 (2017): 90–124, doi:10.2979/histmemo.29.2.05.

39. "Защита" [Defense], Санкт-Петербургского института истории РАН [Saint Petersburg Institute of History of Russian Academy of Sciences], February 18, 2016, http://www.spbiiran.nw.ru/защита-25/ Elena Kuznetsova; "Zashchita s generalom Vlasovym" [Defense with

General Vlasov], *Fontanka: Peterburgskaia internet-gazeta*, March 2, 2016, http://www.fontanka. ru/2016/03/01/173/, in Mark Edele, "Fighting Russia's History Wars: Vladimir Putin and the Codification of World War II," *History and Memory* 29, no. 2 (2017): 90–124, doi:10.2979/histmemo.29.2.05..

40. Interview by email, March 2019.

41. Interview by video call, July 2020. For more detail on the case see Gabrielle Spiegel, "Scholar-in-Exile Finds a Temporary Haven," *Perspectives on History* (American Historical Association), September 1, 2012, https://www.historians.org/publications-and-directories/perspectives-on-history/september-2012/scholar-in-exile-finds-a-temporary-haven].

42. "New Russian Gulag Museum Recreates Soviet Terror," BBC News, October 30, 2015, https://www.bbc.com/news/world-europe-34675413; Neil MacFarquhar, "Critics Scoff as Kremlin Erects Monument to the Repressed," *New York Times*, October 30, 2017, https://www.nytimes.com/2017/10/30/world/europe/russia-soviet-repression-monument.html.

43. Joshua Yaffa, *Between Two Fires: Truth, Ambition, and Compromise in Putin's Russia* (New York: Tim Duggan Books, 2020), 210–211.

44. Tom Balmforth, "Perm's Big Chill," Radio Free Europe/Radio Liberty, March 20, 2015, https://www.rferl.org/a/russia-perm-liberal-bastion-no-more/26911622.html.

45. Mikhail Danilovich and Robert Coalson, "Revamped Perm-36 Museum Emphasizes Gulag's 'Contribution to Victory,'" Radio Free Europe/Radio Liberty, July 25, 2015, https://www.rferl.org/a/russia-perm-gulag-museum-takeover-contribution-to-victory/27152188.html. For a detailed study of the politics and history surrounding the museum and its takeover, see Joshua Yaffa, *Between Two Fires: Truth, Ambition, and Compromise in Putin's Russia* (New York: Tim Duggan Books, 2020), 210–246.

46. Tanya Lokshina, "Dispatches: Russia's Growing Intolerance for Dissent," Human Rights Watch, April 28, 2016, https://www.hrw.org/news/2016/04/28/dispatches-russias-growing-intolerance-dissent.

47. For a full timeline and details of the case see "The Dmitriev Affair," https://dmitrievaffair.com/timeline-1997-2018/; "EU Statement on the Case of Yuri Dmitriev," Delegation of the European Union to the Council of Europe, May 27, 2020, https://eeas.europa.eu/delegations/council-europe/79970/eu-statement-case-yuri-dmitriev_en; "Russia: Rights Researcher's Trial Raises Serious Concerns," Human Rights Watch, July 21, 2020, https://www.hrw.org/news/2020/07/21/russia-rights-researchers-trial-raises-serious-concerns; Andrew Higgins, "He Found One of Stalin's Mass Graves. Now He's in Jail," *New York Times*, April 27, 2020, https://www.nytimes.com/2020/04/27/world/europe/russia-historian-stalin-mass-graves.html.

48. "Russia: Rights Researcher's Trial Raises Serious Concerns," Human Rights Watch, July 21, 2020, https://www.hrw.org/news/2020/07/21/russia-rights-researchers-trial-raises-serious-concerns.

49. Yuri Zarakhovich, "Putin Plays Follow the Leader," *Time*, January 18, 2002, http://content.time.com/time/subscriber/article/0,33009,195071,00.html, in Cheng Chen, *The Return of Ideology: The Search for Regime Identities in Postcommunist Russia and China* (Ann Arbor: University of Michigan Press, 2016), 83.

50. Stalin's popularity has fluctuated since 2003, when results are available; in March 2003, for example, 53 percent of respondents thought he had played either an "entirely positive" or "mostly positive" role in Russian history, compared to 45 percent in March 2011, 54 percent in March 2016, and 70 percent in March 2019. The percentage of respondents who thought he played either a "mostly negative" or "very negative" role has dropped consistently in recent years, from 35 percent in March 2011 to 19 percent in March 2019. See "Stalin's Perception," Levada Center, April 19, 2019, https://www.levada.ru/en/2019/04/19/dynamic-of-stalin-s-perception/.

51. "ВЫДАЮЩИЕСЯ ЛЮДИ" [Outstanding People], Levada Center, June 26, 2017, https://www.levada.ru/2017/06/26/vydayushhiesya-lyudi/ (according to the most recent polls at the time of this writing in 2021).

52. "National Identity and Pride," Levada Center, January 25, 2019, https://www.levada.ru/en/2019/01/25/national-identity-and-pride/.

53. Shaun Walker, *The Long Hangover: Putin's New Russia and the Ghosts of the Past* (New York: Oxford University Press, 2018), 32.

54. Svetlana Prokopyeva, "Russia's Immortal Regiment: From Grassroots to 'Quasi-Religious Cult," Radio Free Europe/Radio Liberty, May 12, 2017, https://www.rferl.org/a/russia-immortal-regiment-grassroots-to-quasi-religious-cult/28482905.html.

55. Svetlana Prokopyeva, "Russia's Immortal Regiment: From Grassroots to 'Quasi-Religious Cult," Radio Free Europe/Radio Liberty, May 12, 2017, https://www.rferl.org/a/russia-immortal-regiment-grassroots-to-quasi-religious-cult/28482905.html; Peter Hobson, "How Russian Authorities Hijacked a WWII Remembrance Movement," *Moscow Times*, May 6, 2016, https://www.themoscowtimes.com/2016/05/06/how-russian-authorities-hijacked-a-wwii-remembrance-movement-a52776.

56. Peter Hobson, "How Russian Authorities Hijacked a WWII Remembrance Movement," *Moscow Times*, May 6, 2016, https://www.themoscowtimes.com/2016/05/06/how-russian-authorities-hijacked-a-wwii-remembrance-movement-a52776. Dmitriyev is not related to the Karelia-based historian Yuri Dmitriev.

57. Shaun Walker, "Russian War Film Set to Open amid Controversy over Accuracy of Events," *The Guardian*, November

23, 2016, https://www.theguardian.com/film/2016/nov/23/russian-war-film-set-to-open-against-controversy-over-accuracy-of-events.

58. Christopher Woolf, "Russia Chooses Myth over History in New WWII Movie," Public Radio International, October 15, 2016, https://www.pri.org/stories/2016-10-15/russia-chooses-myth-over-history-new-wwii-movie.

59. Tom Balmforth, "Soviet WWII Legend of Panfilov Guardsmen Debunked as 'Fiction,'" Radio Free Europe/Radio Liberty, July 12, 2015, https://www.rferl.org/a/soviet-wwii-panfilov-guardsmen-fiction/27123430.html.

60. Елена Рыковцева, "Тяжелое расставание с мифом," Radio Free Europe/Radio Liberty, July 20, 2020, https://www.svoboda.org/a/27138620.html.

61. Anna Dolgov, "Russian Archives Cast Doubt on Legends of Soviet War Heroes," *Moscow Times*, July 9, 2015, https://www.themoscowtimes.com/2015/07/09/russian-archives-cast-doubt-on-legends-of-soviet-war-heroes-a48026; Ola Cichowlas, "To Be Great Again, Russia Resurrects Soviet Legends," *Moscow Times*, December 1, 2016, https://www.themoscowtimes.com/2016/12/01/to-be-great-again-russia-resurrects-soviet-legends-a56380; David Filipov, "Russia's Culture Minister Says Anyone Who Questions This Tale of Soviet Bravery Is 'Filthy Scum,'" *Washington Post*, November 28, 2016, https://www.washingtonpost.com/news/worldviews/wp/2016/11/28/one-surefire-way-to-be-called-scum-in-russia-expose-a-heroic-world-war-ii-story-as-a-myth/.

62. Matthew Luxmoore, "Russian Minister Says Authenticity of War Legend beyond Dispute, 'Amoral' to Dig Further," Radio Free Europe/Radio Liberty, December 3, 2018, https://www.rferl.org/a/russian-minister-says-authenticity-of-war-legend-beyond-dispute-amoral-to-dig-further-/29635477.html.

63. Mironenko was removed as director and demoted, but he continued working at the archive and told one journalist he had wanted to change positions. Peter Hobson, "Battle in the Archives—Uncovering Russia's Secret Past," *Moscow Times*, March 24, 2016, https://www.themoscowtimes.com/2016/03/24/battle-in-the-archives-uncovering-russias-secret-past-a52254; Tom Balmforth, "Russian Archive Chief Out after Debunking Soviet WW II Legend," Radio Free Europe/Radio Liberty, March 17, 2016, https://www.rferl.org/a/mironenko-state-archive-chief-removed-from-post-panfilov-legend/27619460.html; "Meeting with Head of Federal Archive Agency Andrei Artizov," President of Russia website, April 4, 2016, http://en.kremlin.ru/events/president/news/51635.

64. "Director of WWII Propaganda Film Receives 'Historical Accuracy Award,'" *Moscow Times*, December 8, 2016, https://www.themoscowtimes.com/2016/12/08/director-of-28-panfilovtsy-gets-award-for-historical-accuracy-a56470.

65. "Kremlin Backs Culture Minister Who Labelled Soviet Revisionists 'Scum,'" *Moscow Times*, October 5, 2016, https://www.themoscowtimes.com/2016/10/05/kremlin-backs-culture-minister-on-wwii-myth-a55610.

Chapter 9

1. Frank Dikötter, *How to Be a Dictator: The Cult of Personality in the Twentieth Century* (New York: Bloomsbury, 2019), x

2. Interview in Seoul, October 2015.

3. "Kim Jong-il 'Has Nightmares of Being Stoned by His People,'" *Chosun Ilbo*, March 28, 2011, http://english.chosun.com/site/data/html_dir/2011/03/28/2011032801124.html, in Victor Cha, *The Impossible State: North Korea, Past and Future* (New York: HarperCollins, 2012), 446. The report was based on an interview with Chung's son, Chung Mong-joon, who was promoting his autobiography and preparing to run for the presidency at the time.

4. See, for example, David Zucchino, "Iraq's Swift Defeat Blamed on Husseins," *Baltimore Sun*, August 11, 2003, https://www.baltimoresun.com/news/bal-iraqcollapse0811-story.html; Martin Chulov, "Gaddafi's Last Moments: I Saw the Hand Holding the Gun and I Saw It Fire," *The Guardian*, October 20, 2012, https://www.theguardian.com/world/2012/oct/20/muammar-gaddafi-killing-witnesses.

5. Frank Dikötter, *How to Be a Dictator: The Cult of Personality in the Twentieth Century* (New York: Bloomsbury, 2019), x.

6. Frank Dikötter, *How to Be a Dictator: The Cult of Personality in the Twentieth Century* (New York: Bloomsbury, 2019), xiii.

7. Lisa Wedeen, *Ambiguities of Domination: Politics, Rhetoric, and Symbols in Contemporary Syria* (Chicago: University of Chicago Press, 2015), 6, 146–147 (emphasis in original). For more on the use of mass rallies and spectacle to enforce a leader's power see also Ruth Ben-Ghiat, *Strongmen: From Mussolini to the Present* (New York: W. W. Norton & Company, 2020), 104–105.

8. Václav Havel, *The Power of the Powerless* (London: Vintage Classics/Penguin Random House, 2018), 14–15.

9. Václav Havel, *The Power of the Powerless* (London: Vintage Classics/Penguin Random House, 2018), 21. Timur Kuran calls this behavior "preference falsification" and notes the difference between private and public opinion. Timur Kuran, *Private Truths, Public Lies: The Social Consequences of Preference Falsification* (Cambridge, MA: Harvard University Press, 1997), 89–90.

10. Of course, the Kims have relied on more than their cult of personality to stay in power. Over more than seven decades ruling the country, successive leaders had developed a range of tools. They co-opted the elite, rewarding senior party officials and high-ranking military officers, and purging anyone suspected of disloyalty. Kim Jong Un reportedly had his

own uncle Jang Song Thaek executed by antiaircraft machine guns as an example to others. Access to information was strictly controlled and all citizens were required to undergo long hours of political education every week. A fearsome security apparatus and networks of informers stifled any traces of dissent. See Daniel Byman and Jennifer Lind, "Pyongyang's Survival Strategy: Tools of Authoritarian Control in North Korea," *International Security* 35, no. 1 (2010): 44–74, http://www.jstor.org/stable/40784646.

11. Anna Fifield, *The Great Successor: The Divinely Perfect Destiny of Brilliant Comrade Kim Jong Un* (New York: PublicAffairs, 2019), 60–61. For a detailed account of Kim Jong Un's childhood and early life see Anna Fifield, *The Great Successor: The Divinely Perfect Destiny of Brilliant Comrade Kim Jong Un* (New York: Public Affairs, 2019), and Jung H. Pak, *Becoming Kim Jong Un: A Former CIA Officer's Insights into North Korea's Enigmatic Young Dictator* (New York: Ballantine Books, 2020).

12. John Delury, "Reform Sprouts in North Korea?," *YaleGlobal Online*, July 26, 2012, https://archive-yaleglobal.yale.edu/content/reform-sprouts-north-korea.

13. *Kim Jong-il: Biography*, vol. 1 (Pyongyang: Foreign Languages Publishing House, 2005), 4.

14. Anna Fifield, *The Great Successor: The Divinely Perfect Destiny of Brilliant Comrade Kim Jong Un* (New York: PublicAffairs, 2019), 68.

15. Details of the propaganda campaign and emergence of the "Footsteps" song are from Anna Fifield, *The Great Successor: The Divinely Perfect Destiny of Brilliant Comrade Kim Jong Un* (New York: PublicAffairs, 2019), 43, 65–71.

16. Anna Fifield, *The Great Successor: The Divinely Perfect Destiny of Brilliant Comrade Kim Jong Un* (New York: PublicAffairs, 2019), 69.

17. *Anecdotes of Kim Jong Un's Life* (Pyongyang: Foreign Languages Publishing House, 2017), 4, in Anna Fifield, *The Great Successor: The Divinely Perfect Destiny of Brilliant Comrade Kim Jong Un* (New York: Public Affairs, 2019), 64–65.

18. "Kim Jong Il Issues Order on Promoting Military Ranks," Korean Central News Agency, September 27, 2010, in Anna Fifield, *The Great Successor: The Divinely Perfect Destiny of Brilliant Comrade Kim Jong Un* (New York: PublicAffairs, 2019), 76.

19. Kim Jong Un, "Let Us March Forward Dynamically towards Final Victory, Holding Higher the Banner of Songun," April 15, 2012, in Kim Jong Un, *Towards Final Victory* (Pyongyang: Foreign Languages Publishing House, 2016), 37–39, 41, 48.

20. "North Korea: Who Would Dare to Piggyback on Kim Jong-un?," BBC News, March 24, 2017, https://www.bbc.com/news/world-asia-39361984.

21. Experts disagree on the significance and implications of Kim's *Byungjin* line; see, for instance, Choe Sang-hun, "North Korea Vows to Keep

Nuclear Arms and Fix Economy," *New York Times*, March 31, 2013, https://www.nytimes.com/2013/04/01/world/asia/north-korea-vows-to-keep-nuclear-arms-and-fix-economy.html; Max Fisher, "North Korea's Nuclear Arms Sustain Drive for 'Final Victory,'" *New York Times*, June 29, 2017, https://www.nytimes.com/2017/07/29/world/asia/north-korea-nuclear-missile.html?referer=https://t.co/RbrfVKlpdd%3famp=1; B. R. Myers, "A Note on Byungjin," Sthele Press, July 30, 2017, https://sthelepress.com/index.php/2017/07/30/a-note-on-byungjin-b-r-myers/.

22. Christine Kim and Jane Chung, "North Korea 2016 Economic Growth at 17-Year High despite Sanctions—South Korea," Reuters, July 20, 2017, https://www.reuters.com/article/uk-northkorea-economy-gdp/north-korea-2016-economic-growth-at-17-year-high-despite-sanctions-south-korea-idUKKBN1A6083; Eric Talmadge, "North Korea's Creeping Economic Reforms Show Signs of Paying Off," *The Guardian*, March 5, 2015, https://www.theguardian.com/world/2015/mar/05/north-korea-economic-reforms-show-signs-paying-off.

23. "Speech of Kim Jong Un at Conference of Ideological Workers," Korean Central News Agency (KCNA), February 27, 2014, in Benjamin Katzeff Silberstein, "Kim Jong Un's Congress Report: More Economic and Social Controls on the Horizon," 38 North, February 9, 2021, https://www.38north.org/2021/02/kim-jong-uns-congress-report-more-economic-and-social-controls-on-the-horizon/.

24. David O. Shullman, "Protect the Party: China's Growing Influence in the Developing World," Brookings Institution, January 22, 2019, https://www.brookings.edu/articles/protect-the-party-chinas-growing-influence-in-the-developing-world/.

25. Ruediger Frank, "The 7th Party Congress in North Korea': A Return to a New Normal," 38 North, May 20, 2016, https://www.38north.org/2016/05/rfrank052016/#_ftn3.

26. Ruediger Frank, "The 7th Party Congress in North Korea': A Return to a New Normal," 38 North, May 20, 2016, https://www.38north.org/2016/05/rfrank052016/#_ftn3.

27. Justin McCurry, "'A Gift for the American Bastards': North Korea's Kim Fires Back at Donald Trump," *The Guardian*, July 5, 2017, https://www.theguardian.com/world/2017/jul/05/a-gift-for-the-american-bastards-north-koreas-kim-fires-back-at-trump; John Delury, "Kim Jong-un Has a Dream. The U.S. Should Help Him Realize It," *New York Times*, September 21, 2018, https://www.nytimes.com/2018/09/21/opinion/kim-jong-un-moon-economic-development-north-korea-denuclearization.html. For an overview of North Korea's nuclear and missile development see "Chronology of U.S.-North Korean Nuclear and Missile Diplomacy," Arms Control Association, July 2020, https://www.armscontrol.org/factsheets/dprkchron.

28. Adam Cathcart, "Kim Jong-un Syndrome: North Korean Commemorative Culture and the Succession Process," in *Change and Continuity in North Korean Politics*, ed. Adam Cathcart, Robert Winstanley-Chesters, and Christopher Green (London: Routledge, 2018), 13, also quoted in Jung H. Pak, *Becoming Kim Jong Un: A Former CIA Officer's Insights into North Korea's Enigmatic Young Dictator* (New York: Ballantine Books, 2020), 87.

29. "DPR Korea 2013: Humanitarian Needs and Priorities," United Nations Office for the Coordination of Humanitarian Affairs, August 15, 2013, https://reliefweb.int/sites/reliefweb.int/files/resources/OFD-DPR%20 Korea15Aug.v2.pdf.

30. Daniel Tudor and James Pearson, *North Korea Confidential: Private Markets, Fashion Trends, Prison Camps, Dissenters and Defectors* (Clarendon, VT: Tuttle Publishing, 2015), 78–79.

31. Adam Cathcart, "Kim Jong-un Syndrome: North Korean Commemorative Culture and the Succession Process," in *Change and Continuity in North Korean Politics*, ed. Adam Cathcart, Robert Winstanley-Chesters, and Christopher Green (London and New York: Routledge, 2018), 15; "Kim Jong Un Visits Construction Site for Victorious Fatherland Liberation War Museum," Korean Central News Agency, February 21, 2013, http://www.kcna.co.jp/item/2013/ 201302/news21/20130221-37ee.html, in Suzy Kim, "Specters of War in Pyongyang: The Victorious Fatherland Liberation War Museum in North Korea," *Cross-Currents: East Asian History and Culture Review*, E-Journal No. 14 (March 2015), http://cross-currents.berkeley.edu/e-journal/issue-14.

32. Descriptions of the exhibits are from *Victorious Fatherland Liberation War Museum* (Pyongyang: Foreign Languages Publishing House, 2014), 3, 108–109, 123–125.

33. *Victorious Fatherland Liberation War Museum* (Pyongyang: Foreign Languages Publishing House, 2014), 123–125. Analysts concluded the ICBMs displayed in the parade were almost certainly mock-ups; see "Chronology of U.S.-North Korean Nuclear and Missile Diplomacy," Arms Control Association, July 2020, https://www.armscontrol.org/ factsheets/dprkchron].

34. "Kim Jong Un Visits Construction Site for Victorious Fatherland Liberation War Museum," Korean Central News Agency, February 21, 2013, http://www.kcna.co.jp/item/2013/201302/news21/20130221-37ee.html, in Suzy Kim, "Specters of War in Pyongyang: The Victorious Fatherland Liberation War Museum in North Korea," *Cross-Currents: East Asian History and Culture Review*, E-Journal No. 14 (March 2015), http://cross-currents.berkeley.edu/e-journal/issue-14.

35. As is discussed in chapter three, historian Adam Cathcart concludes that there was a series of killings carried out in the area by Communists, Christians, and other anti-regime elements, but explains, "This was

a case of Koreans killing Koreans in the fog of war, not an American attempt to wipe out an entire county of communists through medieval methods." AFP, "Lessons in Loathing at North Korea's Museum to 'US Atrocity,'" France 24, June 7, 2018, https://www.france24.com/en/20180607-lessons-loathing-north-koreas-museum-us-atrocity.

36. Jean H. Lee, "For North Koreans, the War Never Ended," *Wilson Quarterly*, Spring 2017, https://www.wilsonquarterly.com/quarterly/trump-and-a-watching-world/for-north-koreas-the-war-never-ended/; also quoted in part in Jung H. Pak, *Becoming Kim Jong Un: A Former CIA Officer's Insights into North Korea's Enigmatic Young Dictator* (New York: Ballantine Books, 2020), 88.

37. Jean H. Lee, "For North Koreans, the War Never Ended," *Wilson Quarterly*, Spring 2017, https://www.wilsonquarterly.com/quarterly/trump-and-a-watching-world/for-north-koreas-the-war-never-ended/.

38. Interview in Washington, DC, September 2020.

39. "Kim Jong Un Visits Sinchon Museum," KCNA, November 25, 2014, http://www.kcna.co.jp/item/2014/201411/news25/20141125-01ee.html; "Kim Visits Sinchon Museum, Calls for Stronger Ideological Education," *Daily NK*, July 24, 2015, http://www.dailynk.com/english/read.php?cataId=nk01700&num=13361.

40. AFP, "Lessons in Loathing at North Korea's Museum to 'US Atrocity,'" France 24, June 7, 2018, https://www.france24.com/en/20180607-lessons-loathing-north-koreas-museum-us-atrocity; see also "Lessons in Loathing at North Korea's Museum to 'US Atrocity,'" AFP News Agency/YouTube, June 7, 2018, https://www.youtube.com/watch?v=AQsR-e7fD7E.

41. Andray Abrahamian, *Being in North Korea* (Stanford, CA: Shorenstein Asia-Pacific Research Center, 2020), 98.

42. "Kim Jong Un—Speeches at the 7th Party Congress," National Committee on North Korea, May 9, 2016, https://www.ncnk.org/sites/default/files/content/resources/publications/KJU_Speeches_7th_Congress.pdf.

43. John Delury, "North Korea in 2020: In Search of Health and Power," *Asian Survey* 61, no. 1 (2021): 74–82, https://doi.org/10.1525/as.2021.61.1.74.

44. "Kim Jong Un's 2018 New Year's Address," National Committee on North Korea, January 1, 2018, https://www.ncnk.org/node/1427.

45. Colin Zwirko, "Kim Jong Un Oversees Opening of Yangdok Hot Springs and Ski Resort," NK News, December 8, 2019, https://www.nknews.org/2019/12/kim-jong-un-oversees-opening-of-yangdok-hot-springs-and-ski-resort/?t=1576168453144.

46. Jung H. Pak, *Becoming Kim Jong Un: A Former CIA Officer's Insights into North Korea's Enigmatic Young Dictator* (New York: Ballantine Books, 2020), 92 (emphasis in original).

47. Laura Bicker, "Why Kim Jong-un Is Waging War on Slang, Jeans and Foreign Films," BBC News, June 7, 2021, https://www.bbc.com/news/

world-asia-57225936; Benjamin Katzeff Silberstein, "Kim Jong Un's Congress Report: More Economic and Social Controls on the Horizon," 38 North, February 9, 2021, https://www.38north.org/2021/02/kim-jong-uns-congress-report-more-economic-and-social-controls-on-the-horizon/.

48. Seul-gi Jang, "A Deep Dive into N. Korea's New 'Anti-Reactionary Thought' Law," *Daily NK*, December 15, 2020, https://www.dailynk.com/english/deep-dive-north-korea-new-anti-reactionary- thought-law/; Seul-gi Jang, "Exclusive: Daily NK Obtains Materials Explaining Specifics of New 'Anti-Reactionary Thought' Law," *Daily NK*, January 19, 2021, https://www.dailynk.com/english/exclusive-daily-nk-obtains- materials-explaining-specifics-new-anti-reactionary-thought-law, in Benjamin Katzeff Silberstein, "When Sherlock Holmes Left Pyongyang: Surveillance and Social Control in North Korea, 1954–2021" (Doctoral diss., University of Pennsylvania, 2021).

49. Jean H. Lee, "In North Korea, Learning to Hate U.S. Starts with Children," Yahoo News/Associated Press, June 23, 2012, https://www.yahoo.com/news/north-korea-learning-hate-us-starts-early-120658377.html.

50. Christopher Richardson, "'Be Prepared!' Reflections on the North Korean Children's Union," *Sino-NK*, June 13, 2013, https://sinonk.com/2013/06/13/be-prepared-reflections-on-the-north-korean-childrens-union/.

51. Kim Jong Un, "Letter to Those Attending the Fourth Conference of Primary Officials of Kim Il Sung Socialist Youth League, September 18, 2014," in *Young People, Be Vanguard Fighters Who Are Unfailingly Faithful to the Party's Revolutionary Cause of Songun* (Pyongyang: Foreign Languages Publishing House, 2015), 4–5. The full name of the organization at the time was the Kim Il Sung Socialist Youth League; it was renamed the Kimilsungist-Kimjongilist Youth League in 2016, and then the Socialist Patriotic Youth League in 2021, and caters to members aged fourteen to thirty.

52. Anna Fifield, "North Korea Begins Brainwashing Children in Cult of the Kims as Early as Kindergarten," *Washington Post*, January 16, 2015, https://www.washingtonpost.com/world/asia_pacific/for-north-koreas-kims-its-never-too-soon-to-start-brainwashing/2015/01/15/a23871c6-9a67-11e4-86a3-1b56f64925f6_story.html?utm_term=.faadc26e95ea.

53. United Nations, "Report of the Detailed Findings of the Commission of Inquiry on Human Rights in the Democratic People's Republic of Korea," February 7, 2014, https://www.ohchr.org/EN/HRBodies/HRC/CoIDPRK/Pages/ReportoftheCommissionofInquiryDPRK.aspx.

54. Interview in Pyongyang, May 2016.

55. United Nations, "Report of the Detailed Findings of the Commission of Inquiry on Human Rights in the Democratic People's Republic of Korea," February 7, 2014, https://www.ohchr.org/EN/HRBodies/HRC/CoIDPRK/Pages/ReportoftheCommissionofInquiryDPRK.aspx.

56. 려사 고급중학교 *3 [History for High School Year 3]*
     (Pyongyang: 교육도서출판사 [Educational Books Publisher], 2015), 135.

57. *Chinese Characters Middle School Year 3* (Pyongyang: 교육도서출판사
     [Educational Books Publisher], 2015), 26.

58. *Chinese Characters Middle School Year 3* (Pyongyang: 교육도서출판사
     [Educational Books Publisher], 2015), 61.

59. 려사 고급중학교 *3 [History for High School Year 3]*
     (Pyongyang: 교육도서출판사 [Educational Books Publisher], 2015),
     157–159.

60. Interview in London, May 2017.

61. Andray Abrahamian, *Being in North Korea* (Stanford, CA: Shorenstein
     Asia-Pacific Research Center, 2020), 69.

62. Mina Yoon, "Who Do North Koreans Think Started the Korean War?,"
     NK News, January 8, 2014, https://www.nknews.org/2014/01/who-do-
     north-koreans-think-started-the-korean-war/; also quoted in part in
     Andray Abrahamian, *Being in North Korea* (Stanford, CA: Shorenstein
     Asia-Pacific Research Center, 2020), 69.

63. KCNA, "Supreme Leader Kim Jong Un Looks Round Revolutionary
     Battle Sites in Mt Paektu Area," KCNA Watch, December 4, 2019,
     https://kcnawatch.org/newstream/1575410542-830764720/supreme-leader-
     kim-jong-un-looks-round-revolutionary-battle-sites-in-mt-paektu-area/
     ?t=1575414437917&t=1575657354947.

64. Colin Zwirko, "New North Korean Film Stresses Military Path after
     Standing Up to U.S. in 2019," NK News, January 15, 2020, https://www.
     nknews.org/2020/01/new-north-korean-film-stresses-military-path-after-
     standing-up-to-u-s-in-2019/?t=1604328378647.

Chapter 10

 1. Chris Buckley and Keith Bradsher, "Marking Party's Centennial, Xi
     Warns That China Will Not Be Bullied," *New York Times*, July 1, 2021,
     https://www.nytimes.com/2021/07/01/world/asia/xi-china-communist-
     party-anniversary.html.

 2. Xi Jinping, "Remember the Past and Our Martyrs, Cherish Peace, and
     Build a New Future," September 3, 2015, in Xi Jinping, *The Governance of
     China*, vol. 2 (Beijing: Foreign Languages Press, 2017), 484.

 3. Nectar Gan, "Why Xi Jinping's the Man for Me: Vladimir Putin
     Highlights Birthday Party with 'Good Friend' from China as Sign of
     Growing Closeness," *South China Morning Post*, June 6, 2018, https://
     www.scmp.com/news/china/diplomacy-defence/article/2149585/
     why-xis-man-me-putin-highlights-birthday-party-good.

 4. Victory Day was an official holiday in 2015 but did not become an annual
     remembrance day like the Nanjing Massacre Memorial Day and Martyrs'
     Day on December 13 and September 30, respectively; see Jin Kai, "With
     New National Days, China Strikes at Japan," *The Diplomat*, February 28,

2014, https://thediplomat.com/2014/03/with-new-national-days-china-strikes-at-japan/; Andrea Chen, "First National Martyrs' Day Remembers Those Who Sacrificed for China," *South China Morning Post*, September 30, 2014, https://www.scmp.com/news/china/article/1604473/first-national-martyrs-day-remembers-those-who-sacrificed-china. Howard French writes that the government also commissioned the construction of a $6 million full-size replica of a Chinese warship that was sunk by Japan; see Howard W. French, *Everything under the Heavens: How the Past Helps Shape China's Push for Global Power* (London and Melbourne: Scribe, 2017), 20.

5. Vincent Chang argues that the framing of the war has shifted under Xi Jinping from the previously dominant trope of "national victimization" to "national victory" and "national greatness." Vincent K. L. Chang, "Recalling Victory, Recounting Greatness: Second World War Remembrance in Xi Jinping's China," *China Quarterly*, 2021, 1–22, doi:10.1017/S0305741021000497.

6. Xi Jinping, "Remember the Past and Our Martyrs, Cherish Peace, and Build a New Future," September 3, 2015, in Xi Jinping, *The Governance of China*, vol. 2 (Beijing: Foreign Languages Press, 2017), 484–485.

7. Yufan Huang, "Cheers and Jeers as Students Watch Victory Day Parade," *New York Times*, September 3, 2015, https://www.nytimes.com/live/china-military-parade/; Hannah Beech, "The World's Next Superpower Announces Itself with an Epic Parade," *Time*, September 3, 2015, https://time.com/4021131/china-parade-beijing-military-world-war/.

8. Nicholas Kristof, "Looking for a Jump-Start in China," *New York Times*, January 5, 2013, https://www.nytimes.com/2013/01/06/opinion/sunday/kristof-looking-for-a-jump-start-in-china.html. For an overview of the arguments, see also Wen-Ti Sung, "Is Xi Jinping a Reformer?," *The Diplomat*, March 5, 2014, https://thediplomat.com/2014/03/is-xi-jinping-a-reformer/. Xi Jinping holds three titles as leader of China: general secretary of the Chinese Communist Party, president of the People's Republic of China, and chairman of the Central Military Commission. He became general secretary, his most important position, and chairman of the Central Military Commission on November 15, 2012, and assumed the presidency on March 14, 2013.

9. Xi traveled to Guangdong province, where he gave the speech, from December 7 to 11, 2013. His remarks were circulated among party officials afterward, but not published in state-run media; see Chris Buckley, "Vows of Change in China Belie Private Warning," *New York Times*, February 14, 2013, https://www.nytimes.com/2013/02/15/world/asia/vowing-reform-chinas-leader-xi-jinping-airs-other-message-in-private.html. As vice president in 2010, Xi also warned against attempts to "distort and smear the party's history"; see, for instance, Andrew Higgins, "In China, a Long Path of Writing the Communist Party's History," *Washington Post*, May 26, 2011, https://www.washingtonpost.com/world/

in-china-a-long-path-of-writing-the-communist-partys-history/2011/05/16/
AGDfMECH_story.html.

10. "Xi Jinping's Speech at the Seminar for Members and Alternate Members
of the New Central Committee to Learn and Implement the Spirit of
the 18th CPC National Congress," January 5, 2013, "习近平：历史不可
虚无," 中国日报, November 20, 2016, https://china.chinadaily.com.cn/
2016-10/20/content_27123201.htm, in Sergey Radchenko, "Putin and
Xi Eye the Soviet Collapse," *Asan Forum*, March 19, 2020, http://www.
theasanforum.org/putin-and-xi-eye-the-soviet-collapse/#15.

11. Sheena Chestnut Greitens identifies "ideological security" as a crucial
component of regime security and writes that "Xi Jinping appears to
believe that the lack of ideological fidelity; corruption from within; and
insufficient control over the coercive apparatus were among the principal
factors that doomed Soviet communism." See Sheena Chestnut Greitens,
"How Does China Think about National Security?," in *The China
Questions II*, ed. Carrai, M., J. Rudolph, and M. Szonyi (Cambridge,
MA: Harvard University Press, 2022), 2.

12. Chung-yue Chang, "Study History, Be Close to the People," *China Daily*,
July 9, 2013, http://www.chinadaily.com.cn/opinion/2013-07/09/content_
16749701.htm.

13. "Document 9: A ChinaFile Translation," ChinaFile, November 8, 2013,
http://www.chinafile.com/document-9-chinafile-translation.

14. "Symposium on Academic Discourse for Chinese History Research
Held in Beijing," Chinese Social Sciences Today, May 7, 2014 http://
english.cssn.cn/whatsnew/conferences/201405/t20140507_1150997.
shtml?COLLCC=380557967; "国史研究话语权建设学术研讨会在京举
行," *Social Sciences Today* (CASS Special Edition), no. 244, April 25, 2014,
http://cass.cssn.cn/keyandongtai/xueshuhuiyi/201404/t20140425_1124561.
html.

15. *Qiushi*, June 12, 2021, http://www.qstheory.cn/zt2015/lsxwzy823/index.
htm.

16. Details and quotes are from Lou Chi-kuei, *The Five Heroes of Wolf's Teeth
Mountain* (Peking [Beijing]: Foreign Languages Press, 1977).

17. Kiki Zhao, "Chinese Court Orders Apology over Challenge to Tale of
Wartime Heroes," *New York Times*, June 28, 2016, https://www.nytimes.
com/2016/06/29/world/asia/china-hong-zhenkuai-five-heroes.html.

18. Josh Chin, "In China, Xi Jinping's Crackdown Extends to Dissenting
Versions of History," *Wall Street Journal*, August 1, 2016, https://www.
wsj.com/articles/in-china-xi-jinpings-crackdown-extends-to-dissenting-
versions-of-history-1470087445.

19. Kerry Brown and Simone van Nieuwenhuizen, *China and the New
Maoists* (London: Zed Books, 2016), 139. "Leftist" in this context refers
to proponents of CCP orthodoxy including central control over the
economy; for more on the complexity of such labels see Jennifer Pan and

Yiqing Xu, "China's Ideological Spectrum," *Journal of Politics* 80, no. 1 (2018): 254–273, https://doi.org/10.1086/694255].

20. Zhang Yu, "Leftists and Rightists Battle Over How to Interpret Stories of China's Revolutionary Past," *Global Times*, January 13, 2016, http://www.globaltimes.cn/content/963420.shtml.

21. "Full Text of Wang Lihua's Moving Court Statement in Defence of Guo Songmin," Red Song Society, May 13, 2015, www.szhgh.com/Article/cdjc/zhenqi/2015-05-13/84347.html, in Kerry Brown and Simone van Nieuwenhuizen, *China and the New Maoists* (London: Zed Books, 2016), 141–142.

22. Luo Yi, "Listening to the Trial of *Spring and Autumn Annals* at Haidian District Court—A Documentary of the Case File Created by the Five Heroes of Langya Mountain," Utopia website, May 21, 2015, www.wyzxwk.com/Article/zatan/2015/05/344581.html, in Kerry Brown and Simone van Nieuwenhuizen, *China and the New Maoists* (London: Zed Books, 2016), 143.

23. Kiki Zhao, "Chinese Court Orders Apology over Challenge to Tale of Wartime Heroes," *New York Times*, June 28, 2016, https://www.nytimes.com/2016/06/29/world/asia/china-hong-zhenkuai-five-heroes.html.

24. Xi Jinping, "Speech at a Medal Presentation Ceremony Marking the 70th Anniversary of the Chinese People's Victory in the War of Resistance Against Japanese Aggression," Xinhua, September 2, 2015, in *Qiushi* 8, no. 1 (January–March 2016).

25. Verna Yu, "The Death of a Liberal Chinese Magazine," *The Diplomat*, July 19, 2016, https://thediplomat.com/2016/07/the-death-of-a-liberal-chinese-magazine/.

26. Interview in Beijing, February 2018. While the timing of the takeover coincided with Hong Zhenkuai's court case and the controversy over the Langya Mountain case, it should be understood in the context of the shrinking space for public debate more broadly under Xi Jinping; see Jude Blanchette, *China's New Red Guards: The Return of Radicalism and the Rebirth of Mao Zedong* (New York: Oxford University Press, 2019), 147.

27. "China Makes Defaming Revolutionary Heroes Punishable by Law," Reuters, April 27, 2018, https://www.reuters.com/article/us-china-lawmaking/china-makes-defaming-revolutionary-heroes-punishable-by-law-idUSKBN1HY14N.

28. Interview in Beijing, February 2018.

29. Interview in Beijing, March 2018.

30. Perry Link, "China: The Anaconda in the Chandelier," *New York Review of Books*, April 11, 2002, https://www.chinafile.com/library/nyrb-china-archive/china-anaconda-chandelier.

31. "Chinese Lecturer Fired for Raising Presidential Term-Limit in Class," Radio Free Asia, May 21, 2018, https://www.rfa.org/english/news/china/lecturer-05212018105710.html.

32. Chris Buckley, "China Warns against 'Western Values' in Imported Textbooks," *New York Times*, January 30, 2015, https://sinosphere.blogs. nytimes.com/2015/01/30/china-warns-against-western-values-in-imported-textbooks/.

33. "10 Institutes Established to Study Xi's Thought," Xinhua, December 14, 2017; "China's Xi Calls for Tighter Ideological Control in Universities," Reuters, December 29, 2014, https://www.reuters.com/article/us-china-universities/chinas-xi-calls-for-tighter-ideological-control-in-universities-idUSKBN0K70TI20141229; "CPC to Promote Patriotism among Intellectuals," Xinhua, August 4, 2018, http://www.xinhuanet.com/english/2018-08/04/c_137367370.htm; "China to Enshrine Xi's Thought into State Constitution amid National 'Fervor,'" Reuters, January 19, 2018, https://www.reuters.com/article/us-china-politics/china-to-enshrine-xis-thought-into-state-constitution-amid-national-fervor-idUSKBN1F812P.

34. Interview in Beijing, March 2018. This was a reference to Deng Xiaoping's warning in 1978 about the emergence of "forbidden zones" during the Cultural Revolution, when he said, "Some people found it safer to stop using their heads and thinking questions over." Deng Xiaoping, "Emancipate the Mind, Seek Truth from Facts and Unite as One in Looking to the Future," December 13, 1978, in *The Selected Works of Deng Xiaoping*, vol. 2 (1975–1982), https://dengxiaopingworks.wordpress.com/2013/02/25/emancipate-the-mind-seek-truth-from-facts-and-unite-as-one-in-looking-to-the-future/.

35. Interview in Beijing, March 2018.

36. "Xi Jinping: rang lishi shuo hua yong shishi fayan, shenru kaizhan Zhongguo renmin kang-Ri zhan-zheng yanjiu" [Xi Jinping: let historical facts speak, deepen the research on the Chinese people's War of Resistance against Japan], Xinhua, July 31, 2015, http://www.xinhuanet.com//politics/2015-07/31/ c_1116107416.htm, in Vincent K. L. Chang, "Recalling Victory, Recounting Greatness: Second World War Remembrance in Xi Jinping's China," *China Quarterly*, vol. 248 (Supplement S1), 2021, 1–22, doi:10.1017/S0305741021000497.

37. Xi Jinping, "Rang lishi shuohua yong shishi fayan, shenru kaizhan Zhongguo renmin kangRi zhanzheng yanjiu" [Let history speak and use facts to deepen and open research on the Chinese people's War of Resistance against Japan], CPC News, July 31, 2015, http://cpc.people. com.cn/n/2015/0731/c64094-27393899.html, in Rana Mitter, *China's Good War: How World War II Is Shaping a New Nationalism* (Cambridge, MA: Harvard University Press, 2020), 93.

38. Vincent K. L. Chang, "Recalling Victory, Recounting Greatness: Second World War Remembrance in Xi Jinping's China," *China Quarterly*, vol. 248 (Supplement S1), 2021, 1–22, doi:10.1017/S0305741021000497. On the starting point of the war, Rana Mitter notes that there were "perfectly reasonable historiographical arguments for an earlier start date," with

Huang Meizhen, for instance, arguing that the conflict should be viewed as the beginning in 1931 in a 1987 essay, but he concludes that the decision to move to the "fourteen-year" framework was taken for "political rather than scholarly reasons." Rana Mitter, *China's Good War: How World War II Is Shaping a New Nationalism* (Cambridge, MA: Harvard University Press, 2020), 90–92.

39. Kinling Lo, "Textbooks Change: China's War against Japanese Aggression Lasted 14 Years Instead of Eight," *South China Morning Post*, January 10, 2017, https://www.scmp.com/news/china/policies-politics/article/2060939/chinas-education-ministry-extends-timeline-war-against, in Rana Mitter, *China's Good War: How World War II Is Shaping a New Nationalism* (Cambridge, MA: Harvard University Press, 2020), 90.

40. *Zhongguo Lishi* [Chinese History], Grade 8, vol. 1 (Beijing: Renmin jiaoyu chubanshe [People's Education Press], 2017), in Vincent K. L. Chang, "Recalling Victory, Recounting Greatness: Second World War Remembrance in Xi Jinping's China," *China Quarterly*, vol. 248 (Supplement S1), 2021, 1–22, doi:10.1017/S0305741021000497.

41. Interview in Beijing, March 2018.

42. 楊鈺, "壓縮的文革歷史與擴張的愛國教育, 中國歷史教科書70年變遷," *The Initium*, September 10, 2020, in Zheng Wang, "The Past's Transformative Power," *Wilson Quarterly*, Fall 2020, https://www.wilsonquarterly.com/quarterly/the-ends-of-history/the-pasts-transformative-power/.

43. "教育部办公厅印发《中小学贯彻落实〈新时代爱国主义教育实施纲要〉重点任务工作方案》的通知—加快构建一体贯穿、循序渐进的爱国主义教育体系," Ministry of Education of the People's Republic of China, July 6, 2020, http://www.moe.gov.cn/jyb_xwfb/gzdt_gzdt/s5987/202007/t20200706_470591.html in Zheng Wang; "The Past's Transformative Power," *Wilson Quarterly*, Fall 2020, https://www.wilsonquarterly.com/quarterly/the-ends-of-history/the-pasts-transformative-power/. For more on the function and content of patriotic education in China see Karrie J. Koesel, "Legitimacy, Resilience, and Political Education in Russia and China: Learning to be Loyal," in *Citizens and the State in Authoritarian Regimes: Comparing China and Russia*, ed. Karrie J. Koesel, Valerie J. Bunce, and Jessica Chen Weiss (New York: Oxford University Press, 2020), 264–271.

44. Tetsushi Takahashi, "Chinese Tourists Flock to Communist Party 'Holy Sites,'" *Nikkei Asia*, September 22, 2020, https://asia.nikkei.com/Business/Travel-Leisure/Chinese-tourists-flock-to-Communist-Party-holy-sites; Bloomberg News, "China Stirs Up Patriotism by Sending Tourists to Mao's Old Haunts," Bloomberg, September 29, 2019, https://www.bloomberg.com/news/features/2019-09-29/china-red-tourism-promotes-communist-sites-to-boost-xi-s-economy; "习近平：革命传统教育基地不

要贪大求洋," *People's Daily*, July 19, 2016, http://politics.people.com.cn/n1/2016/0719/c1001-28565660.html.

45. Bloomberg News, "China Stirs Up Patriotism by Sending Tourists to Mao's Old Haunts," Bloomberg, September 29, 2019, https://www.bloomberg.com/news/features/2019-09-29/china-red-tourism-promotes-communist-sites-to-boost-xi-s-economy.

46. "China's 2019 'Red Tourism' Revenue Tops 400 bln Yuan," Xinhua, May 19, 2021, http://www.xinhuanet.com/english/2021-05/19/c_139956421.htm.

47. "Across China: 'Red Tourism' Makes Uniform-Renting a Hot Business," Xinhua, November 9, 2018, http://www.xinhuanet.com/english/2018-11/09/c_137594743.htm.

48. Bloomberg News, "China Stirs Up Patriotism by Sending Tourists to Mao's Old Haunts," Bloomberg, September 29, 2019, https://www.bloomberg.com/news/features/2019-09-29/china-red-tourism-promotes-communist-sites-to-boost-xi-s-economy.

49. Zheng Wang, "The Past's Transformative Power," *Wilson Quarterly*, Fall 2020, https://www.wilsonquarterly.com/quarterly/the-ends-of-history/the-pasts-transformative-power/.

50. Lulu Yilun Chen, "Chinese Technology Moguls' Latest Obsession: Red Tourism," Bloomberg, June 25, 2019, https://www.bloomberg.com/news/articles/2019-06-25/chinese-technology-moguls-latest-obsession-red-tourism.

51. Sheera Frenkel and Cecilia Kang, *An Ugly Truth: Inside Facebook's Battle for Domination* (New York: HarperCollins, 2021).

52. David Lague and Jane Lanhee Lee, "Why China's Film Makers Love to Hate Japan," Reuters, May 25, 2013, https://www.reuters.com/article/us-china-japan-specialreport/special-report-why-chinas-film-makers-love-to-hate-japan-idUSBRE94O0CJ20130525, in Howard W. French, *Everything under the Heavens: How the Past Helps Shape China's Push for Global Power* (London and Melbourne: Scribe, 2017), 21.

53. Zheng Wang, "The Past's Transformative Power," *Wilson Quarterly*, Fall 2020, https://www.wilsonquarterly.com/quarterly/the-ends-of-history/the-pasts-transformative-power/.

54. Rebecca Davis, "China Aims to Become 'Strong Film Power' Like U.S. by 2035, Calls for More Patriotic Films," *Variety*, March 3, 2019, https://variety.com/2019/film/news/china-strong-film-power-by-2035-wants-more-patriotic-films-1203153901/; Zeng Yuli, "China's Filmmakers Fine-Tune Patriotism for a New Generation," *Sixth Tone*, December 13, 2019, https://www.sixthtone.com/news/1004833/chinas-filmmakers-fine-tune-patriotism-for-a-new-generation.

55. "Abominable: A DreamWorks Movie, a Map, and a Huge Regional Row," BBC News, October 18, 2019, https://www.bbc.com/news/world-asia-50093028; Scott Tong, "Hollywood, U.S. Navy Accused of Caving to Chinese Censorship Standards," Marketplace, November 21, 2019, https://

www.marketplace.org/2019/11/21/hollywood-u-s-navy-accused-of-caving-to-chinese-censorship/; David S. Cohen, "'Transformers': A Splendidly Patriotic Film, If You Happen to Be Chinese," *Variety*, July 3, 2014, https://variety.com/2014/film/columns/transformers-age-of-extinction-patriotic-for-china-1201257030/.

56. James Tager, "Made in Hollywood, Censored by Beijing," PEN America, August 5, 2020, https://pen.org/report/made-in-hollywood-censored-by-beijing/.

57. Steve Rose, "The Eight Hundred: How China's Blockbusters Became a New Political Battleground," *The Guardian*, September 18, 2020, https://www.theguardian.com/film/2020/sep/18/the-eight-hundred-how-chinas-blockbusters-became-a-new-political-battleground; Rana Mitter, *China's Good War: How World War II Is Shaping a New Nationalism* (Cambridge, MA: Harvard University Press, 2020), 165–167.

58. Rebecca Davis, "Chinese Research Group May Have Caused Cancellation of 'The Eight Hundred' Premiere," *Variety*, June 15, 2019, https://variety.com/2019/film/news/history-why-eight-hundred-shanghai-cancelled-1203244771/.

59. Interview in Shanghai, March 2017.

60. Steven Lee Myers and Chris Buckley, "In Xi's Homage to Korean War, a Jab at the U.S.," *New York Times*, October 23, 2020, https://www.nytimes.com/2020/10/23/world/asia/china-us-korean-war.html; Guan Ling, "纪念抗美援朝：江泽民高调邓小平淡化的玄机," Duowei News, October 21, 2020.

61. Yang Sheng, "Trade War Reminds Chinese of Korean War," *Global Times*, May 19, 2019, https://www.globaltimes.cn/content/1150664.shtml.

62. "Xi Says China Not Afraid of War in Speech to Mark Korean War," Al Jazeera, October 23, 2020, https://www.aljazeera.com/news/2020/10/23/xi-says-china-ready-to-fight-in-speech-to-mark-korean-war.

63. "Full Text: Speech by Xi Jinping at a Ceremony Marking the Centenary of the CPC," Xinhua, July 1, 2021, http://www.xinhuanet.com/english/special/2021-07/01/c_1310038244.htm; Chris Buckley and Keith Bradsher, "Marking Party's Centennial, Xi Warns That China Will Not Be Bullied," *New York Times*, July 1, 2021, https://www.nytimes.com/2021/07/01/world/asia/xi-china-communist-party-anniversary.html. Xinhua's English translation of the speech opted for milder language than the original, warning that China's opponents would find themselves "on a collision course" with a great wall of steel, rather than cracking their heads open and spilling blood. J. Stapleton Roy notes that the language draws from China's national anthem and suggests the most accurate translation would be: "The Chinese people absolutely will not permit any foreign power to bully, oppress, or enslave us. Those who vainly attempt to do so will bloody their own heads when they collide with a Great Wall of Steel composed of the flesh and blood of over 1.4 billion Chinese

people." See J. Stapleton Roy, "Read Xi's Words in Proper Context," Wilson Center, July 27, 2021, https://www.wilsoncenter.org/article/read-xi-jinpings-words-proper-context].

64. Chris Buckley and Keith Bradsher, "Marking Party's Centennial, Xi Warns That China Will Not Be Bullied," *New York Times*, July 1, 2021, https://www.nytimes.com/2021/07/01/world/asia/xi-china-communist-party-anniversary.html.

65. "Bengbu: Rail Renaissance Set to Bring New Glory," *China Daily*, July 1, 2011, https://www.chinadaily.com.cn/business/2011-07/01/content_12818178.htm.

66. The quotes and details in this section are from interviews in Bengbu in March 2018.

Conclusion

1. E. J. Hobsbawm and David J. Kertzer, "Ethnicity and Nationalism in Europe Today," *Anthropology Today* 8, no. 1 (1992): 3–8, doi:10.2307/3032805.

2. Ivan Zhilin, "Повестка в Сталинград," *Novaya Gazeta*, December 1, 2020, https://novayagazeta.ru/articles/2020/12/01/88187-povestka-v-stalingrad; Matthew Luxmore, "Russia Summons Stalingrad Survivors in World War II 'Genocide' Probe," Radio Free Europe/Radio Liberty, December 12, 2020, https://www.rferl.org/a/russia-summons-stalingrad-survivors-in-world-war-2-genocide-probe/30997288.html.

3. "Unveiling of the Rzhev Memorial to the Soviet Soldier," President of Russia website, June 30, 2020, http://en.kremlin.ru/events/president/news/63585.

4. Shaun Walker, "Angels and Artillery: A Cathedral to Russia's New National Identity," *The Guardian*, October 20, 2020, https://www.theguardian.com/world/2020/oct/20/orthodox-cathedral-of-the-armed-force-russian-national-identity-military-disneyland.

5. "The President Visited the Main Cathedral of the Armed Forces and the Road of Memory Museum Complex on the Day of Memory and Sorrow," President of Russia website, June 22, 2020, http://en.kremlin.ru/events/president/news/63543.

6. Gleb Bryanski, "Russian Patriarch Calls Putin Era 'Miracle of God,'" Reuters, February 8, 2012, https://www.reuters.com/article/uk-russia-putin-religion/russian-patriarch-calls-putin-era-miracle-of-god-idUKTRE81722Y20120208.

7. Vladimir Putin, "The Real Lessons of the 75th Anniversary of World War II," *National Interest*, June 18, 2020, https://nationalinterest.org/feature/vladimir-putin-real-lessons-75th-anniversary-world-war-ii-162982.

8. "Patriotism Is Russia's National Idea, Says Putin," TASS, May 10, 2020, https://tass.com/society/1154865.

9.   "Meeting of Pobeda (Victory) Organising Committee," President of Russia website, July 2, 2020, http://en.kremlin.ru/events/president/news/63591.

10.   "Russian Court Rules That Mass WWII Killings in Zhestyanaya Gorka Were Genocide," Radio Free Europe/Radio Liberty, October 27, 2020, https://www.rferl.org/a/russian-court-nazi-genocide-zhestyanaya-gorka/ 30915672.html; "Russian Court Rules That Mass WWII Killings in Pskov Region Were Genocide," Radio Free Europe/Radio Liberty, August 27, 2021, https://www.rferl.org/a/nazi-killings-pskov-russia/31431523.html.

11.   Andrei Kolesnikov, "A Coercive History Lesson from Vladimir Putin," *Foreign Affairs*, October 29, 2020, https://www.foreignaffairs.com/articles/ europe/2020-10-29/coercive-history-lesson-vladimir-putin.

12.   "Совфед одобрил закон о патриотическом воспитании в школах," RBK, July 24, 2020, https://www.rbc.ru/rbcfreenews/ 5f1ac7ae9a79476580620750; Hannah Alberts, "Next-Generation Fighters: Youth Military-Patriotic Upbringing Bolsters the Russian Military's Manning and Mobilization Potential," CSIS, September 22, 2020, https://www.csis.org/blogs/post-soviet-post/next-generation-fighters-youth-military-patriotic-upbringing-bolsters-russian.

13.   "Russian Lawmakers Seek to Ban Soviet-Nazi Comparisons," *Moscow Times*, May 6, 2021, https://www.themoscowtimes.com/2021/05/06/ russian-lawmakers-seek-to-ban-soviet-nazi-comparisons-a73826.

14.   "Russia Claims Soviet Army 'Liberated,' Not Invaded, Poland During WWII," *Moscow Times*, September 17, 2021, https://www. themoscowtimes.com/2021/09/17/russia-claims-soviet-army-liberated-not-invaded-poland-during-wwii-a75074; see Twitter post by @MID_ RU on September 17, 2021, https://twitter.com/MID_RF/status/ 1438768364353114115.

15.   Felix Light, "Russian Court Orders Closure of Renowned Rights Group Memorial," *Moscow Times*, December 28, 2021, https://www.themoscowtimes.com/2021/12/28/ russian-court-orders-closure-of-renowned-rights-group-memorial-a75674

16.   "Remembering Is Knowing Open Lesson," President of Russia website, September 1, 2020, http://en.kremlin.ru/events/president/news/63983.

17.   "Russian Duma Passes Bill Introducing Five-Year Prison Sentences for Insulting WWII Veterans," Radio Free Europe/Radio Liberty, March 17, 2021, https://www.rferl.org/a/russia-insulting-world-war-two-veterans-crime-navalny/31155861.html; Steven Lee Myers, "Shutting Down Historical Debate, China Makes It a Crime to Mock Heroes," *New York Times*, November 2, 2021, https://www.nytimes.com/2021/ 11/02/world/asia/china-slander-law.html. The law was strengthened in both countries in March 2021 so that it was now considered a criminal offense punishable by up to five years in prison in Russia and three years in China.

18. Anton Troianovski, "Russia Expels European Diplomats over Navalny Protests, Defying the West," *New York Times*, February 5, 2021, https://www.nytimes.com/2021/02/05/world/europe/aleksei-navalny-russia-court.html.

19. Andrew E. Kramer, "In First Interview from Jail, an Upbeat Navalny Discusses Prison Life," *New York Times*, August 25, 2021, https://www.nytimes.com/2021/08/25/world/europe/navalny-jail-prison.html.

20. Yi Wonju, "N.K. Leader Accuses 'Hostile Forces' of Intensifying 'War Drills for Aggression,'" Yonhap News Agency, July 30, 2021, https://en.yna.co.kr/view/AEN20210730002052325.

21. Josh Smith and Cynthia Kim, "North Korea's Kim Calls U.S. 'Our Biggest Enemy' in Challenge to Biden," Reuters, January 8, 2021, https://www.reuters.com/article/us-northkorea-politics/our-biggest-enemy-n-koreas-kim-says-u-s-policy-doesnt-change-with-presidents-idUSKBN29D2YA?il=0.

22. Colin Zwirko, "Kim Jong Un Suits Up in Military Uniform for Never-before-Seen Portrait," NK News, January 7, 2021, https://www.nknews.org/2021/01/kim-jong-un-suits-up-in-military-uniform-for-never-before-seen-portrait/.

23. Elizabeth Chen, "The 2021 Party History Study Campaign Stresses Revolution and Sacrifice," Jamestown Foundation, June 18, 2021, https://jamestown.org/program/the-2021-party-history-study-campaign-stresses-revolution-and-sacrifice/, "百年初心成大道 万里征程作雄行," *People's Daily*, December 24, 2021, http://paper.people.com.cn/rmrb/html/2021-12/24/nw.D110000renmrb_20211224_1-01.htm

24. Cate Cadell, "China Launches Hotline for Netizens to Report 'Illegal' History Comments," Reuters, April 11, 2021, https://www.reuters.com/world/china/china-launches-hotline-netizens-report-illegal-history-comments-2021-04-11/; Jun Mai, "China Deletes 2 Million Online Posts for 'Historical Nihilism' as Communist Party Centenary Nears," *South China Morning Post*, May 11, 2021, https://www.scmp.com/news/china/politics/article/3132957/china-deletes-2-million-online-posts-historical-nihilism.

25. Joseph Brouwer, "The Historical Nihil-list: Cyberspace Administration Targets Top Ten Deviations from Approved History," *China Digital Times*, August 16, 2021, https://chinadigitaltimes.net/2021/08/the-historical-nihil-list-cyberspace-administration-targets-top-ten-deviations-from-approved-history/.

26. "Xi Focus: Xi Stresses Carrying Forward Great Spirit of Resisting Aggression," Xinhua, September 4, 2020, http://www.xinhuanet.com/english/2020-09/04/c_139340869.htm.

27. Laura He, "China's Korean War Propaganda Movie Smashes Box Office Record," CNN, October 4, 2021, https://www.cnn.com/2021/10/04/business/battle-lake-changjin-china-box-office-intl-hnk/index.html.

28. "Xi Focus: Xi Stresses Carrying Forward China's Volunteers Army's Spirit in War to Resist U.S. Aggression and Aid Korea," Xinhua, October 20, 2020, http://www.xinhuanet.com/english/2020-10/20/c_139452337.htm.

29. "Xi Focus: Xi Jinping and China's Anti-Poverty War He Commands," Xinhua, October 17, 2020, http://www.xinhuanet.com/english/2020-10/17/c_139447364.htm; "China Creates Poverty-Alleviation Miracle in Human History," *People's Daily*, October 6, 2020, http://en.people.cn/n3/2020/1006/c90000-9766952.html; "Xi Focus: Chronicle of Xi's Leadership in China's War against Coronavirus," Xinhua, September 7, 2020, http://www.xinhuanet.com/english/2020-09/07/c_139349538.htm; Rana Mitter, *China's Good War: How World War II Is Shaping a New Nationalism* (Cambridge, MA: Harvard University Press, 2020), 261.

30. "Xi Focus: Chronicle of Xi's Leadership in China's War against Coronavirus," Xinhua, September 7, 2020, http://www.xinhuanet.com/english/2020-09/07/c_139349538.htm; Zheng Wang, "The Past's Transformative Power," *Wilson Quarterly*, Fall 2020, https://www.wilsonquarterly.com/quarterly/the-ends-of-history/the-pasts-transformative-power/; Cai Xuejiao, "China to Add State-Approved COVID Content to School Curricula," *Sixth Tone*, October 30, 2020, https://www.sixthtone.com/news/1006369/china-to-add-state-approved-covid-content-to-school-curricula.

31. "Full Text: Resolution of the CPC Central Committee on the Major Achievements and Historical Experience of the Party over the Past Century," Xinhua, November 16, 2021, http://www.news.cn/english/2021-11/16/c_1310314611.htm.

32. "在新时代新征程上赢得更加伟大的胜利和荣光," *People's Daily*, November 12, 2021, http://paper.people.com.cn/rmrb/html/2021-11/12/nw.D110000renmrb_20211112_2-03.htm.

33. "Full Text: Resolution of the CPC Central Committee on the Major Achievements and Historical Experience of the Party over the Past Century," Xinhua, November 16, 2021, http://www.news.cn/english/2021-11/16/c_1310314611.htm

34. Jeremy Page and Trefor Moss, "South China Sea Puts Beijing in a Corner," *Wall Street Journal*, July 13, 2016, https://www.wsj.com/articles/south-china-sea-ruling-puts-beijing-in-a-corner-1468365807, in Orville Schell, "To Forget or Remember? China's Struggle with Its Past," *Washington Quarterly* 39, no. 3 (2016): 143–157, doi:10.1080/0163660X.2016.1232641,

35. Orville Schell, "To Forget or Remember? China's Struggle with Its Past," *Washington Quarterly* 39, no. 3 (2016): 143–157, doi:10.1080/0163660X.2016.1232641.

36. Jessica Chen Weiss, *Powerful Patriots: Nationalist Protest in China's Foreign Relations* (New York: Oxford University Press, 2014), 3.

37. Simon Schama, "Simon Schama on America's History Wars, Race and the Flag," *Financial Times*, July 8, 2021, https://www.ft.com/content/c304ace0-3a1f-4e8d-8de1-8a4e62a9f7b6.

INDEX

For the benefit of digital users, indexed terms that span two pages (e.g., 52–53) may, on occasion, appear on only one of those pages.